FORT WORTH LIBRARY
3 1668 05059 2457

W9-CEI-312

ROSEANNEARCHY

Dispatches from the Nut Farm

Also by Roseanne Barr

MY LIVES

ROSEANNE: MY LIFE AS A WOMAN

ROSEANNEARCHY

Dispatches from the Nut Farm

Roseanne Barr

GALLERY BOOKS
New York London Toronto Sydney

Gallery Books
A Division of Simon & Schuster, Inc.
1230 Avenue of the Americas
New York, NY 10020

First Gallery Books hardcover edition January 2011

Designed by Jaime Putorti

Manufactured in the United States of America

10 9 8 7 6 5 4 3 2 1

Library of Congress Cataloging-in-Publication Data

Roseanne, 1952–
Roseannearchy : dispatches from the nut farm / Roseanne Barr.—1st Gallery Books hardcover ed.
p. cm.
1. American wit and humor. I. Title.
PN6165.R667 2011
814'.6—dc22 2010027413

ISBN 978-1-4391-5482-3
ISBN 978-1-4391-6007-7 (ebook)

This book is dedicated to those I love and to those who love me. May we always think for ourselves and continue to rebel against the Confederacy of Dunces who now rule the earth.

Contents

Foreword

by Bill Pentland

I had no idea, when I carefully pored through the shallow cardboard box of Roseanne's hand-scribbled ravings in 1973, I would one day be writing the foreword to her third book. This is somewhat of a literary hat trick for me: As a nine-year-old boy, I received my first rejection letter from Rod Serling; years later, as a young cub reporter, I witnessed the first burgeoning seeds of the Watergate scandal. But commenting on the inner workings of Roseanne's mind is something else entirely.

The scathing diatribes you'll find herein are very much like the tracts in that cardboard box that she hesitantly allowed me to view almost forty years ago. She was shy and protective of her writings then; a motley collection of handwritten essays, thoughts, poems, and rants scribbled on random scraps of napkins, notebook paper, and colored memo pads, and stashed under an unused bunk in our eight-by-forty-six-foot trailer. We had recently moved up in the world—a young hippie couple vacating their mountain cabin, pump, and outhouse for the relative luxury of a 1956 Alma trailer, complete with electricity, working lights, a refrigerator, and, wonder of wonders, indoor hot water on demand! No longer would we have to tramp into two feet of snow to fill a galvanized bucket with water from our hand pump to heat on the stove. It was only natural, now being comfortably ensconced, that Roseanne could free up the time to pursue her passion of writing and telling the world specifically what was wrong with it.

Writing came naturally to this early Roseanne; punching a time clock did not. She found the restrictions of steady employment a drain on her muse. How else could one explain her predilection for wearing corporate baseball uniforms to her job as a fancy restaurant hostess or her insistence that I punch in on her time card to do her dishwashing shifts for her? How else to explain her excitedly watching, from behind a kitchen door, poet and singer Rod McKuen munching a biscuit at her very own hostess station? She later told the staff that he ordered "a glass of water, please. By the sea, by the sea, by the beautiful sea . . ." The staff cracked up and a monster was born; that day, she learned she could do better in life tossing off sarcastic one-liners than ever holding a steady job.

And she was in good company. Georgetown, Colorado, was nothing if not filled with the most eclectic ragtag band of Bohemian misfits and social renegades this side of Prague. Head chef Andy Ivory would often cook in the nude, reluctantly wearing an apron only to keep boiling grease from splattering his genitalia. Six-foot-eleven Stretch might tell us about the young ghost in his room the night before, and One-Armed Carlos would bus a table with his single appendage ten times faster than a busboy with twice the armage. Mad polka music would fill the bar on Sunday evenings and the suds would flow; with my frosty mug stashed in the ice-cream freezer, I washed the Texan-spattered dishes earmarked for Roseanne.

Georgetown was a little like Greenwich Village then, a little like Nome, and a little like Dodge City. Artists, writers, exiles, and hooligans of every conceivable stripe were drawn there, taking low-paying jobs to keep a roof over their heads and their hopes alive. I believe this milieu of total creative anarchy made a firm and lasting impression on Roseanne, who was all of nineteen years old. We fancied ourselves "Alpine Bohemians," and not the white trash we would have appeared to most people. Then again, it's hard to avoid the "white trash" label when you live in a trailer and have to bring your sewer pipe inside at night to keep it from freezing, or steal change from a motel cigarette machine to buy hamburger meat.

But bit by bit, Rosie began to morph into a housewife, and we finally decided to tie the knot in 1974—after seeing *The Exorcist,* we were convinced that Satan had possessed us. We came to the realization that although Alpine Bohemia was nice, eating was nicer. We got tired of scraping for pocket change and composting garbage and fixing our VW with chicken wire. We aspired to own a home without wheels one day; we wanted to have kids without having to borrow money from a paycheck-cashing service to cover the maternity bills; we wanted a TV with a picture you could actually see instead of the static that passed for entertainment at 9,000 feet above sea level. We even dreamed that someday we might own a Sony Trinitron!

Therein followed our next life course, which was to admit defeat as hippies and crawl to Colorado Springs, where I would finally pursue the civil service career my father had been pitching to me for years. We took out a loan, bought another trailer, and began what would become for Rosie five years of self-imposed agoraphobia and scattergun childbearing. We had three children in thirty-nine months (again with the "white trash" labels!), eventually moving to Denver and plunking down $25,000 on our first real home. Thus began our inexorable descent into mainstream establishment Amerika. We traded in our patched blue jeans for new Levi's, patchouli for Obsession, our Gremlin for a Ford Country Squire station wagon. I went to work for the U.S. Postal Service, while Roseanne stayed home with the kids and slowly went insane (or sane, depending on your frame of reference).

For five years, we played Ward and June Cleaver, and I foolishly believed we were just living life. But apparently Roseanne was recording every synapse, meltdown, revelation, and resurrection to create the persona that would become Roseanne Barr/Connor. Somewhere, around the time our youngest left diapers and I left the graveyard shift, Roseanne had what I viewed as a psychotic break. She began to explore radical feminism and Wicca, and went to work at a women's collective bookstore, staffed by the angriest bunch of ball-bustin' babes I had ever met in my sheltered white-bread Lutheran upbringing.

Frankly, I was threatened by her involvement in women's studies; my only interest in the feminist movement at that time was seeing a picture of Gloria Steinem in that Playboy bunny outfit. Of course, it didn't help that Roseanne's rad-lib sister, Geraldine, was living with us. Geraldine and I were in a constant battle for Roseanne's soul then; I wanted Rosie in the kitchen, barefoot and pregnant, and I suppose Geraldine had some silly idea about Rosie having an identity outside of our suburban Denver home. (Geraldine would provide the basis for the character of Jackie and her love/hate friction with Rosie's husband, Dan Connor.)

Roseanne would eventually try stand-up and incorporate the people in our lives into her routine, eventually evolving the template that became one of the most accurate portrayals of a blue-collar family in history. Although our three kids were the primary models for Becky, Darlene, and D.J., Rosie would weave real details, peccadilloes, accents, clothing, etc., from actual people she knew. One of our hillbilly trailer park neighbors provided Roseanne with some great grist for the Connor mill, with her backwoods Kentucky accent, lanky protofeminine swagger, and the chutzpah to praise her four-year-old daughter's hot-dog-eating abilities. "You just keep on doing that, darlin', and you'll never have want of nothin'," she would say. "Men just love that, I don't know why." You can't write stuff like that, but you can sure as hell absorb it and splinter it off into another five or ten characters. Not to mention the subliminal feminist ramifications!

Roseanne continued with radical stand-up, alienating every white male within a 2,000-mile radius (a talent she maintains to this day, incidentally). As the threatened male-dominated Denver clubs began to close their doors to her, she instead branched out as a fledgling producer and integrated herself into the Denver art scene. But as her stand-up became more mainstream, more and more of our daily workaday lives melded themselves into the Becoming Roseanne Connor Family. By couching a radical feminist doctrine in a safe, chubby housewife, she was able to go inside the stereotype and eventually, I truly believe, enact real, measurable change into the consciousness of the average American woman.

While this has been a generally positive development, Roseanne's persona unfortunately spawned its own Moriarty. While it talks like Roseanne Connor, the leviathan Sarah Palin is busy going inside her own stereotype as well. I only hope that when they remake *The Dead Zone,* they cast Tina Fey in the role originally played by Martin Sheen. You really can't blame the Palin phenomenon on Roseanne, I guess, but I'll bet Ms. Palin would have presented herself differently had there never been a Roseanne Connor.

Eventually, destiny came to Roseanne in the form of Johnny Carson. Her five-minute monologue on *The Tonight Show* fired the opening salvo in the real war of the sexes. A new sheriff was in town and, baby, she was loaded for bear. The Friday night her monologue aired, I was driving across the moonlit Wyoming tundra with our three kids asleep in the back in what was to become our last "normal" year of life in Denver. Things would change very soon, and they would change hard. Overnight success has its own agenda. There is no preparation for this, no support group, no legend, no diagrams; you simply hold on to the barrel as you cascade over the falls. In 1988, shit would come in so fast and so hard that it is only now, twenty years after the fact, that I can even get my head around it.

When Roseanne first exploded across the national consciousness, the tabloids began their crazy dance. One has to live through shredding one's billing statements, peeling off prescription bottle labels, separating booze bottles from the regular trash, and erasing planted calls off answering machines to fully appreciate the horror of the microscope. But it can be fun, too. When NBC and Fox aired their competing (and unauthorized) "Roseanne" biopics, we gathered around the television, panning the actors who had been cast to play our extended family.

Roseanne has written of her creative struggles with ABC in prior works, but *I was there and I saw what she did.* She not only talked the talk, she walked the walk. Much of the Hollywood establishment simply viewed her as a spoiled brat, an 800-pound gorilla, a histrionic, salivating she-bitch. And she is. The reason Roseanne prevailed is because Roseanne Connor *was* Roseanne Barr, and no one understands that better than she. She knocked the network suits on their asses by the simple virtue of presenting the truth. I can only hope someday the rest of the world will catch up to what she was saying all along.

For nine years, Roseanne Connor held forth on her bully pulpit; Roseanne Barr has held forth a lot longer than that. Within these pages, she will once again regale you with her unique vision, her misanthropy, and her general intolerance of slack-jawed, drooling dunces. You will learn of her impending decline into her golden years and of smelling like pee, her obsessions with serial killers, conservatives, Satan, and blaming everything on everyone else. Pure vintage Rosie, and the final maturation of those scraps of Rocky Mountain paper. Read this book and enjoy once again that special descent into the catacombs of her mind. It's all here; you just have to look for it.

And don't be afraid.

ROSEANNEARCHY

Dispatches from the Nut Farm

Introduction

The first thing I asked myself after making everyone I know check around to see if they could get me a book deal was, *Why the hell am I thinking about writing another book?* After all, everywhere you look, some pouty intellectual is whining about how we live in a postliterate age, which means that nobody reads anything longer than a text message, and even those are just a few dumb-ass abbreviations strung together—LOL (laugh out loud), LMFAO (laughing my fucking ass off), ROFLMAO (rolling on floor laughing my ass off), TTYL (talk to you later), or LOLSTC (laughed out loud scared the cat!).

Now here I am, almost fifty-eight years old, being completely honest with myself as I begin to approach middle age (LOL), full to the brim with wisdom, grandmotherly love, and the kind of gas that only a whole head of roasted garlic can generate, so you, dear reader, are in for a treat. I wanted to write the kind of book that I'd like to read, but my publishers, who just got bought again (this time by a Chinese hedge fund or something), told me that trashy crime novels full of lurid sex and gory details that forensics freaks love to revel in are just rotting on the racks. So I went straight to Plan B: a timely, eclectic book by a Baby Boomer that even younger people could take home and read, if they could in fact read after coming up through our skool systom (ROFLMAO).

Speaking of younger people, my five kids (I used to be pro-life), who think of me as a Mominatrix who has somehow always managed to both cruelly neglect them and butt into their lives too much, are glad I'm writing it. In fact, my whole formerly estranged extended family is happy about it. I think it's because it'll give them a chance to really consider my words carefully, get to know me all over again, and then see if there's anything in here that would give them grounds to sue me. God love 'em.

I know damn well that there are a lot of people who *never* really got to know me and still don't like me, but this really isn't a book about ex-husbands. Some people are almost incurable hardcases, and despite the fact that legions of Roseannethropologists have determined that I've done our desperately diverse, dynamically dysfunctional culture way more good than harm, some folks just won't let me live down that night all those years ago when I started the National Anthem too high, and ended up sounding like a screechy but brittle blend of battlefield surgery and a pterodactyl with its tit in a wringer. I've said I'm sorry a million times! I know this is a Christian nation and all that, but can't they at least consider forgiving me after all these years? Talk about going the extra mile: I'm a Jew and I dressed up like Hitler and baked little burned people cookies to atone for my poor performance! What more can I do, for Christ's sake?

I know that there are a lot of books out there right now by well-known people in the comedy business, people who are utterly brilliant and have timely, relevant things to say—funny things, poignant things that go straight to the heart after tickling the funny bone. Some of these talented figures, many younger than I, have enjoyed big success on TV more recently than I have, and they're getting rave reviews. I'm not too proud to say that I hate those people. But I can't let the jealousy I feel for them and my inability to focus keep me from trying to show them up and get out there and have my say, too!

I just know this book will be wildly successful and well received because I'm someone who surrounds myself with positive energy and light, someone who doesn't let negative, demoralizing words like *failure* or *disappointment* or *exercise* even begin to creep into her life. I learned an important, valuable lesson years ago, when I used to smoke three or four packs of cigarettes a day: I am no quitter! I do whatever it takes to make things work—to make them fulfilling and joyous.

Hell, you want to see determination? I'll take my son's college money (I don't think he's college material anyway, but let's just keep that between us), give it to my personal assistant when she gets out of rehab, and have her buy thousands of these sons of bitches, ten at a time. I don't need Oprah's Book Club; I'll spend myself into the goddamn poorhouse, buying my own books by the truckload, and then get me one of them government bailouts! See what I'm saying? Those rookies at Goldman Sachs will come to *me* and ask how to work this free market ba-ziz-ness up in here!

I do hope you like it, though—yes, *you*, who are reading my words at this moment, this very moment, the only one we really have. Okay, there's this moment, too, but you know what I mean. Think of this book as a big, fun, shiny fridge that you can open at three in the morning when your pill wears off and you realize your nightmare was more fun than your real life and you're looking for something tasty to read. Open this book and the light will come on, and you can just stare into it, like a clueless zombie who doesn't give a damn about low fat or fiber or cholesterol or corn syrup or blood pressure or any of that other crap the science nerds try to scare us into caring about—then you can just start grabbing at things, unwrapping them, smelling them, trying some of this or that. Don't think of the slabs and slices and chunks of words as chapters that unfold in a logical manner or reveal some artfully woven plotline or ironclad womanifesto. Logical shmogical! Think of it more like "Hey, this chocolate-covered strawberry really tastes good with a mouthful of bean-and-cheese burrito! Now, where's the rest of that pumpkin pie?" (I just made myself hungry.)

Anyway, thanks for buying my book, my friend! Eat hearty, and we'll start our walking program next week—next week for sure. Till then: Bon appétit!

■

IRONY ALERT: Upon reading any and all parts of this book that deal in matters religious and political or any other areas that have traditionally caused humor-challenged people with arguably "traditional values" to burn bigmouthed women at the stake, please be aware that I reserve the right as a comic, a satirist, and a citizen of the nation that proudly proclaims itself the freest on earth to say things that should probably not be taken literally enough to make a nut job like *you* (you know who you are) feel justified in attacking me. Just as I discourage you from menacing or inflicting bodily harm on your spouse, your kids, your pets, your neighbors, or complete strangers who don't look, act, think, dress, or believe exactly as you do, I urge you to keep an open mind and a sense of humor in reading this book.

I extend this invitation to the "journalists" and the "media," too, as you guys always seem to take my jokes and report them as if they are serious news. Of course, I know that you cannot tell the difference, and I admit that I like to fuck with you all the time. But the last straw was when I was out with Michael Moore for his "Slacker Uprising" tour of colleges, and I used this joke onstage: "I voted for George Bush because he is way more 'educationably orientated' than that Kerry guy"—despite the fact that I got a huge laugh, the local Cleveland paper reported that I said: "George Bush is more education oriented than is John Kerry." I fumed at this act of satanic brilliance and deceit—enough is enough. You can fuck with me, but don't fuck with my jokes, you bastards!

Yours, for a free and peaceful world for all living things to keep living in,

Roseanne Cherrie Barr

Postintroduction

What the Hell . . . Let's Go!

Writing another book is like having another baby, they told me, except with a baby you get screwed only at the *front end* of the deal. I wanted to write this book for a few reasons, and one is that I still have a story worth telling. Part of it has already been told, but the saga continues, as they like to say in comic books and zillion-dollar movies about adventurers and sorcerers and tales that challenge the imagination. The part that lots of folks who know me, or know of me, have probably heard starts with a fat, little Jewish girl growing up in Mormon Utah with chronically broke, disappointed parents who warned their daughter that if she didn't cut down on the calories and the wiseass comments, she would end up a poor, fat, lonely, bitter old spinster. Man, am I glad they were wrong about the *poor* part!

Anyway, long story short, I'm guessing that if you're reading this right now, it's probably because of *Roseanne,* the TV show about the fat, sassy little girl who had become a fat, sassy woman with a husband and kids, all of whom found themselves in a family that doesn't quite get how brilliant they are. It's like the horse that's pulled the cart of everything that's come after it. I shouldn't brag, because it's been awhile since the show that made me famous aired on prime-time television; but it's funny how the more time passes, the more *Roseanne* is proving to have been ahead of its time. Whether addressing working-class issues, gender equality, or changing family models, we took a pretty hard look at an America that was in need of a pretty hard look. It's been more than a decade since we stopped making the show, which still airs all over the place in syndication, and we're still grappling with the same issues that were brought to light back then.

I often open my stand-up act by telling the audience that I know what they're thinking (because I'm psychic): "Roseanne, what has a *has-been* of *your magnitude* been up to recently?" Obviously, I'm able to take a joke, but really, I'm grateful that there's always been a pretty steady stream of opportunities for me to dive into in showbiz. TV people, who figure lightning can strike again, still pitch me ideas; I've gone around the world with my stand-up act; the phone rings and the emails pile up—but something keeps me from jumping into any real big projects with both feet. And it's not just because I'm busy raising my awesome but (I hope, temporarily) surly teenage son.

I have found that after all is said and done, having my say and doing it for free is my therapy for poststardom soul retrieval. Losing your soul is the cost of fame and fortune, I found. It will become severely compromised when you realize that you must remain silent about the worst things on earth. You will need drugs, alcohol, sex scandal, and incessant shopping to help you stay "above the fray" so that your conscience doesn't bother you anymore. After buying everything on earth that one can buy, visiting exotic places, and meeting princes and idols, all I found myself wanting was to be able to say exactly what I wanted to say when I wanted to say it. There are, sadly, almost no women, famous or infamous, who can afford to do this, or who have the education, brains, or courage to do this, either—and there never have been. Which brings me to my website, Roseanneworld.com, and the blogging habit that inspired me to write another book.

I was the very first celebrity blogger, and I remain the only one to this day who advocates the return of the splendid guillotine for class criminals and pedophile priests. My blogging has gotten me into some uncomfortable positions on occasion, but it's the place where I go to unload, upload, and fire back at the shitstorm of absurdity and horror that the media unloads on me, and the rest of us, every day. I shoot from the hip and bitch about people, places, and things; I pontificate and react and panic; I praise and criticize and encourage people, and sometimes fight with them; I turn them on to worthy organizations and causes, and talk about the things I think are the most important issues in our lives. Some days I go on at length about all kinds of strange, esoteric, metaphysical musings, and sometimes everything I write sounds like New Age jibber-jabber. I've expressed myself, reversed myself, defended myself, made people laugh, made people think, pissed people off, engaged in feuds, made new friends, made peace, given advice, asked for advice, and some of what I write is just pure Roseannearchy; channeled from Goddesses on High.

I've asked the world to cut the bullshit. The world can be a better place in a hurry. I don't have forever, and sometimes it really pisses me off!

I have spent the majority of my life researching information about solutions to the world's problems. I got interested in doing this at a young age, when I first discovered that I had an Imaginary Friend with whom I could spend most of my time discussing how to fix such a cruel and crazy world as this one. My Imaginary

Friend was "God." (Now I know that She was actually an Inner Self-Helper—something all dissociatives possess.)

She was always available to discuss my thoughts and fears, and later, when I could finally read (at about six years of age), She led me to find a lot of answers in old books found in my grandmother's bookcase, at school, and downtown at the Salt Lake City Public Library, which became my home away from home once I got a library card. I grew up in a city that actually prized knowledge and education and books, despite being so fundamentalist Mormon.

I sometimes wondered if I was from a special tribe, the Tribe of Librarians or Book Lovers. My passion for books and for reading took up the first twenty years of my life. I read an average of five books a week, and most of them were about what people wrote on the subject of God, which I would then discuss with my Imaginary Friend. Sometimes I would test Her, just to see if She actually existed or if She was merely a figment of my imagination. I would open my mind wide, and ask Her a question; and each and every time, without exception, I found that merely opening a book, *any book*, to *any page*, would provide an answer of some kind to those questions I asked of Her.

Currently, I own my own library of sorts. I have collected more than twenty-five hundred books. They are mostly about God, written by people with varying points of view from every corner of the world. Most of the books call Her a He, but I am able to ascertain what is meant, despite that *semantic error*. God is a She, and here is my proof of that fact: I was made in Her image, which I found in the mirror where I went as a child to speak with Her. She was Me, and yet I was not Her—that blew my mind, and continues to do so. I'm a mystic, and find myself excited at the theory of physics that says the universe itself functions as a sort of mirror of consciousness. Of course, this does not surprise me at all, as I have always known that to be true.

If a Roseannethropologist comes along someday, and figures out how and where I was shaped by the odd world I found myself in, and how I did some shaping of that world myself, she'll have plenty of ground to uncover. Your Domestic Goddess grew up in Utah during the '50s and '60s. It was such a fun-house mirror of sorts, where I saw the "Truth" completely reversed by women. I heard them talk constantly about how weak men were, how disloyal, cruel, misogynistic, and devoid of empathy. Yet they also talked constantly about how, if the apelike human male were molded correctly by them, could become more female, and therefore more human, then they, the women in my childhood sphere, could then rest well, assured that their Frankenstein monster would dutifully support them in the manner in which they wished to live.

As they attempted to remake all the males in the family, their oldest daughters were deemed to be their indentured servants and often the targets of their rage. They would never miss an opportunity to instruct me on how I needed to be groomed and dumbed down enough to get a husband of my own someday to mold into a guilt-controlled provider of my own. It was a perverted patriarchal world that I grew up in, and one that I wanted and *needed* to be free of.

How I did that—and keep doing it—is my story.

Preface

Right Is Wrong, and We Need to Straighten It Out

Does this sound familiar: "Where does some old show-business spoiled brat get off blabbing her opinions about politics and economics and religion and the way the world should work?" I'd like to telepathically air-smack people who say that, right in their cake hole! To anybody who asks me who I think I am to tell political bigwigs, captains of industry, and religious honchos where to get off, I answer: Who do I *have* to be? I am the Domestic Goddess, you impertinent creature, you!

Please listen to me, and listen to me good. I'm also your sister, your granny, your friend with the big mouth and the heart of gold; for some of you, I'm even your favorite TV mom. I'm someone who came out of nowhere, and had to cut through a jungle of old-growth bullshit, using nothing but my mouth for a machete. How many Vegas oddsmakers would have given a fat girl from Utah with a chip on her shoulder a chance of becoming one of the most famous women on the planet for a time? It happened because I was preaching a message that flew in the face of the proper, politically correct behavior that reigned before I flung the door open and came out swinging.

I dropped out of school, got a real education, took myself to the prom, peed in the punch bowl, and got rich doing it. And believe me, they don't *give* big dough away—but they will pay if they're sure you have something people want. And what did people want then that they still want now? They want a plainspoken message from somebody they figure is on their side, somebody who cuts people who think they're better than the rest of us down to size.

The key phrase there is: "on their side." There are more than a few blowhards raking in huge money, who are good at acting like they're "one of you," standing up to those in power. A recent example is the Sarah Palin phenomenon. Note to Sarah Palin: Telling a bunch of powerful men and their brainwashed lemming lackeys what they want to hear but doing it in a spunky, folksy manner does *not* make you a maverick! I got especially turned off when I saw some footage of Sarah P. in church, where along with some mundane, provincial happy talk about how super it was to be this congregation's particular brand of Christian, she gave a rodeo-style shout-out to her son, who was shipping off to Iraq with his unit. It was *so* cheerleader! I mean, seriously, it was like he was going up the road to play the rival high school in football. And this was from the pulpit at church! It really demonstrates the truth that politics and religion in the United States work like the twin grips of a pair of pliers on a critical mass of the masses.

I have a feeling that before Dick Cheney and Cowboy George decided that the poor Iraqis hated our freedom so much that we had to go kill a bunch of them, Sarah P. couldn't have found wherever her heavily armed son was headed on a map, even with both hands. But enough about Sarah, our geopolitically challenged, national pom-pom girl, who walked off the job she ran for and was elected to complete. I'm ticked off at Oprah for giving her so much attention as it is. Let's move on to the bigmouthed men who are so good at spreading their fake populist BS that shouldn't fool anybody, but does.

Now, before any of you Rust Limburg or Sean Cassity disciples and dittoheads tune me out or accuse me of blasphemy, you really owe it to yourself to give it all another look. Everybody knows that we took a wrong turn in this country awhile back, and we can argue for another twenty years about who and what was behind it. But damned if most working people don't agree that *something* happened that didn't lead us in the right direction—it did, however, lead us in the *right* direction (in the political sense).

Regardless of your politics, if you're a fair-minded person, at least hear me out. If there's anybody who loves their country and the American people, it's me! Why wouldn't I? I was able to scrape my way up from *under* the bottom of the barrel to the top of the heap, and I was able to do it by speaking my mind. I got more attention, love, respect, and opportunities to *keep* speaking my mind than a broke-ass, little fat girl from Utah had a right to even dream of having—not to mention a boatload of money and the good things in life that all of that brings. *But* I'm still speaking out and I'm doing it for the same people I always did it for: the ones like me, who felt shut out or different or looked down on or ignored or all of the above.

For working people, average Americans, the hundreds of millions of people who feel like lots of things are passing them by, can we at least agree that life's getting harder instead of easier? People are getting screwed! There are places in this country where one family in three is "upside down" in their homes. They have to pay way more for things than they are worth, and the pile they owe isn't getting smaller, because they're mostly paying interest on their debt. That is damn near slavery!

There was a time when the expression "Home Sweet Home"

embodied an ideal we could all aspire to and attain with hard work and careful planning. Owning your own home and the ground it sat on was a cornerstone of the American Dream. Home was where you put your feet up after a day's work, raised your kids, found comfort and safety. "There's no place like home" wasn't just a line from *The Wizard of Oz*; it was a mantra we believed in wholeheartedly. But when did a home become like a chip in a casino? Where did we make a wrong turn?

Remember the movie *Wall Street*? Michael Douglas played a lizard of a finance big shot named Gordon Gekko—pretty subtle, eh? He was one of the Wall Street elite, a tycoon who loved to say things like "Greed is good." Art imitates life, though, and all that stuff about "trickle-down economics" had been running through the national dialogue for a while (my friend Susan Bublitz, a funny comic, said it meant "the rich piss on the poor"), along with all the rest of that jazz that rich guys used to love Ronald Reagan for saying. They didn't call Reagan the "Great Communicator" for nothing. Personally, I think they called him that because the "Great Bullshitter" was probably rejected as a nickname by the Carlyle Group or at a meeting of the Bilderberg Group or one of those other cabals consisting of ten or so guys who have more wealth, power, and insider information than anyone else.

Granted, Reagan was a likable sort—relaxed and folksy while oozing a grandfatherly vitality, as he simultaneously helped to reverse and dismantle a half century of hard-won social progress. I won't bury you under page after page of bad-mouthing Reagan; the major point I'm trying to make here is the importance of distinguishing facts from opinions. (In that spirit, I offer the title of a book that's a treasury of facts about how Ronald Reagan seldom missed an opportunity to steer resources away from public services and into private pockets: *The Man Who Sold the World: Ronald Reagan and the Betrayal of Main Street America*.) The middle class has been shrinking like the dollar, union membership, and our standing in the world (with a few brief spurts of growth) ever since the Reagan era. Given the facts, how can the windbags on the extreme right justify describing the president who slashed public services and even took the solar panels off the roof of the White House as the greatest president in recent history? They're as entitled to express their opinions as the rest of us—freedom of speech is, after all, one of America's founding principles. But it's up to the public to discern fact from opinion and make up its own mind.

Religion—yep, I'm going there—and allowing people of diverse faiths to practice their beliefs without fear of persecution is another defining quality dating back to the birth of our nation. I grew up with religion on steroids—two religions, in fact. Being a nominal Mormon among Mormons, but also, inescapably, a Jew, really affected me. I was in a hyperspiritual environment, where people would regularly insert phrases like "The Lord" *this* and "God" *that* and "The Devil" *such and such,* in the most mundane, casual conversation. It still comes so naturally to me to think and talk in the manner of my childhood. That was some powerful indoctrination. A lot of my attitudes and actions have either been because of those conflicting influences or in rebellion against them. As I get older, I can see where there's overlap in what used to seem like two totally different religious cultures. One thing I know: Patriarchy runs deep in both systems.

I'm loving the show *Big Love* right now. It's almost spooky to watch so much of that "Utah thang," as I affectionately call it, play out on television. Watching it reminds me a lot of what it was like when I lived there—what with the rampant xenophobia and homophobia that led to my little brother's nose being broken nine times by devout Mormon classmates by the time he was nine years old, either for looking Jewish or being effeminate. The Mormon influence is still out there, big-time.

Religion needs to be less about believing things and more about beholding things—sharing and healing and bringing people together, not separating them. When I hear people say they have a need to connect with something bigger than themselves, one of the voices in my head says, *How can you* not *be connected with something bigger than yourself? You're part of everything!* I look at my young grandsons, for example, and just the pure physical fact that these little guys are in the world—living, growing, thinking, using language, and finding their way—is *profound*! They're setting out on a life that's as big and deep and wide as they can feel and experience, and *that* is amazing enough for me. I'm not so sure that they need a great big belief system injected into their mostly pliant minds right now, or ever. I'm breaking with tradition; I just tell them to be kind to one another and polite to other people, and they'll turn out just fine. Mostly, I just like to have fun with them.

I look out at what's left of the natural world, and it is as mystical and beautiful as it was when I ran around in the mountains of Colorado doing my 1970s Wiccan, natural-woman thing. When I remember how complex and awesome is nature's machinery, the planet's place in a vast solar system that contains such precision of motion, I still feel a huge sense of awe for it all. Just to be quiet and behold and respect its greatness seems so much more appropriate than to impose a big net of dogma that supposedly makes everything more meaningful.

Instead of knocking myself out trying to understand or rationalize a bunch of holidays (holy days?) with their symbolism and oh-so-deep, arcane significance, I'm a little less quick to chase that merry-go-round and more apt just to dig the seasons and the real turning points in the year, which are less about myth and interpretation and more about *real* signposts on our trip around the sun. Why believe a bunch of Bronze Age stuff we can't prove when we have dependable occurrences to believe in, like the summer solstice—the day with the most light and the least dark? No believing required, nothing to argue about. Or the vernal (spring) and autumnal equinoxes—the balance of day and night—perfect, predictable, and plenty spiritual *and* scientific for me. I guess we were all pagans way back when—observing, accepting, and respecting the natural world—and that wasn't such a bad thing.

In looking at the world in all its scary glory, people often see it as a backdrop on which to pin their religious beliefs, like a giant billboard, and then insist that other people accept those beliefs as fact. For example, the Creationist movement points to the universe, to life itself, as proof that there's a creator, one that they just happen to know a whole lot about and want to "share" with you. Before you know it, you're on an ideological conveyor belt. That mental assembly line has you going from "Wow, the vastness of space!" and having a sense of wonder about life on earth straight to talking about the blood of Christ, living in the Last Days, and taking dictionaries out of schools because they contain words that are unacceptable to certain Christians. I'm not bitching about Christians; I'm righteously bitching about fundamentalists of all stripes, anywhere, who insist that there's just one way to live, and that way is strictly in accordance with their ancient religious texts—as they interpret them, of course.

Speaking of ancient religious texts and who does the interpreting, can you believe that there's a movement under way to write a revised Bible that's more about "free market principles"? There are people who think that there's way too much "help the poor" and "love thine enemy" talk, along with a whole lot of other stuff that they feel is way too "liberal" and "entitled" to be in a proper, what, capitalist Bible? Yikes!

This all goes back to my premise: People are getting screwed—from both sides: politics and religion. Let's face it; religion *is* politics. Right-wing Christians, who deny the fact that Jesus was basically a Jewish liberal from *way* back east, have hijacked his teachings to suit their political beliefs. Jesus did an awful lot of talking about caring for the poor and sick, and he warned us about judging one another while not being perfect ourselves. But these facts are conveniently overlooked in service of a new interpretation of the Christian tradition that better suits the conservative agenda. We all know that the extreme religious right is losing a little of its clout, but changing the Bible to be more "conservative" is absurd.

I'm not letting Jews off the hook, either, when it comes to twisting and politicizing something that should bring peace and unity. For some, unquestioning support of the Israeli government serves as a litmus test for Jewish people. I ain't buying it! I'm militant in my support of peace and cooking down militarism. There's defense, and then there's the insane policy of beating your plowshares into swords and acting threatened and victimized when you've got the biggest life-threatening shithammer in the world on your side.

I'm for taking an Armageddon break. I have to; I have little grandsons whose future I need to consider. In fact, I'm taking a small step back from magical thinking of all kinds: religion, astrology, New Age pseudosciences—and let me tell you, it's not easy. Like I said, my spiritual "rearing" in Utah—Hillbilly Israel, a hybrid modern-pioneer theme park with cheerful hymns, a few pervs per block, and some polygamist families scattered around to keep us guessing—had a profound impact on me. (As I say in my act, my family really stuck out in Utah: We had only the *one mother*!) But seriously, folks, I have some crackpot religious, messianic, paranoid tendencies in my blood. Add to that my hippie, Wiccan, radical feminist, multiple personalities, and the Kaballah razzmatazz, and I'm a gushing fountain of symbology from Scientology to Roseannethropology. But I've been making a little more room for things that work whether you believe in them or not and using plain old common sense to identify those things that almost everybody can agree are stubbornly true.

We're here on earth for a finite amount of time. Life can be good when people are kind to one another and try to work things out when there's conflict. Except for the fundamental belief in kindness (the Golden Rule), religion gets pretty complicated and calcified and can really create more division between people than we need in a crowded world with real problems that probably won't be prayed away. I think we need to live and let live, get over ourselves, and do away with the thinking that life is not enough for us as it simply unfolds every day. Why fixate on the stuff we can't prove, like the existence of prophets or messiahs or angels or devils? I don't think any of it makes a gorgeous sunset any more gorgeous, or the wine any more delicious, or the kids any cuter. Why can't we love and cherish what we *can* see and know? Can't we just start with the basics—appreciating life and helping to make it better for everybody—without insisting on the existence of some elusive deeper meaning?

This fresh outlook is part of my brilliant, new program of trying to lead what great spiritual masters and adepts from all disciplines and sects call a less-dumb-ass life. I'd like to provide you, free of charge, with a coping tool, as they call such things in "workshops" and support groups and the like. It's called Dynamic Laziness. And it's not easy for a recovering hyper–control freak with ADD and *tri*polar disorder to practice; you have no idea what an incredible struggle it is for me to leave things alone for a minute. Sometimes, for me, not throwing a tantrum is what running a marathon or swimming the English Channel must be like for others of a less-challenging emotional nature—a descriptive term I like a lot better than "completely crazy," which I've often been called. I've also been called a drama queen, an apt description for my behavior throughout much of my life—until I had an epiphany one day in the form of a simple, undramatic realization: Dynamic Laziness is my salvation.

Sure, panic and rage still felt natural and came in handy whenever I felt the need to generate a much larger reaction than was called for or would be helpful. But those emotions just weren't providing the warm, "fully engaged with life" kind of self-Tasering experience I'd come to expect from expressing them. Like losing interest in sex, the ambivalent afterglow was almost gone. Sure, there was the revulsion and fatigue and remorse. But instead of that "roll over and have a cigarette" feeling of satisfaction, it was more like I wanted to be put on a respirator and covered gently with a plus-size morphine patch. Getting too mad or freaked out really feels like work now, and uses up more of what's left of me than I need to be burning up with useless wear and tear. Now that I have embraced Dynamic Laziness, if I desperately feel compelled to make bile and blood and adrenaline gush through my arteries like torrents of churning, pressurized BS spurts from Glenn Beck's blowhole, I'll simply go for a walk/blog.

■

I've gotten in touch with my inner tired old Jewish woman. Like me, she's in her late fifties, and she really feels it—as they say, "It ain't the year, it's the mileage." Now, whenever smoldering anger or panic rises up inside me, the tired old Jewish woman within says, "For *this* you'll risk a heart attack?" In fact, the prospect of most any kind of physical or emotional exertion gets tossed on the cost-benefit scale these days. And usually, I think: *Anger, shmanger*—I'm getting too mature for that. And by *mature,* I mean tired and lazy.

I know I used to drive people around me a little crazy sometimes (which is like saying Stalin used to get grouchy and mess with people—an understatement, to say the least). In addition to tormenting my poor, witless husbands, I put a lot of unnecessary mileage on my ticker. Not good! And I know there were days when my children probably felt that living with the awful realization that I wasn't dead yet almost wasn't worth the effort they didn't put into looking for jobs. At times like that I decided that I needed to focus on trying to like them more often, too.

These insights come to me during meditation, when I sit quietly and let my churning thoughts drain out of me, like old bong water on Willie Nelson's tour bus or the fat at a Beverly Hills liposuction clinic. It's not easy to let go of these thoughts; they are always there, pushing me to do and achieve, reminding me that life is short, like Tom Cruise, that these nails aren't going to chew themselves, that the new tabloids are out today, possibly with women fatter than I am on the cover. It's so hard to sit still and do nothing while a suffering world calls out for my help to heal it, and then eat crab legs and hear God Herself speak to me through cheese and fulfill what's left of my grand destiny, and then watch forensics shows until my son comes home from school and gives me that special look, that mix of contempt and condescension that only a mother can recognize and bask in. It's a rich, full life. And it's time to enjoy it.

So beware of the two-headed monster of politics and religion. Listen to your inner compass. We all have an inner compass. Mine's right there next to my inner pie detector and my dashboard full of panic buttons. Seriously, we have some kind of hardwired internal voice that says, *Don't be a dumb-ass,* which I can often hear in there saying things like *Have another glass of wine!* and *I hate women who lose weight for a living and are skinny and rub everybody's face in it.* Heed that clarion call. Don't be a dumb-ass!

Moving from prescribed dogma to a truth-based approach to life has been a work in progress for me. That extra layer of religion that was lacquered on me as a kid wasn't easy to slough off—being a Jew *and* a Mormon was a full-time job. Navigating between those two monuments to rigid, patriarchal arm-twisting wasn't exactly like rowing my boat gently down the stream.

I used to think there was a world of difference between Jewish and Mormon belief systems, but the latter sure has done a lot of borrowing from its predecessor. In Judaism you're made to think you're betraying your people if you don't trudge dutifully along the road of persecution and guilt and suffering that's always in the rearview mirror and just around the bend for God's chosen people. Even the happy songs are in a minor key. Mormonism isn't much different. Both religions revere a prophet who trudged through the desert or the mountains with his people to some kind of promised land—it's Zion *this* and Hebron *that*, and a whole lot of energy goes into begetting. Let's face it: A lot of the heavy lifting involved in begetting is assigned to the women. The Hebrews were no strangers to polygamy, and there's an inordinate amount of emphasis on breeding in their faith—same with the Mormons, of course. In their case, it's extra strange because they believe God just had the one son, but the average old Mormon daddy can crank out as many as his wives can send down the chute.

Anyway, Judaism and Mormonism against the backdrop of 1950s and '60s Republican Utah was my crucible. With those two judgmental, busybody monoliths yelling in my face from down the centuries and up the street, I had to pull my head in like a turtle and strain to hear the inner voices that I figured were casually acquainted with "the real me." No wonder I needed a Greek chorus of multiple personalities to stand up to the legions of patriarchs, who, whether in sandals or cowboy boots, never tired of letting me know I needed to show plenty of respect for their odd doctrines, and that I definitely needed to know my place as a woman and stay in it. I guess they didn't know whom they were dealing with. I had three words for them and I shouted them over my shoulder as soon as I had a chance to get on up the road: "So long, suckers!"

Chapter 1

Chosen and Humbled

I knew at a young age that I loved being the center of attention, singing and dancing and making my family laugh and lifting their spirits—that way I could avoid having to talk to them almost completely. They were hairy and smelled like herring, garlic, and onions, and shrieked at one another in loud, shrill tones.

But they were a great audience, and to me that pretty much made up for the fact that I had to be around them all the time. I never really bonded with them, or with anyone on earth, really, until I had children of my own, who now wish I would just shut up and leave them alone. But I can't, not now, not after all I have been through.

Almost everyone in my family was musical and played an instrument and sang and loved to show off, so I was no stranger to it. During my brilliant and audacious performances, my family constantly remarked that they thought I sang like Shirley Temple, only way better and a lot more adorably, and that my dancing made hers look contrived and boring. I humbly accepted their assessments and believed them to be true.

After all, my own grandmother, Mary Bitnam, had left her town of Aborniki, Lithuania, to move to the United States after being accepted at the Salt Lake City Conservatory of Music, so she knew something about the arts! She played the mandolin and other stringed instruments and sang soprano. She performed at weddings and bar mitzvahs until she married her husband, Ben Davis, whose father was Utah's only kosher butcher.

She encouraged me to sing and dance and tell jokes every Friday night, Shabbat, in the windowsill of her living room after everyone had gorged on her brisket. She also talked about God all the time, and the importance of being honest and obedient to Him, so I figured that she was honest with me about my singing and dancing talents.

My family would laugh and clap, adoring everything that came out of my mouth and every move I made—every twirl, every note, every word I said. I was the first grandchild, niece, and daughter in my extended family, and therefore I was spoiled rotten until I became dissociative and narcissistic enough to imagine myself to be "special" as well as "chosen."

It did not occur to me at a young age that empty flattery is actually quite toxic and would one day be my complete downfall.

Each Friday night, I persisted in writing, producing, as well as directing my all-time favorite performer (myself) in one showstopping number after another. During my more than one-hour-long act, I did not consider it a *proper* performance unless I had laughed, danced, sung, and cried. "Sarah Bernhardt" was what my audience of family members proudly called me.

As the first granddaughter in a Jewish-American, first-generation, post-Holocaust Utah family typically does, I looked to show business as a way to move up the socioeconomic ladder and climb all the way out of Salt Lake City. Utah was a pretty weird place, and nowhere was weirder than my own family's apartment building, which housed survivors from Auschwitz and Bergen-Belsen who moved to the States after being sponsored by my grandparents and who were also part of my audience every Friday evening.

I once asked Mrs. Rose, one of my grandmother's tenants, what the numbers tattooed on her arm were for, and she told me that it was her phone number. My grandmother and Mrs. Rose would watch the Eichmann trial on television, and while they watched, I was told to stay out of the living room. I kept asking why I couldn't join them until one day, being a nosy and headstrong little girl, I barged in and saw the most graphic and disturbing images of bodies starved and heaped upon others, and from that point on I greatly feared human beings.

My grandmother tried to explain that I should always be "proud" of being hated for being a Jew. And I became so "proud" of being Jewish that I made it my mission to straighten God out by detailing what I felt were Her shortcomings in the many one-on-one conversations I had with Her in the mirror. If I hadn't had the refuge of my showbiz fantasies and my conversations with God to occupy me, who knows what more damage I could have done to myself and to others.

When I was between the ages of three and six, I always got the message from my family that I was the most talented star ever. Fueled by their praise that I was better and more talented than Ms. Shirley Temple herself, whom I watched on TV and idolized, I copied her every move, pressing my fingers into my cheeks in an attempt to create dimples and constantly begging my mom to curl my hair into ringlets. But after I lost all the adorable baby part of my baby fat and only had the fat part left, they all gleefully and fickly moved on to encouraging the show business aspirations of my younger, lighter, and perkier cousin, Debbie Aaron.

I became a has-been at age six. My family started to tell me then that if I really wanted to be a singer and dancer on old "Broad Way" someday, I needed to lose some weight. That really depressed me and made me eat more. Instead of just losing twenty pounds and solving my problems forever, I got fatter and fatter, and retreated deeper and deeper into my fantasies of stardom. The more I did so, the worse my neurosis grew. I knew that I was the most important person on earth, and yet it seemed that I was now alone in that knowledge. Was it possible that everyone around me failed to see the superhuman being who walked in their midst? Of course, they were all God's chosen, too, but I was not just *chosen,* I was also special! I couldn't be the only one to recognize the fact that I held the keys to the universe and had total control of all things in it, could I? Didn't that make me crazy?

I asked God, "Doesn't this just mean I am crazy, if no one believes that I am Your One True Messenger here on earth?"

And God spoke to me, like She always did, and She thus spaketh: "Fuck them, my child, if they cannot take a joke!"

I said, "But it's not a joke to me, Lord. I have vowed to do Your bidding and be Your servant in order to glorify myself so that I can then give You the credit at the awards shows! When all I want to do is to glorify Thy name and do Thy bidding, why hast Thou made that so damn hard for me? Shouldn't being the Messiah of mankind mean anything to people?"

"Fuck them, Roseanne, if they can't take a joke. Thus I have spoken and thus I am that I am. See ya!" Bored, God vanished, and left me there talking to myself again, trying to figure out how to fix the entire world alone.

I fantasized that I would one day graciously accept the deafening applause of my peers and the various awards they would practically force on me. From the stage and before all the cameras, I would humbly admonish the adoring crowd to quiet down just enough to hear me clearly gasp out my gratitude to God for allowing really dumb people like them the rare good taste to recognize a genius such as me. Eventually, all the accolades would become tedious, I reckoned, but ever the giver, I would bear up and go along with the program in order to inspire others to know that God might someday love them, too, if they would only love me enough.

Soon after I turned six, my mother and father moved us away from Bubbe Mary and closer to Mormon culture. I loved Mormon culture because there is a lot of singing and dancing in it. Happy songs not in minor keys! It was great at first. I still longed to sing and dance, despite the fact that my audience had moved on, so I signed up for lessons at Dorleen's Dance Studio. After I had taken only four classes, my parents told me they could not afford to pay the dollar a week for those lessons that I really wanted and prayed for every night.

During one dancing lesson, my friend's big brothers stood on the sidewalk outside, looking through the huge glass window, as they laughed and screamed, "Look at Tubby Roseanne dancing!" Humiliated, I told my parents, and my mom asked Dorleen to please put up a curtain to keep the boys from doing that to me, and she did.

But soon after, having thought things through clearly in her Mormon woman way, Dorleen told my parents she didn't want me to continue taking lessons from her, as I caused a "ruckus." My mom told me this when I was in my fifties, long after I had wasted all that time blaming my parents for being so cheap.

After Dorleen decided I was too much of a distraction, I would stand outside her studio at four o'clock each Wednesday with the boys, and peer through the curtainless window at my very tiny and slim neighborhood friends, as they shuffle-ball-changed their thin asses back and forth over the boards. My friend's brother told me that it was no fun to watch the girls if I wasn't in there anymore. He said he liked to laugh at the fat jiggling on my legs. So the boys stopped coming around, and when it was just me watching through the window, Dorleen put the curtain back up.

I vowed that they would one day envy me after I became a huge star, which I would do no matter what it took to get there—no matter what asshole I had to marry, and despite the fact that I could not scare up one dollar a week with all the talent I had. The talent of two Shirley Temples! I knew it was up to me to blaze a new trail for females like myself, the fat wallflowers who were emotionally bruised by the indifference of others. I pitied those who could not see how great I was. I would show them.

Because my mother wanted to assimilate more than anything else, she began to take me to church with our Mormon neighbors around this same time. My mother spoke in the Mormon church about how, at age two, I had fallen on my face and contracted Bell's palsy. Mom would talk about how she summoned the Mormon priests to pray for me, and how they "healed" my face by laying their hands on me. She would finish her talks by saying she wanted to become a Mormon and planned to do so one day soon. Then she would play the piano.

The Mormons loved her talks and they loved me. I sensed my imminent reinvention. I began to sing and dance and talk about being healed in front of another appreciative audience of people whom I couldn't stand to be around when I was not performing. But what the hell, it was stage time, and I have to admit that I loved the fact that they all seemed to talk to God all the time, too.

The main thing we young Utah Mormon girls cared about back then was the Lord, and the Lord's policies. Near the top of the Lord's policies was that the state of Utah was to be kept stone-cold sober, and therefore all decent Mormons were to vote NO on Proposition 3: to allow alcoholic beverages to be bought in bars.

The news on television told us repeatedly that the prophet of our church wanted us all to vote against that proposition. He said that if the gentiles (the Jews) had their way, our neighborhoods would become overrun with prostitutes and criminals.

In addition to obeying the Lord's wishes, we young girls busied our minds with the homemaking arts so that we one day could trap a man and get him to do exactly as we wanted. The intense programming about finding a husband and having babies grossed me out terribly, but I knew I had to act like it was the greatest thing going because if I didn't I would have even less to talk about with these girls I was stuck being around. They all loved to sing and dance, too, and once a year, each little Mormon church would put on its own "road show," a wonderfully fun little hour and a half of performing all over the city in other Mormon churches.

My mother tried like hell to fit in with the dominant culture, like Jewish people have done for years and have still never done right! She played the piano for the road shows and tried to insist that I be a part of them, too. I tried to fit in with the Mormon girls but always failed in the end. I think they felt sorry for me, not being able to cut it in the boy-meets-girl love story that they were all living, what with the being fat, dark, and having no ass thing, and mostly thinking of myself as too "special" to be subservient to men. I remember how excited everyone was when we finally got Barbie dolls, which everyone really wanted because then they could start dating in their minds, which led to planning weddings, which led to having babies, the most fun of all dolls.

Had I not started talking to God at a really young age I would have been incredibly lonely. And because God was my best and only friend, I felt protective of Her. I was able to clearly see for myself that people did not really mind their godly p's and q's. They said God could see everything we thought and did, but then they would do a whole bunch of things they knew God didn't want them to do and then lie about doing them, as if God couldn't see through that bullshit!

They thought they could hide from God and from people who *saw* them hiding from God, as if they were invisible—like ghouls, I thought—as if God couldn't see for Herself what hypocritical assholes they were. For me, who *actually* knew God and talked to Her personally every single day of my life, this was just further proof that I was *different* as well as *special* and *chosen.*

I always asked other kids if they talked to God, too, so that I could figure out just how different, special, and chosen I indeed was. They always said that they talked to God to ask Him to give them stuff or to forgive them for things they were caught doing. Nobody conversed with God to figure out how to save the world with Her (His) help like I did.

When I asked if God answered when they talked to Her (Him) no two answers were ever the same. This is where it started getting weird. Some of them said, "Well, He will in the fullness of time," and some said, "He's tellin' me not to worry about getting even with my grandpa, 'cause the Lord punishes sinners and they go straight to hell for all eternity." Or "What are you talkin' about? You mean, like tellin' me to vote against liquor by the drink or somethin'?"

"Oh, just forget it," I would finally say, confirming that I was different and chosen and special, just as I had suspected.

My mother would have joined the church in a second if not for her mother and my father. Although my father was basically a socialist and an atheist, he still insisted that we remain Jewish. My dad would always say he didn't believe in God, that God was just a concept that weak people needed. When asked if the Jews were weak people, he would always say the same thing: "The Jews survived Hitler, so no, they are not weak."

He refused to let us have Christmas, either. He told me the

reason we didn't celebrate was because "Santa is an anti-Semite." I prayed to God that Santa would bring me a Barbie doll even though I was a Jew. One Christmas, the entire community of our Mormon neighbors brought us bags and bags of toys and food, and a Christmas wreath, so that we could be "embraced" and "included" at that special time of the year. I loved it because I got a Barbie doll! I immediately made her into a spy who parachutes behind enemy lines to save the Jews in Germany. I did this by dropping her out of the windows with a piece of cloth tied around her neck.

When playing Barbie dolls with the other Mormon girls, I would get so bored with the inevitable dating and wedding-planning story lines that were the subject of every playdate that I would say, "Why don't we play a game where Barbie parachutes behind enemy lines to save the Jews?" The Mormon girls would try to be nice while ignoring me and say, "You have to be Ken." I hated being Ken, because all Ken could ever say was, "When will we be having our wonderful wedding, Barbie dear?" I tried to give Ken some balls by having him say, "Barbie, why don't you and I parachute behind enemy lines and save some Jews from the Nazis before our wedding?" But the Mormon girls would just ignore Ken, and emasculate him by telling me to shut up. There was really nothing for Ken or for me to do or say after that, and I would just go back home to my Torah and my books about the Holocaust and the Nazis. Or I would walk back to my grandmother's apartment (about two miles away), and we would play gin rummy and talk about God and the Bible.

When we girls played "house" in the neighborhood, I liked to play the part of the mother; if we played "school," I wanted to be the teacher; if we played "hospital," I wanted to be the nurse. I never wanted to be the daughter, the student, or the patient. Those parts were so boring. You didn't get to really boss people around, and I loved to do that because I knew I had all the answers—and if I didn't, well, my buddy God sure did, and I could get them out of Her as needed.

Everyone said I was too bossy and they didn't like to play with me. Their fat, nosy moms would tell mine that I needed to "get along" better with others. So, of course, my mom would make me crawl across the street and beg to play "paper dolls" or "babies" with the other little girls. Playing the daughter was the only role I was allowed after I had been banished for bossiness and had to beg my way back into their circle. Whichever girl was taking a turn playing the mother would always hold the baby doll and say: "Idn't our baybee just beootieful? She's thee most beootieful baby in the whole wide world, idn't she?"

And then I would have to chime in, "Oh yes, she is just the most beautiful baby there is." I would play along at first, until everything was going smoothly, and then I had to screw it all up by asking, "Mother, could I ask you a question?"

The mother would correct me by saying, "You mean 'Mother, *may* I ask you a question?'"

I would reply, "Yes, sorry, Mother. May I ask you a question?"

"Yes, Sister" (what all mothers call their daughters in Utah), "you may."

"Mother, do we believe in God?"

"Of course we do! God is the Lord and the Lord hath made us this beootieful baybee daughter right here. Now let's dress her up for church. She needs to have her nice warm bath and get on her pretty dress, don't you, honeybaby?"

I would try to sneak in another question: "Mother, does our Heavenly Father talk to us?"

She would then put the lid on the conversation: "Will you please fix a bath for your little sister, and no talking, please?" I would have to go over and pretend to fill up the sink with water. That was so not fun. I would just have to stand there and go "SHHHHHHHISH-HHHH" and pantomime running my hands through it.

Out of all the available futures that I was encouraged to try (teacher, nurse, or housewife), I liked being a housewife the best. I never personally knew any teachers or nurses, but I did know housewives, and I loved that they sat around all day talking. But that, of course, left me with a large existentialist problem: How the heck was I going to get a guy to like me enough to support me for the rest of my life, and adore me enough to build a suburban Taj Mahal for me to live in, when all they did was push me down and call me a fat slob? I was not beautiful, obedient, or thin, as rich men require. Therein lay, and still lies, the veritable rub. As my boyfriend, Johnny, says, "Doll, you're destined for poor guys, because even if you got a rich guy, you'd have to do what he told you to do, when he wanted you to do it, at least part of the time, and trust me, that IS NOT FOR YOU!" He's so right, of course; I realize that now. Having more money than the guy is the way to go for the gal on the go!

I was so lonely looking for peers as a kid, not being able to talk about talking to God with anyone but God Herself. She was the only one who got my sense of humor. I asked her why She had dumped me on a planet with all of these human beings? I knew I was not one of them; rather I was immortal, a goddess myself, and why oh why was I surrounded by idiots?

She said, "Because it's important to Me that you learn to read books! I have hidden great stuff in them for you to find out about Me! Every time you find another of My messages to you in a book, I will come to you and we will discuss it." In the oldest of our holy books, She is called "the Sabbath Queen," "the Shekkinah," "the Bride of God," and yet, I was greatly disturbed that this fact was known by almost no Jew. She Herself told me that I would one day write about Her, and set the record straight!

In order to make sure that we kept up with our Hebrew and Judaic lessons even though we had moved far away from her, Bubbe Mary took it upon herself to invite us over for hotcakes before going to Sunday school at Congregation Montefiore. I did enjoy talking to the Jews about God in Cheder class every Sunday morning, and then talking to Mormons about Her at their church on Sunday afternoon. But I never met other people in either religion who conversed with God like I did.

After Bubbe got her grandchildren back into the Jewish fold, Mama decided to teach my Sunday school class at synagogue in order to be able to afford to send me there. The Mormons charged 10 percent off the top to go to their church, so Mama figured the Jews were offering the better bargain, I guess. Mama was not quite the center of attention at synagogue as she had been in the Mormon church, but the first thing she did as Sunday school teacher was to write and direct a musical for Purim. It was the story of Esther, and Mama allowed me to play the part of King Ahasuerus, who saved the Jewish people. It was the singular happiest time in my childhood. It was good to be the king, although I knew that it would have been much better to be the queen. The king gets to make the final edicts, but only after his wife tells him what to say, as we all know. Anyway, I killed, and had there been an Oscar for youthful performances in a Sunday school play, I would have won it.

Of course, I could never keep my mouth shut or stay out of trouble even then, due to my Tourette's syndrome. I asked the rabbi why we Jews didn't accept Jesus as our savior, and that pretty much put a damper on the whole back-to-synagogue experience. The rabbi did not even want to hear the word *Jesus,* and freaked out, calling my mother in to ask her where I heard such things. (Sometime in the early '70s, things changed, and a Jewish kid could safely mention the guy's name around a rabbi and receive an almost intelligent answer in response.)

Then I asked my Mormon bishop if I could ask him some questions about the Book of Mormon, which, of course, I had read cover to cover more than once. I said, "So, the Native Americans are the new Jews then?" And he told me, "Those were the old Jews of the *Old* Testament. The saints are now the new Jews, and Salt Lake City is the city of Zion. And here in Zion, all of you 'Jews' are 'gentiles.'" I remember thinking, I am a Jew and a gentile, therefore I am chosen, special, different, and *saved*!

I knew that none of the people around me knew God as well as I did. They pretended to *believe*, which I knew was just another way of lying. I knew that God talked to me and I answered Her, and that She listened to me and answered me back—not in my mind, like a lot of crazies, but right there in front of me in the mirror. She told me that would be the way we would communicate for a while, and it was kosher for me to see myself in Her, as I was made in Her image anyway. She would say to me, "Roseanne, let's Me and you figure out a way to help this world be a better place."

Looking back, I cannot believe how brazen I was as a young girl to actually reply, "Your books tell children to pray, and that You will answer their prayers. But many do pray and you *don't* answer their prayers. Now, how can You tell children that You hear their prayers, when You are not lifting a finger to stop the bad things?"

God answered, "I do not have fingers, Roseanne. I am an idea in people's heads only! You guys have the power to make good things happen. You must tell kids out there that they have four fingers to help them get things done, and one thumb to help the four fingers do it. None of my other animals were given that special tool—use it!"

I fell asleep thinking about the good that one person can do. The Lord was my shepherd, and I did not fear death, because I had the magic words. Not the ones every other child I knew said at bedtime—"Now I lay me down to sleep, I pray the Lord my soul to keep. If I should die before I wake, I pray the Lord my soul to take" (ghouls!), but these magic words instead: "Good night, God/Mother."

It was She who came up with the idea that I would become a storyteller in my old age. I discussed with Her for decades what that story would say, how we would tell it.

Chapter 2

Borderline, Bipolar, Paranoid, Obsessive-Compulsive, Jewish, and Mormon

I trusted my intuition and my feelings—until I started seeing a headshrinker at age eight because my intense mental labors to save the world included forgetting what time it was and peeing my pants in school a lot. I should never have been forced to mix with gen pop, as I was too "out there." I had some pretty paralyzing fears, one of which was that something terrible would happen to my parents while they were out on their nightly walk. Singing in my room along with James Brown records (Mr. Brown had replaced Ms. Temple in my fantasies as the Idol that I most wanted to emulate by age eight) was one of the only manageable antidotes to controlling my escalating panic attacks.

I began to work hard to attempt to re-create his dance steps, his voice, and his soulful attitude, even though I knew I was not a black male Christian, I wanted to be.

I also found that doing everything five times was an effective way of handling stress. While my parents were getting ready to leave, I would have the compulsion to ask them five times when they would return. That would be exhausting because they would answer "About an hour" once or twice, and around the third time I asked, they would tell me "Never mind" or "Stop asking the same question over and over," not understanding that I had to do things five times or I would be powerless to prevent the horrific tragedy that could befall all who ignored the Five Rule. My heart would pound in my ears about the fourth time I asked and they refused to answer, so I would open the door as they walked toward the corner and yell it at them again. Sometimes they would say, "We will be right back!" and then I could relax. However, "Get back in there and shut up and close the door!" did not rightly count as one of the five required answers, so I would have to keep asking the question as they rounded the corner and disappeared out of sight.

If they answered five times, I would meld with James Brown's records until they returned: I would go to my room, scarf tied around my neck and sunglasses tilted at a jaunty angle, and sing for about ten minutes over the scratchy records. If the five answers had been mined out of the parents, I could thereafter move on to the next step in my fantasy, talking into my hairbrush microphone, as I interviewed myself in the mirror as Johnny Carson, whom I imitated and idolized. I (as Johnny Carson) would ask myself: "Well, Miss Barr" (he always called me that in my fantasies; but in real life, when I was later a guest on his show, he called me "dear"), "tell the folks at home how you learned to sing, dance, tell jokes, and act so damn well, won't you please?"

If the Five Rule had not been followed, after a few minutes of the James Brown sing-along, I would end up running downstairs, plugging in the iron, and sitting inside the bathroom with the door locked, holding the iron in front of me for protection from the intruders who had killed my parents and would next come in the house and kill me if I didn't have a hot iron as a weapon to keep them from doing so. When my parents inevitably returned from their walk, whether I had received five answers or not, it never occurred to me that I was mistaken in any way; I just thought the inevitable had been delayed till another time. I always had morbid fears, as far back as I could remember.

My fears would paralyze me, and sometimes I would just stand there looking stupid and pee my pants. It was so humiliating.

When they made me start seeing the school shrink about all the pants-peeing stuff, the shrink said my obsessive fears were probably the guilt I had for always wishing that my parents would get hit by a car or killed on their nightly walks. I said I did not want that to happen at all, and that is what I was so afraid *would* happen. She told me that Freud said, "Where there is a fear, there is also a wish," and so I was actually wishing for my parents to be killed! An extra layer of nuts was added to my crazy salad by that goddamn shrink. So, on top of the fear that my parents would be killed, I then had to think that it would be all my fault for fearing/wishing it so! But my parents were never killed by anyone on their nightly walks, thank God! Had they been killed, I would have even more emotional problems than I have as a result of their *not* being killed on their nightly walk.

I admit now that the thought of them getting killed appealed to me a tad because I thought that if I were grief-stricken enough, I might be unable to eat anything, and therefore get thin and become a star. I was screwed too tight for my own good. Falling into the deep end was a comfortably familiar act for me.

Later on, my condition had a name, some obsessive-compulsive disorder Tourette's–type thing about being stuck in a loop of weird thoughts, like many Jewish people are, especially those born and raised in Utah. I had incredible happiness with the magical thinking, and misery with reality, so I hardly bothered with it at all.

At one time, as a young mother, I started to think that I could lose weight and subsequently perform in public by combining my eating disorder with my obsession for doing everything five times. By devising and following a very simple formula that I had worked out over several hundred failed attempts at successful dieting, I would diet my way to stardom and happiness this way: I could never cheat, not even once, and I had to walk, dance, exercise for five hours a day. My menu consisted of one German chocolate sweet roll for breakfast, with black coffee, and one scoop of Dairy Queen ice cream on a regular cone for lunch, and a bowl of lettuce with lemon juice for dinner (five items at five hundred calories). I also smoked five thousand cigarettes a day, but I somehow managed to lose 122 pounds and to keep it off for several years.

I exchanged my compulsion for overeating for a new compulsion of seeking the attention and admiration of men for being thin. I found that when I was thin, men thought I was witty instead of loud, and adorable instead of a bitch. After losing the weight, I really wanted to get out there and become a famous star. I still believed that I was a good singer and dancer, but it was starting to become apparent to me that the real talent I had was in being funny. If I hadn't been thin when I first stepped on a comedy stage, all the fame and fortune which allowed me to buy my own nut farm in Hawaii and drive all over it in my fabulous Kawasaki Mule with my little grandsons never would have happened. We couldn't communicate with turkeys by gobbling over and over, oinking at pigs, meowing at wild cats, harvesting coffee beans, building domes out of macadamia nuts, and growing majestic white pineapple, and believe me, I wouldn't have missed all that for the world! (Note to Kawasaki: Yes, I would appreciate a new, fabulous Kawasaki Mule when my current fabulous Kawasaki Mule wears out!)

Chapter 3

Antisocial or Allergic?

I used to think I was antisocial, but it turns out that I was just allergic.

Note to women: Perfume is something you don for your boyfriend to discover as he disrobes you and draws you near. It is a very intimate thing and not to be used as a way to biologically poison an entire area.

I hate women who wear too much perfume. I think PETA should adopt it as one of their causes. Come to think of it, so should the chemtrail conspiracy folks.

Many of us have a strong negative reaction to perfume. It causes instant migraine headaches in people who are allergic to it, as I am, along with my two sisters, my daughter, and my grandson. I have developed a bit of an immunity over the years, but anything syrupy, flowery, or with a slight aluminum/metal smell makes my head pound like a drum. When I see a woman who is over age sixty approaching, I steer clear of her, particularly if she's wearing a matchy-matchy outfit. Invariably, her scent will be too aggressive for my sensitive nasal apparatus. If I see one of these types approaching the elevator I am standing in, I will panic and hold my nose and vacate like the plague is coming at me. I always say something as I depart, too, because I consider it a kind of moral obligation to let these women know that they are making offensive choices. I usually mutter: "Good God, did you have to soak in that cheap cologne to cover up your heinous personal odor or what?" as I leave.

So much about women infuriates me, but nothing as strongly as the grotesque stinking up of oneself by one's own goddamned hand at the behest of Madison Avenue's conspiracy in feminine mind control. Call me crazy, and say I smoke too much medical marijuana and have gone paranoid if you must, but if Madison Avenue can get all these skanky celebs to convince women that covering themselves in stink water makes them sexy and desirable, then they can pretty much control everything that women do and say and think.

Young girls in cheap shoes and short dresses on dates are terrible offenders as well. I got so mad last night at dinner—a good two tables away from the perfumed predator who was causing my temples to pound at ten yards! Keep your stink within a reasonable radius, for Christ's sake! I wanted to stand up in the restaurant and approach the girl and throw my glass of water in her face and tell her that she stunk so badly that I was getting ready to faint. Instead, I ordered another glass of ruby port to calm my fraying nerves and developing headache.

I have nearly attacked many unconscious gay men and overly made-up Jewish women with overly large buttocks balanced on six-inch heels at better stores everywhere who approach me and try to spray fragrance on me when I'm shopping. I have yelled, "I do not want to smell like Britney Spears, okay?" or "Musk scent is taken from the whale's asshole—wake up, idiot!" or something to that effect when out trying to help our economy by innocently perusing handbags and shoe sales, my shopping passion. If they assault and spray/mark me from the side or behind, I must run to the lav and wash, wash, wash it off, and then run to the nearest bar and drink, drink, drink away the headache (a cure I devised while quite young).

As a child, I used to immediately see double and get the urge to vomit whenever I smelled my grandmother getting ready for Saturday synagogue. The rest of the time I loved being around her, unperfumed at her home, where she taught me how to cheat at gin rummy, fixed me snacks featuring mayo, and tried to get me hooked on *Perry Mason* reruns. While she was entranced in *Perry Mason*, I would gleefully sneak into her bedroom and snoop through all her things. She always had green Doublemint gum in her purse, which she kept in the third drawer of her bureau. I would yell, "Can I get some gum out of your purse?"

She would yell back, "Vut?" and I would ask again. She would say, "Go ahid, but leaf mine uzzer tings alone in dere."

"Okay," I would yell again.

"Huddy up and come out heuh, ve ard gittink veady fur da trial now!"

"Coming!" I would yell again as I stuck four pieces of gum in my mouth and snapped up the purse, covered it back up with the linens, and closed the drawer. I learned early on, while gleefully snooping through her stuff, to avoid her perfumes because as soon as I touched them, I would get a bad headache, and then I would go lie down on the floor of her closet, because it was dark and cool in there, and just ten minutes of that would alleviate the pulsing in my temples.

Once when lying in her closet recovering from the fragrance, I found homemade wine in a jar next to the box containing my dead grandpa's old shoes. I began to take little nips of it, and found it to be simply dee-lish. It actually helped with the headaches caused by smelling the fragrances on her vanity! Another few minutes would pass, and then she would yell for me: "Shana!" (This is one of my Hebrew names and what she called me.) Off I would run to hear her explain how Perry Mason really mattered almost as much as the Law of Moses.

Later, around age eight, when I could finally read, I more closely examined the bottles that she kept on her vanity table for synagogue, turned over on her gloved index finger and then dabbed behind her ears and wrists before grabbing her matching purse and hat. I saw that the stuff was called "toilet water." I was dumbfounded. I remember thinking, Who in their right mind would dab water from the toilet on themselves after they had just bathed and put on clean clothes? It was just one more thing about the world that made no sense at all! I figured then that dousing yourself with toilet water must be pleasing to God in some way, and the resulting migraine seemed to fit in with the whole "God is wrathful" thing that Rabbi Cardin was fond of pushing weekend after weekend.

Yom Kippur was actually my favorite Jewish holiday. I liked it, I figure now, because no perfume was worn in synagogue on this most High Holy Day, because no vulgar display of wealth or status was allowed, so that the community could enjoy a day of mourning to the fullest. Rabbi Cardin explained that by getting women to wear signs of wealth and status, Satan was encouraging them to covet their neighbor's wealth, thereby tempting the Evil Eye. As everybody in the know knows, you do not want to activate the Evil Eye of a bunch of Jewish women if you fear the shame of hell at all! Of course, on all the other days of the year, coveting wealth and tempting the Evil Eye were all but ignored. But on this one day, we could wipe out a year's worth of bad karma from having done those things, so there was no perfuming and no fucking around at all!

No one wore perfume to services on Yom Kippur, so it became the most tolerable Jewish holiday. There was no headache, but there was the usual weeping, gnashing of teeth, beating on the breast, and tearing the clothing over your heart kind of holiday celebration of groveling and begging God to stop bothering the Jewish people. All of the holidays were about who killed our people, when and where, and what kind of food goes with each of those massacres. I hated the whole religious kit and caboodle at such a young age, and still often wonder where the line of demarcation is between suffering from regular mental illness and just being Jewish.

But, truth be told, they always served hotcakes to break the fast afterward, and no migraine or jealous Jehovah could hope to ever dissuade me from my appreciation and dedication to those! Free pancakes are worth everything to me to this day, and are the final irrefutable proof that there is a God indeed, and that She is just! (The only good part of getting old, by the way, is the half-off offer of pancakes to seniors from the International House of Pancakes.) I see now that as a girl, in many ways, I mistakenly confused God's doings for my own allergic reactions. Whoa! Sorry about that! Now I realize that God is good and has nothing to do with suffering or with humanity at all in any way. She lives inside of the wind and the trees, especially the cacao tree (chocolate), and doesn't really feel all that flattered when people insist on tormenting themselves and others to impress Her.

The Shabbat headaches began to show up daily around the time that my mother started working at the Fort Douglas PX in Salt Lake City. There she would spray every kind of scent in the world on herself on her breaks. She was able to buy many things at a great discount as an employee there, and most of the things she bought were perfume and scarves and lipsticks to wear to work, and some household items to help me keep a clean and proper house as her homemaking protégée, since I was the oldest daughter. Before my mother had to get a job, she just smelled nice like Pine Sol and my dad's Old Gold unfiltered cigarettes that he smoked sixty of per day.

When Mama went to work, all hell began to break loose at our house. I had to pick up all the slack, cooking and cleaning and beating Mama's kids for her, as well as waiting on my dad in her place. My mother accused me of faking the headaches I would get when she came home after work smelling of Tabu/Jungle Gardenia/Evening in Paris to get out of washing the dishes. The nose knows, though, and throughout the entire process of making the conscious connection between migraines, scent allergies, and overly sweetened wine, I have learned to classify people on smell alone. Here is a list I compiled for your reading pleasure:

- **Gay males** who show too much of their chests also overdouse themselves with expensive stink water. I avoid sharing air space with them, too, as I have had to learn the hard way how to protect myself.
- Almost invariably, for some reason, the **overweight person** is a huge offender, even though dressed in the muumuu or bowling shirt and sweatpants, they still manage to make up for looking bad by trying to smell good and are therefore a huge nuisance.
- In fact, the only people who do not reek of perfumery are **lesbians,** ever the proverbial canary in the cultural mine. In San Francisco, these right-on women actually add this to the bottom of the various flyers they pass out announcing the newest gathering of conspiracy theory speech events; "THIS IS A FRAGRANCE-FREE EVENT." Though I adore lesbians, unfortunately, they all seem to smell of coconut

products, which make me itchy, though not quite migrainous.

- **Lesbian rabbis,** though, seem to smell much like their straight male counterparts, of strong, fried onions, and Right Guard Spray Deodorant, which is just plain off-putting, though nontoxic.
- **Little children and early teens** smell the best to me. Of course, that is if they have not shit their pants, and have showered after gym class. This, of course, is rare, as any mother of an infant or preteen knows.
- Attending Hollywood functions makes me nauseous not only due to the grotesque displays of vulgar wealth that tempt me to cast the Evil Eye, but also due to the fact that there is no greater offender to those with olfactory allergies than that of the **Hollywood publicist,** whose overdependence on perfumes in order to disguise the stale cigarettes and nervous sweat of manic-depressive desperation is unparalleled in offensiveness in the civilized world.
- Also, **makeup artists** of either sex are deadly. I must bring my own (Shannone) with me to gigs and photo shoots, because most makeup artists in Hollywood really pour it on and stink to high heaven. Plus, their incessant name-dropping and gossiping about young stars with three names, none of whom I have ever heard, is a bore. Although not quite as bad as when they are New Age and talk Oprahtic about angels and positive thinking and all that bullshit.

I used to think I avoided the above types because I was prejudiced and neurotic, but I have since accepted that all of that was just me overly second-guessing and judging myself. I was actually just allergic.

- Lest I be accused of leaving **myself** out, let me say that honestly I know that I smell like the proverbial old, Jewish, Lefty Granny—like pee, sardines, and garlic. My boyfriend is at home with my smells. Perhaps that is because he is old and Serbian. Some, perhaps all, **older male Serbs** smell like leather, paprika, and pancake syrup, which just happens to be a huge turn-on for me, so it works out well for us both.

Chapter 4

The Curse of the Cute Cousin

I had longed to star in commercials since I was a little girl on the stage. They always seemed to me to be the best thing on television. Frequently funny or accompanied by catchy little jingles, they depicted people who seemed so happy—unless they had indigestion or constipation or a pounding headache, which was illustrated by an animated hammer hitting a drawing of a cerebral cortex. To this day, the commercials are what I remember best of watching television as a child (besides the Eichmann trial, *The Ed Sullivan Show,* and Jackie Gleason's shows). I loved that Ed and Jackie did their shows' commercials themselves!

So I was overcome with jealousy when my cousin Debbie and her brother, David, were cast in a Dr. Ross dog food commercial in the early '60s. I never quite got over it, either.

Their mother was a natural blonde with dimples, and David and Debbie had dimples, too. They were adorable because they didn't look Jewish at all. David and Debbie lived on the east side of town because their dad was in Formica counter sales. My dad sold crucifixes and 3-D pictures of Christ door-to-door to Mexicans on welfare, so we lived on the west side. The Aarons were everything my side of the family wasn't. They were the perfect, modern, assimilated Jewish family.

Debbie sang and danced and impersonated Shirley Temple like I did, but she was thin and bubbly and I was fat and morose, so you do the math. David and Debbie always got to find the *afikomen* (the special matzoh, wrapped in linen and hidden for kids to find and then use to extract ransom money from the adult who led the service) *every* Passover, too, because their grandfather, Uncle Ben, always led the Seder every year, and he shamelessly let them do it. I always hated him secretly for that, too. It was horribly unfair, since my grandmother did all the preparation and the cooking and the buying of every single piece of the whole Passover affair, and she had seven grandchildren of her own who deserved a chance to find the goddamn *afikomen,* too! I seemed to be the only person who was ever upset about this.

My own mother said, "It is just something nice we let Uncle Ben do every year." And I asked, "Well, how come no one does anything nice for Bubbe Mary? She does all the work!" I was actually thinking more of myself and my jealousy of Debbie than I was about the division of labor in my family, but my mother, ever the patriarchal apologist, said, "We do nice things for men because they lead the services!" as if I was slow-witted regarding everything that life is really about. I had to sit there year after year and watch David and Debbie get the fifty cents, and it burned me up.

I vowed that I would do anything to get my crack at starring in a television commercial someday, including developing some form of talent to make people pay even brief attention to me. That talent shit is the real hard part of the whole thing. Although it really doesn't seem to matter—anyone can sing and dance to a drum machine and recite ridiculous lyrics about how being sexy matters more than anything on earth except money. I am now convinced that talent is secondary to distribution in show business.

When I used to sit in front of the television set watching Miss Dinah Shore in her sparkling gowns sing about the glories of Chevrolet, I was so in awe of her tiny waist. I remember thinking that she probably had to squeeze into several girdles to look that thin. It never occurred to me as a child that some women just have tiny waists! All the women in my family were bumpy around the middle and would force their flesh inside restricting boned contraptions. My grandmother told me that a good corset is not only the foundation for making a waist but the foundation of good posture needed for musicality itself. The "cors-a-let" that she wore when dressed up squeezed her fat out of her middle, down into her butt, and up into her back. But the creation of a waist made her a more confident woman, so who was I to doubt her?

I remember hating Miss Shore's singing because vibrato reminds me of howling cats. But I knew that this was the "talent" she had to trade on in order to be afforded the great privilege of selling things for big companies. So I used my talent to write two hundred and sixty excellent jokes and one-liners for my act, got "discovered," and then my dreams came true—I was chosen to do a Pizza Hut commercial, which went on to win every single award that advertising offers, including the Cleo, the veritable Peabody of commercials and commercialism, and I knew I had arrived. Right after that ad, I got a job as "Mrs. Ralphs" for Ralphs food stores in California.

The many men and women who wrote the commercials for the average housewife (played by me) about the transcendental Ralphs Shopping Experience told me that my "input" was welcome. And I was thrilled to give it; I could say whatever I wanted to say and rewrite the commercials to make them more comical—

and do it for free without credit. I now understand that means "appropriating uncompensated intellectual property." I learned this too late, when later I could afford some big-time Hollywood lawyers. The hours and hours of enjoyment I gleaned from the hours and hours of drinking and stewing in my own juices after hearing that the "input" I had freely offered had won Cleo awards and made money for others, and that I had not even been included, thanked, or even courteously notified that something I wrote got somebody I met once a pretty nice home, were so worth it. I was unable to keep my big mouth shut, however, and was soon fired when it became all too apparent to the people at the top that Mrs. Ralphs was a loud, lefty feminist and not a liberal career woman.

Similarly, after mutilating the National Anthem, the sponsorships I had landed for a children's cartoon and line of toys were revoked. I was called to New York and told to my face by Dennis Somebody, as head of the ABC Saturday morning children's programming, that as a marine he was personally offended at my rendition of the Anthem, and was canceling my cartoon, and was replacing it with the Teenage Mutant Ninja Turtles. I destroyed my own dream with my big mouth and my lack of respect for authority and decency. I have learned my lesson. I would like another chance to sell a product on TV, but the truth is that I probably cannot get any endorsement deals or my own commercial, ever, because everyone is afraid that I will not be able to control shooting off my big mouth, or perhaps I'll start too high again (one way or another) and proceed to ruin another sacred tune on television. They're probably right, because this comedian thing is sort of a spiritual Tourette's syndrome, seriously! However, incurable optimist that I am, I still have a feeling that I can make millions starring in "before" ads for weight-loss products and Prozac, and "after" ads for Depend adult diapers.

Chapter 5

A Tale of Two Bubbes

Almost every word of the following story is true, except one or two things.

My two grandmothers, or *bubbes,* as we in the Jew trade call them—my mom's mom, Mary Davis (formerly Bitnam-Davidovitz) and Fanny Barr (formerly Katz-Borisofsky), my dad's—were way larger than life; they both knew it and so did everybody around them. They impressed and affected me in ways I still recognize and rediscover to this day. I still see them in my mind's eye, watching me from the wings in my fleeting roles as everything from hippie hitchhiker to Bel Air benefactress, from tradition-bound matriarch (sort of) to rebel at the barricades. No wonder I've been called the Queen of the Mixed Message by lots of people in my life. (Mixed message? Hey, I'm just passing it along; don't shoot the messenger.) They, along with my mother, all very different types of Jewish women, lived in Salt Lake City, Utah, and formed the kaleidoscope of my early spiritual training, and also my feminism.

My allergy to ambergris (a perfume ingredient) colored my entire worldview, so Yom Kippur was the only tolerable, migraine headache–free childhood Jewish holiday for me. Most Jews in the world have obviously been similarly imprinted by an allergy to whale vomit (ambergris), or something like it, because Yom Kippur is the one and only day that most of the world's chosen people attend synagogue. Most of us share not just weird allergies, or the unceasing craving for carbohydrates, but the fear that not repenting for the things we did the other 364 days of the year will really come back to kick our ass if we omit groveling for God's forgiveness on Yom Kippur. That's our holy "get out of jail free" card. Jews are so brainwashed that even though the majority of us are closet atheists, we wouldn't think of not getting together to kiss God's probably nonexistent ass on the High Holy Days.

According to Bubbe Mary, my Orthodox Jewish grandmother, Simchat Torah, *not* Yom Kippur, is the most important Jewish holiday, because it's the day Moses came down from the mountain with "the Law." She loved the Law and discussed it with me all the time. Whether it was the Laws of Moses, which, of course, had to be obeyed, even though they were intolerable or ridiculous and incoherent, or the law of averages—she clearly cheated in order to win every single hand of gin rummy that I ever played with her. Her interest in keeping certain laws and cheating others included an immense admiration for the "practice" of law by one Perry Mason, America's supreme TV lawyer back in the pre–Judge Judy days. If Bubbe had only lived to see the day when Judge Judy, a feisty, female, gavel-wielding Member of the Tribe, unseated the non-Jewish Oprah Winfrey as the queen of daytime TV's ratings, she would have died of JOY! Bubbe Mary was quite a virulent anti-non-Semite.

Born of elite, Lithuanian, Jewish parents, Bubbe Mary classified everything into two groups, Jewish and Goyische. Many Jews, including Bubbe Fanny, fell under her "Goyische" listing. Bubbe Mary was the "Lady Chairman" of the Talmud Torah Committee, whose sacred task it was to make sure each child at synagogue knew about Simchat Torah. In order to do this mission justice and represent properly for Moses, she "conducted herself like a lady," and coordinated and designed gorgeous ensembles that she sewed herself. Bubbe Mary was an expert seamstress, and that ability had brought her to America, where she was hired for work in a sweatshop at age sixteen, and promptly enrolled herself at the Salt Lake City Conservatory of Music as well. She sang Yiddish songs and Rudy Vallée songs, played the ukulele and the mandolin, and entertained at bar mitzvahs in her spare time before she became an old woman whose friends died before she did.

She applied a fraction of these skills in order to look fantastic, while passing out the traditional Hershey's milk chocolate candy bars to the children on their way out the door after Simchat Torah services at Congregation Montefiore, the Sephardic synagogue we attended. She explained to me that the chocolate bars were not only Kosher and ordained by Heaven and the Rabbinical Council of America, but were also given to us in order to help us make the symbolic connection in our young minds to the sweetness of the Law. So, in other words, the sweetness of Moses receiving the tablets from God Almighty was synonymous with receiving an entire large bar of milk chocolate from Bubbe's white-gloved hand, and huffing it by oneself, unshared with other siblings or parents. Ah, how those wonderfully rich commandments really sealed the deal for us chocolaty chosen children, as well as laid the groundwork for our future type 1 diabetes.

Almost as much as *lusting* for the candy bar, I *coveted* (two separate sins) her typical couture outfit for Simchat Torah. There was the navy dress with the white collar and three-quarter-length white cuffed sleeves that had fifty or sixty tight rows of pleating down the bodice front, with a smart belt that had a rhinestone buckle, white hat with net, and gloves, worn with open-toe woven blue wedgies with cork heels and tiny little patent leather bows, tied neatly above the open peekaboo tips, where three, perfectly manicured, red nails were encased under the black-lace toe of the hose covering her foot. It was quite a post–French Revolution, educated-proletariat kind of look, which I adored.

I inherited her gold dress with the brown embroidered neckline and pockets that I still own to this day, and wore in her honor on my first trip to the Wailing Wall in Jerusalem. There, I told The God that I would never ask It for another thing, but instead, as a responsible adult created in Its image, I would now begin to solve my own problems and accept things for what they are, and not as a symbol of something else. Declaring myself a peer of God was the most spiritual thing that I have ever done, and of course, as you might imagine, I topped it all off with a delicious Hershey's milk chocolate candy bar.

As a preteen girl, I wanted to dress as twins with Bubbe Mary because I just loved her clothes, but she never wanted to do the whole matching grandmother-and-granddaughter-outfit-making and -wearing thing that was so popular with our Mormon neighbors, which was a huge disappointment to me. My clothes never were nice or right for me, and that was largely due to the fact that I was close to being the only overweight girl in the land of Zion (SLC). I had to shop from one rack in the basement of ZCMI, where there were only ever *two* size 14 dresses in the space marked "for chubbettes." The store would not even have *had* a size 14 rack, except for the fact that my other grandmother, Bubbe Fanny, worked there as a salesperson, and she would order a couple of dresses for her chubby granddaughter each season and put them on layaway for me! That brings me to Bubbe Fanny.

Bubbe Fanny was born in Kansas City, Missouri, to parents of Russian Jewish descent. Her father, Joe Katz, left Russia at age nine, after his father, whose death by pogrom, otherwise called "natural causes" for the Jews back then, he witnessed. His mother walked herself, Joe Katz, and eight other children out of Russia to Poland after that. And Joe then walked his way to Spain, earning a living by the shoemaking skills his father had taught him, later sailing for South Africa as a merchant marine. After landing in the USA years later, he proceeded to walk from New York to Kansas City, Missouri, where he found gainful employment, by dressing up like a blindman and selling pencils on the street.

He married a fat Jewish woman there, who gave birth to little, dimpled, kinky-haired, wide-nosed, round Frances (Fanny) Katz, who was a working-class hero, did not believe in God, was not educated or refined, but in a weekend could crochet a slipcover or an afghan to cover and warm the Statue of Liberty. When I was sixteen and turned hippie, discussing Marx with her, she told me she would have been happy to carry a rifle in the revolutionary forces against the czar had she lived in Russia back then. She said, "I'm a Bolsha-whatever, too! Those dirty bastards sitting there eatin' caviars, while the people starved all around them, should roast in hell, if there *is* one." Fanny's father, Joe Katz, used to call her a whore because she didn't keep kosher and she dyed her hair red. She loved Spam, ham and eggs, shrimp, and all the other delicacies that disgusted Bubbe Mary, who agreed with Joe Katz that only a Jewish whore would defile her overweight and diabetic body by ingesting nonkosher meats.

Leftist and rebellious, Fanny enjoyed every moment of her life, despite the misery she had lived through: an abusive father and husband, and the tragic loss of two of her preschool-age children—and she did it all without any prayers, ever. She had no superstition in the least. Once when I was out walking with her, and we happened upon a cemetery, which she insisted we cut through, I repeated a learned Jewish law, "We are not allowed to go into cemeteries!" Fanny replied, "Hey, it's not the dead ones we have to worry about." That sentence remains the funniest one I can recall from my entire childhood, and also the most freeing. It broke through the fear I had been taught by Bubbe Mary's adherence to the Law, which had been shoved down my throat every day of my life since I learned how to speak.

Fanny laughed every prohibition away, and drank beer, too! Those things were bad enough, according to Mary, but worse than all of that, Bubbe Fanny wore pants! Also a seamstress, she sewed them herself, using Butterick patterns, which Bubbe Mary found "Goyische." The wearing of pants was on par with the eating of pork by-products—outrageously scandalous to her. "What kind of a Jewish woman wears pants to show off her *tochas*? Francis has no class at all!" she would say, shaking her head. "No class at all!" And Bubbe Fanny's summation of Bubbe Mary: "She is just stuck up and doesn't know how to have any fun in life."

Fanny stood on the opposite side of tradition, was resourceful, had huge dimples when she laughed, and didn't have a self-righteous bone in her big, honest, round body. Once, a few old biddies were talking some prissy diet talk, while daintily picking around some snacks and talking about how they couldn't eat this or that because it would put weight on them, and you just knew they were aiming their remarks in her direction. "Not me," said Fanny, grabbing one of these and one of those. "I never seem to gain a pound!" It was true! She managed to keep herself right around a nice, healthy, two hundred and thirty pounds her entire adult life, which she lived deep into her seventies, enjoying every bite of it! She was a role model for me and was the perfect antidote for all the uptight, repressed, tradition-bound women I saw almost everywhere I looked in the Utah of the 1950s and '60s.

■

Bubbe Mary voted Republican in every election from school board to president, and would make Bill Kristol look liberal. She loved Nixon! She did not accept evolution as a reality in the least, and she was quite vocal about the duties of the Jewish woman to run the entire world, as required by Jehovah. I'm not sure where that's written, exactly, but I'm *down* with that (as the kids say), so who cares? Her politics never grabbed me, coming of age in the '60s as I did, BUT (and it's a big BUT—hey, no big-butt jokes!) I think it was her unshakable belief in the power of women and her confidence that it was up to them to straighten out this crazy world that instilled a lot of that same gutsy confidence in me. Bubbe Mary was a damn force of nature!

Even though Bubbe Mary was a rogue capitalist, she dropped every spare dime and quarter into a blue and white tin charity box that she kept in her pantry, right next to the jars of gefilte fish and red beet horseradish. She once explained to me that being a Jew meant being someone who gives charity. I asked if we give charity to those who are not Jews, and she said, "We give to our own first." I remember asking her, "If there is any left over, do we then give that to non-Jews?" Her answer: "There is never anything left over." That was that.

Next to the charity tin sat the cans of Campbell's soup, green beans, stewed tomatoes, and corned beef. Then the rows and rows of Ritz crackers, matzoh, kosher salt, flour, sugar, matzoh meal, cornmeal, and instant mashed potato boxes. The entire right side of the pantry was stacked with kosher candles for the Sabbath and memorial candles for the dead. Next to the shelves were the dozen or so barrels of pickles she made herself, out of the cucumbers she grew in her garden, which had an arbor over it, where the grapes that she crushed for her homemade closet winery grew.

Bubbe Fanny had grown up in the Midwest and was the Queen

of the Casserole, and she also made pickles. Where Bubbe Mary made the very garlicky kosher pickle, Bubbe Fanny made the bread-and-butter pickle, which Bubbe Mary used to say was completely "Goyische," as was the casserole, and everything that Bubbe Fanny did or said. Things were to be cooked in a pot, not a Pyrex oven dish!

Bubbe Fanny said that Bubbe Mary was "old-fashioned" and a "religious fanatic," and that her pickles were too "heavy" and caused diarrhea. Our favorite food at Bubbe Fanny's house was a frozen Salisbury steak in a plastic pouch that we took out of the freezer, dropped into a boiling pot for eight minutes, and then cut open with scissors and placed atop a lovely white slice of sandwich bread, washed down with a fabulous cream soda, bread-and-butter pickles, and potato chips. This was so modern, which was what we called everything that wasn't Bubbe Mary–like.

Bubbe Fanny also infuriated and upset Bubbe Mary by joining a bowling league with other women who wore pants and were not Jews, and most of all by becoming involved with a man named Roy, whom she had met downtown, where she worked as a salesclerk. Roy "enjoyed a cocktail" and was from New Orleans, Louisiana. Wearing pants, working as a clerk, eating nonkosher foods, and bowling all receded into the background as colossal social errors next to this seditious turn.

Both of my grandmothers, however, were in complete agreement with each other in the worship of the homemade noodle, which was an important thing to know how to make in our very fat extended family. Now that I am menopausal, I have gotten into making the world's best noodles. I use my grandmothers' recipes, but I roll the dough out very, very thick—it takes the noodles at least six hours to dry out. My noodles are like plump, beige knapsacks; two of them are an entire meal, I swear.

For no extra charge, I gladly include the recipe here in this book as a special bonus to you, my dear readers! (You are so very welcome!) Just call me Bubbe Roseanne! *Ot azoj kocht men di lokshn!* (How to cook noodles.)

Lokshn (Noodles)

1½ cups flour
½ cup water
1 egg
1 tablespoon sunflower oil

Place flour in a mixing bowl. Make a well in the center, and add water, egg, and oil. Mix with clean hands, kneading into a smooth dough. Roll dough into a rectangle. When dough dries, sprinkle with flour, roll out flat, and cut into strips. Cook in boiling salted water and drain. Can be used for soups, kugels, or as a side dish.

■

After my father presented Bubbe Fanny with the choice between giving up living with the man she loved or seeing her own grandchildren, she chose to elope to Wendover, Nevada, with Roy and become Mrs. Fanny Charbenau. This way, she explained, they were no longer living in sin (sleeping together). Daddy was feeling outsmarted and quite abandoned by his mother and her choices. Instead of giving up the goy, she had married him. He was screaming at the top of his chain-smoking lungs about how Bubbe had tricked him. My mother said, "Well, you told her the issue was living in sin, so she made it legal. You should have said the issue was that she shouldn't have sex with a goy! But you didn't; you said, 'You cannot live in sin and be a good grandmother,' so . . . you got what you wanted!"

Buoyed by Mama's explanation of his triumph over his mother's sinfulness, Daddy started to go over to her house for breakfast every day on his way to work, and grew closer to Roy. We kids hardly ever got to go over to Fanny's house, because Fanny worked and bowled and made crafty things out of old beer cans and then sold those things at craft fairs to raise enough money to go on fishing trips with Roy. Bubbe Fanny had totally transcended the entire scope of Judaica in everyone's mind on the more fundamentalist side of our family by baiting a hook and catching, gutting, and cooking a rainbow trout out in the woods in a silver bullet camper pulled by a goy named Roy in a big truck. He was enjoying showing our Bubbe how the other half lives, inducting her into the secret and exotic world of the cowgoy.

He adored her and would say, "Here come those big dimples and that smile that Roy loves to see!" She laughed easily, and told off-color jokes now and then, too, that made *him* laugh. His sister told my sister that his first wife had died of cancer after years of fighting it, and he had nursed her through it all until the end. Bubbe Fanny made him laugh, and that gave him a reason to live. Bubbe told Sis that Roy was different from all other goys—he was nice and sweet and there was none of "that Jesus crap." He reminded her of her primitive ancestors, and the way they lived in harmony with their conflicts, joyfully roasting a "kid" in its "own mother's milk" as the carefree goys still do to this day.

Like Bubbe Fanny, I found the cowgoys a loving bunch, flirting with women in open adoration, and not in the lecherous way typical of our own menfolk. Listening to the way Jewish guys talk, I could never believe that their lecherous ways would work so well on the shiksas. I was incredulous—until I left home and saw for myself that Jewish guys act differently with shiksas than they do with Jewish girls. Most of the Jewish guys I met when I left home thought I was a shiksa, so I was privy to the truth about how much nicer they are to "chicksas" than to Jewish women. They don't really like us Jewish chicks because we are stronger than they are, and they like to act like the Big Man and not the Little Boy. We *like* taking care of the Little Boy, though, for the most part.

The Big Man thing is, of course, all an act, as every Jewish woman knows. Mostly, we do not like our own men that much, either, and find them to be whiners and blamers and big, hairy, suckling, and arrogant babies who give next to nothing back. These things are true, of course, but when they get with a shiksa, they fall all over themselves to keep her. She is the one they drop us for, their true and secret ideal of womanhood. They do not realize that no woman really likes them all that much once she gets to know what a bunch of whiners they are, and so, once they get dumped for a smarter, richer Jewish guy, they keep trying to get with newer, thinner, dumber shiksas, and that takes some money when you look like a Dustin Hoffman. It's quite complicated.

Though I sleep with goys, marry and divorce them, work with them, and have borne their children, make no mistake: I am a Jew and will always be a Jew because I cannot NOT be a Jew. It is an inescapable matrix. Feminist Jews argue against patriarchy while honoring it. Liberal Jews argue against elitism yet practice separatism. Progressive Jews take the words of old men wandering around in the desert six thousand years ago as good modern advice. There is no way out for any of us.

I want to be whatever it is that everybody else is not, like every other Jewish woman. I am part rebel and part joker, like my *bubbe* Fanny was, and part student of the Torah, like my *bubbe* Mary. I am an enigma; I contain multitudes.

Sleeping with someone is the most important thing in the world to many, many women, who find great joy in being awakened by a snoring, sweating bed hog whose toenails are too long and whose base urges are aimed in their general vicinity or particular direction. I prefer to fart alone in comfort and in style. But women had to marry a man in order to sleep with him in those olden days. You had to pay for your physical pleasures, meager as they were, with fertility and pain. One had to force oneself to become uncomfortably familiar with terms like "pistons," "cylinders," and "tight ends," and the other endless little inconsequential subjects of the male—the mutant species with whom we have nothing whatsoever in common. The rogue element. The Y chromo. The Damned.

■

When Bubbe told Sis (and Sis later told me) that she "never enjoyed sex so much before, in my entire marriage to Sam Barr," it made me hurl hot spittle and vomit across a gorgeous lace-covered tabletop. I said, "Why are you telling me this when I will no doubt be attempting to overeat later?" The thought of Bubbe on top of Roy or vice versa was a horrid vision, one that would be followed by an entire mental slide show of grotesque horrors, catalogued by my "Morbid Thought Disorder," which began at age three, after viewing Holocaust films and photographs on Bubbe Mary's TV.

The goyim with their bright smiles and high hopes were gods to me. I loved being around them because they never talked about the real world, ever, and were always baking and eating cookies. Eating cookies that you bake with your grandmother is one of the greatest social steps one must experience in order to grow up into a decent world citizen, in my opinion. Bubbe Mary may have shown her love for us by making fantastic cheesecakes and sponge cakes and angel food cakes and killer apple strudels with hand-rolled homemade phyllo dough, as well as the Holy Chocolate Bar of Mosaic Law, but her cookies were abysmal. Those awful hamantaschen with the figgy prune inside are not pleasing to the palate until one is well into her diabetic sixties, just for the record!

Those cookie-baking Mormon mothers who surrounded us might not have had a conscious thought in their heads that wasn't tranquilized away by the largely Mormon-owned pharmaceutical companies, but they did possess the good sense and the incredible awareness to add a bittersweet chocolate chip or two, and crushed pecans, and some peanut butter to the basic vanilla cookie batter. They were so very modern, and unsaddled with the burden of six thousand generations of suffering grandparents hauntingly stuck to them like glue, like we Jewgaboos were. Mormons seemed carefree, with only about one hundred years' worth of suffering, marching, and freezing ancestors to leave survivor's guilt behind. I knew that I would rather marry their cousins than mine because I was not tribal at all by the age of three, despite the witches and warlocks who tried to program and indoctrinate me into the Jewish cabal of sado-spirituality and carbo-slavery to Jumpin' Jehoshaphat Jehovah.

Bubbe Fanny was so incredibly, modernly Jewish to me, what with the boily-bag dinners, and the high-heeled sandals, and the cool furniture, lamps, and art brought back from Korea by her soldier son, my father's brother Larimore. (Bubbe Mary, on the other hand, would remark, "Jewish people do not join the army. They are doctors, lawyers, and accountants.") After Larimore's return from Korea, many lovely Korean people became Bubbe Fanny's new west-side neighbors, and like all of the people who lived in Bubbe Fanny's vicinity, they loved her, because she made people feel welcome, with casseroles, or crocheted hot pads, or a plate of some of *her* homemade cookies, which were the "Ding Dong Daddy Hot Dog Diggity Bestest in the Westest" little round mouthfuls of heaven from the loving hand of "The Hostess with the Mostest," Fanny Barr Charbenau! She was the first to add butterscotch bits, pecans, milk chocolate, *and* semisweet chocolate chips into a lovely little vanilla cookie. And it was she who made the pineapple upside-down cake with the newfangled coconut crisp on top and underneath. So back off, back up, and step off, bitches!

Even though the Koreans loved her, they did hold handkerchiefs over their noses when they visited her home. We thought their homes stunk, too, and were incensed that they thought the same thing of us. Apparently, we smelled worse to them than they did to us, or else they were just less polite or less dissociative than we were, because at least we would not tip our hand by placing perfumed handkerchiefs under our noses when we visited them. Instead, we would put the perfume directly on our upper lip, and everyone thought we had colds when we repeatedly sniffled during our warm and welcome cross-cultural visits. After a time, we all started to smell alike, as that is what assimilation is all about, I think.

Nobody really liked Bubbe Mary. It was not just the smell of garlic, fried onions, and dill that turned people off. She had hardly any friends, aside from Dora Gallenstein, with whom she would monitor the comings and goings of other Jewish women of our community, judging whether or not they were conducting themselves as ladies should. Mostly, she had no friends because she was mad all the time, at the injustice of the injustices against small business owners in America. At one point, she had to build a bathroom for each of the apartments she rented out to tenants instead of forcing them to all co-op just one bathroom among three apartments, and that stuck in her craw. Barry Goldwater, Bubbe's favorite candidate of all time, would see to it, if elected America's first Jewish president, that the principles of Ayn Rand, Bubbe's psychic mentor, would become law someday, in a proper world where might makes right and the weak are silently grateful for the crumbs they are allowed.

I once witnessed her slap a six-foot-three policeman across the face, right in front of me, my sister, and my pregnant mother, who almost fainted. My mother said, "Mama, the cops will hurt you."

"They don't hurt a lady in America!" Bubbe insisted.

Mom said, "If you assault them they will!"

Bubbe Mary, who had pulled the boots off a dead German soldier in order to have shoes when she was only nine years old, was in need of having her files updated. Learning to respect police authority ran counter to her ideas about being an American citizen. She believed that in America being a business owner meant the police were your personal servants. It took Mama screaming in her face about being nicer to people or she would get smashed down one day soon by forces stronger than she, who saw old women as marks and as easy pickings, whom they could get away with hitting over the head and robbing, especially those old, fat Jewish ladies who had money sewed in their coats and mattresses, to get through to her.

Mama would also remind Bubbe that it was the pharmacist in her hometown of Aborniki, Lithuania, who Bubbe's mother, Rifka (whom I was named for), trusted, who poisoned Bubbe's twelve-year-old twin brothers, who both died in agony as a result, in one of many pograms. (Sometimes, for no reason at all, fortunes change and the wind blows through the world, scattering us here and there, battered and dazed.) We need to fit in better and get along with our neighbors, Mama said. Mama had a way with threatening words. Bubbe subsequently attempted to make a more genteel change in her outward behaviors from that day forward. She stopped cheating people out of the return of their damage deposits when they moved out of her rental apartments—although she kept cheating me at gin rummy.

One fine day, boys and girls, a man named Anderson the Handyman (who later became Anderson the Fugitive) rented a room from Bubbe Mary in "Mary's Manor" and befriended her, offering his tasteful services in the grooming of the rosebushes, about which he knew everything. He told Bubbe Mary that he had a lot of rosebushes himself back in Florida, where he used to live before he decided to leave his life of golf and roses and leisure to come to Salt Lake City and write his book about how he left Florida for Utah to live among the drunk and the poor there. He was quite tan and elegant in his golf shirts and penny loafers and sunglasses. Nobody we knew wore sunglasses; everybody around us wore big hats and squinted instead.

Bubbe was used to a less erudite clientele, comprising mostly drunken older men and a drunken old woman or two—all, of course, white. Leo Sheritude, a leathery-faced Basque gentleman whose bumpy, brown, freckled bald head topped off a huge belly and scrawny chicken legs, lived in the apartment above the one that was next to Bubbe's apartment. There he sat, perched on a stinky pillow in his stinky boxer shorts and knee socks and T-shirt, with his cane tucked between his legs, chewing tobacco, drinking Greek wine, eating peanuts and Spanish olives and spitting the pits out onto the roof, and looking out the window, 24/7, 365 days a year, in protective watch of us little girls. Like our own guardian angel, he would croak out his warnings to us like a crow, "Stay away from him—that one is trash!" Or "Stay away from the little girlies!" he would warn the many deviants among Bubbe's tenants. His voice had the quality of a running motor and a hammer hitting a steel anvil. Had Leo not been forced into the old folks' home that same year, after breaking his hip, perhaps Anderson would never have grown so close to Bubbe or to Mama. Maybe then the end of Judaic patriarchy would never have come to my family, and I might by now have ended up some Midwestern rabbi's fat and gregarious wife, who baked, solved the problems of other women in her community, and was able to talk about the Torah day and night, as per my girlhood fantasies. Damn!

Leo recuperated from his injury, and three months later came back with his walker, wearing his hospital accoutrements, begging Bubbe Mary to let him come back. It was very sad for us that she had to send him away again in an ambulance.

By then Bubbe was completely overcome with the charms of the gentleman of leisure who paid a handsome thirty dollars a month for room and board, each month promptly on time and with a good attitude, and a gift! Anderson knew about roses, which were her passion, and part of the reason that my English name is Roseanne. He could fix things, too, which blew my grandma's mind, having lived around Jewish male "biblical scholars" (and gamblers) her whole life, who preferred arguing points of holy law, like whether a man actually lived inside a real whale or if that story was, perhaps, almost inconceivable as it may seem, only an allegory, to screwing on door handles and moving around hoses.

This Anderson guy was handsome, like my great-grandfather—chiseled cheekbones like Paul Newman with blue eyes like Newman's own—although very short and slight. He could have played the role of Tom Cruise's better-looking, equally short, older brother in some Hollywood movie. The poor man had no experience with women like the women I was raised by. He fell through a rabbit hole of sorts into a world under the visible one.

Bubbe was so enamored of this guy, she was beginning to *assimilate.* She told my sister that since she had gotten to know Anderson, her tenant, who was a very nice and handsome, educated man—though a goy—she felt that perhaps she had been wrong in her assessment of all goyim being worthless drunks and idiots, and now that she had met such a nice and handsome one, she figured the actual truth of things might just be that the goyim are very, very much like the Jews, surprising as that sounded. We never thought those words could ever come out of her mouth; we laughed, amazed. We used to get such a perverse-reverse thrill out of listening to Bubbe's stories about her hatred of goyim. She would offer great little gems of wisdom, such as this one: "Dogs are actually smarter than goyim, as a dog will not lay in his own shit. He crawls away or at least turns his little head. But a drunk goy will just fall asleep with his face in dreck, vomit, or pee." Sis asked her if maybe now she could understand how Bubbe Fanny might have fallen in love with one of *them*. Her wonderful, particular take on that was this: "Anderson ain't no fisherman; he is all class, highly refined, and educated."

I think she loved him because he talked to her like an intelligent and well-reasoned person who encouraged her to question her most basic assumptions. He showed her incredible kindness and generosity, too, which were new things to women like her, the plain-looking, workhorse type. My mother is and was a great beauty (which meant, culturally: a Jewish girl with a straight nose)—a charming woman who had big boobs and a small waist, a nice rear end, a lovely smile, a tinkling laugh, and an admiring glance for every handsome man she ever saw. Men loved my mother's charisma. She would reel them in, and they would soon find themselves helplessly jerked around and fixing things in our house. She would charm them up and then turn them down right after they started to believe that she actually found them fascinating.

Anyway, Mom saw that Anderson could fix things, so she flirted with him to get him to come over and help out around the house. I, her ugly, fat daughter, watched her never-ending, romantic sagas, which she continued to rewrite and live throughout all seventy-seven of her years, unfold with amazement. Daddy had no problem with Anderson being in our house at all hours, either. He was just glad that he didn't have to do anything that took away from the hours he spent chewing on his cuticles and saltwater taffy, or scratching his balls, eating éclairs, and palling around with his beloved little dog, Ervin, who chewed taffy, too, and who later, like Daddy, developed diabetes and was put on a special low-carb diabetic diet.

I was unaware of there being any problem with any of this at first, though I noticed that something changed one day, as I eavesdropped on Mama and Bubbe's conversation. They knew I was there, and they knew I was listening, but Bubbe would say, "Shana Rifka, don't listen to what we say now." And usually I wouldn't, but sometimes I would, especially if they were talking about the handsome, mysterious man who could have afforded to live better than he did. I heard Bubbe tell Mama that Anderson had told her once, after he had been drinking a lot, that he was running away from some legal trouble he had back in Florida. Bubbe used the word *fugitive,* which was the name of her second favorite TV show, next to *Perry Mason.*

Anderson went from handsome handyman to handsome indebted servant very quickly after sharing that secret. He mistakenly imagined my grandmother to be a compassionate Jewish woman who could offer safe haven and comfort in some small measure, if only a teaspoon of the milk of human kindness, and not a fascist-leaning rogue capitalist—that was his first terrible mistake. Perhaps he hoped that she would offer him some of the Magic Jewish Woman Chicken Soup that all men would kill and die for.

The Magic Jewish Woman Chicken Soup would indeed work its will and become his restorative medicine. He had never before in his life experienced anything quite so delightful as Bubbe's chicken fat and kosher salt, with globules of provocative noodles and succulently, seductively rounded, juicy, sumptuous matzoh balls, mixed with chicken necks, and four hundred cloves of garlic. He had no idea what it can do for a man. He was nursed back to health after being worked nearly to death as there was much remodeling to be done in our house and Bubbe's fifteen apartments. His workload was comparable to the workload of a typical Egyptian slave building a typical pyramid or two.

In other words, a bit of the handsome bloom was off the rose now, so he had to be initiated into the Mama-Bubbe Drama a tad further, as there was no other living man available or left alive who would allow himself to be taken down that dark path.

To my mother, nothing on earth mattered unless there was a man there to witness it. Her entire generation is like that, and who's to say they were less smart than my generation, who always went out of our way to show men that we could do without them, pick up a tab, and work right alongside them. We, in fact, got stuck with the final payments on everything we had bought together before the divorce, and were foolish enough to demand to be put in our own names, sealing the rotten deal that made us have to pay it all off alone *after* the divorce! NOT TOO SMART, GIRLS! Goin' backward a little there. (However, if you continue to read this book and listen to what I say, then there is still a slight chance that we can turn everything around, reverse this backward slide, and begin to live up to our potential as the world's saviors, and be rewarded with delicious cakes everywhere we ever go around the world!)

Around the same time, above and beyond the manual labor, Anderson's tasks were increased to include making my father jealous of his admiration for my mother. That was a game that Mama loved to play often with my dad. At first, he couldn't be bothered and pretended not to even care that there was another man at the dinner table with his family, sitting next to his wife, in between himself and Mama, who complimented his wife on the way she looked and the way she cooked, all through the meal, night after night. Daddy, Mom, and Anderson ate steak and potatoes, and we kids ate Franco-American spaghetti straight out of the can with a fork, all together, like one big, happy, freako, pre–Jerry Springer family.

Mom loved having a guy mooning over her, whom she could follow around and say, "My, you just put that screwdriver into that little screw and screw it around and around? Wow! Jerry, you need to get a screwdriver!" and then she would giggle. The guy would slobber, Daddy would take his dog out for a walk to buy éclairs, and I would get a migraine headache and dissociate.

I used to wish I were a boy. I would swear that I never wanted to be a woman like my mother. I would fantasize a lot about being a sailor on a boat in Greece. I would also sneak out to the corner store and steal baby food—I liked the Gerber banana pudding and would steal jars of it and run out and eat them real fast, and then throw the empty jars up on the roof of the store and run home. (Yes, I was weird.)

I was jealous of my mother's beauty and her charisma, and thought that she felt embarrassed that I, her oldest daughter, was not a pretty girl at all, but a fat, loudmouthed, nail-biting, decidedly unpretty girl, who picked holes in her skin, and reflected badly on Mama's pretty image of herself and the world of prettiness in which pretty girls like her lived their lives, honing their powers of glamour and enchanting men, casting spells and manipulating their tiny pea-size brains for their own profit and amusement.

Back then, as a kid, I felt sort of sorry for the men who always fell into the pretty trap. Men like pretty women, not fat ones, old ones, smart or funny ones—after a lifetime of trying to deny and disprove those tiring tidbits of truth, I must admit that now. Women have better sexual imaginations than men do, and therefore they can let themselves do things like fall in love with and have sex with a Woody Allen or a Roman Polanski.

Men's imaginations are never quite as broad or juicy as it seems they should be. I have thought of opening a whorehouse for women my age, where you can have a talk with a pirate type who can discuss poetry and economics, and then actually enjoy you sexually, or meet a statesman with whom you can discuss interesting political issues that would lead to some debauchment later, in an undisclosed location. But in reality, not many of those kinds of exciting and stimulating men exist at all. Most likely only actors would be available for hire in my man-bordello and actors are notorious for having no real ideas of their own, sexual or otherwise.

One night at dinner, Mama started in on one of her "special performances." She stood up at the table, directing her words to Daddy, and said, "What is the matter with you? Do you not see this man here, who is in love with me, and thinks I am beautiful and a good cook and a loving homemaker, sitting right here in front of your stupid, fat face?"

My father, with his devastating blackest humor, pushed himself away from the table, and with a laugh, said, "Yes, I see him. I don't care what he thinks or what he does as long as he fixes the shit around here, for free, and I don't have to do it."

I choked down the laughter, as I always did—by thinking about morbid things and feeling humiliated for and by my mother, in front of a handsome, humiliated man.

Some time after that, Anderson removed himself from the table, and from Park Street. Maybe it's because she loved Anderson still, after he was gone, and she thought about the things he had said, that bubbe—sadder, wiser, older, sicker—decided that the old way of the old patriarchs should be replaced, and a new way of thinking was due not only her daughter but also her granddaughter, me. Around that time, she took me aside and told me that she did not believe any part of Judaism, and only "kept up with it to honor the dead who had believed it." Wounded, somewhat, that the superstition and the magical thinking that had gotten me through my life was being dishonored by bubbe, I asked her, "But how can *you* say *you* don't believe that the Torah is the actual Word of God, that every sacred letter is also a number and a code and a musical note, as well? You taught it to me, and you have discussed it with me daily every day of my life with you! You spent your life lying to me about who you are, about who I am, and about how I am to act in this world? How could you have done that?" For another honest moment in her life, she looked hard into my eyes, and said, "We are the Torah. We women are commanded by Hashem to change the story when it is time for the story to change."

Bubbe Mary had become an agnostic and a truthseeker, and Bubbe Fanny had thrown the Jewish matriarchal burka to the ground and run a camper truck over it. Mama proudly keeps up the renovated "Mary's Manor," which has become her life. She has made it into small condos, rented by many of the gays, whom my mother loves, because they will let her stick her big nose into all of their business. My mother, who still reads the Torah every day of her life, and has a very nice Mormon gentleman as a boyfriend, turned bubbe's old apartment into a hospice to shelter someone undergoing chemotherapy at the University of Utah, for free, in honor of her mother. Jewish women are big on the honoring the dead thing. It's a sweet way to wrap up a life; between honoring the dead and giving the evil eye to other living women, another bipolar reality can be lived out in a Jewish way.

At Bubbe Mary's funeral, my sisters and brother and I thought about how to honor her, in a new American way. When Geraldine and I told the rabbi that we, along with our cousin Cindy and our brothers, were going to be our grandmother's pallbearers, he nearly choked on a hairball from his beard, which he damned near swallowed. Bubbe Mary was the first Orthodox Jewish woman to be carried to her grave by her granddaughters, who broke all patriarchal tradition and created a more matriarchal one.

At Bubbe Fanny's funeral we said nothing about religion.

Both were each a new kind of Jewish woman—a Western American Jewish Woman. They gave birth to those of us who created the sixties. And according to our own daughters, we, the daughters of that American Gender Revolution, ruined the entire world.

Chapter 6

Eat, Pray, Love, Conjure Satan

Let me take you back, dear reader, to the exact moment in time that I went from a chubby twelve-year-old girl to a calculating rising star. At that point in my life, like any twelve-year-old, I was fed up with the unfairness of the world. My anger and bitterness had been seething inside me for a good six years by then, ever since I went from being a cute and cuddly little toddler, at the center of attention, to a fat older sister on the periphery. To top it off, my cousin Debbie, who was a year younger than I and so incredibly average and thin and gorgeous and underwhelming in every way, was cast in a television commercial, my life's goal and dream. Yes, *she* and not *I*, the true heir to Shirley Temple–dom.

It was during Passover, of course, when Debbie and David had found the matzoh *again,* and received the fifty cents for it *again,* that our Aunt Blanche, ever the rebel, said we could turn on the TV set, let it warm up for five minutes, and watch the commercial that Debbie and David starred in, which would be coming on at five thirty. My heart fell to my feet as I watched them in black-and-white on the screen, musing about Dr. Ross dog food. I asked Debbie how she got the job, as I knew I was the one made to star in commercials, not her, and was told that her aunt on her mother's side had cast her in it. I became jealous and irate, and I said, "I want to be in a commercial!" I was told that I was too fat, too dark, and not pretty enough to star in Utah's commercials by another of my fat and mustached aunts, Yetta, may the bitch rest in peace.

That became the genesis of my one-woman crusade against everything that sucks. I swore that one day I would undo the patriarchal system of "pretty means skinny!" Debbie, her aunt, Yetta, and all the other forces of evil would not get away with what they had done to me and all the other fat girls in this godforsaken world. I would make "Fat and loud" my war cry, and soon my enemies would be vanquished in the wake of my tidal power.

One day, as I sat in my room crying and snapping the heads off my Barbie dolls with my chocolate-soaked sausage fingers, and perusing a copy of my dad's *National Enquirer,* I saw in the back pages therein an ad for information about acquiring occult powers. I decided that I wasn't going to feel sorry for myself anymore. I was determined not to accept the status quo, and I would do anything, and I mean *anything,* to alter the world to the way I wanted it to be.

I decided to do something that would have a profound impact on my life, something that I would eventually be very ashamed of as an adult. Everything that follows is all true, every single word of it . . .

When you find yourself upset and jealous and bitter, do not, I repeat, do not call on the power of Satan. Once you do a deal with the devil, you will burn in hell with shame and regret. When I was twelve, I summoned Satan and signed my name in blood. I had learned how to do this from the Mormon contingent in my hometown. These people keep records on everything, and the satanic worship sections of their libraries are some of the best. I had done my homework, and decided it was time to make my move.

I would love to explain just how I conjured up Satan and what the books I got from the Mormons taught me, but for obvious reasons I will not publish them here so that other lost and lonely souls don't repeat my mistakes. Obviously, it's easy enough to enter into a binding satanic contract, as every lawyer, politician, and Hollywood star can attest. Backstage at the Oscars is a veritable bloodletting of virgins and goat fucking. I am the first celebrity to admit it, and I believe it is time that all of you knew our dirty little secret.

He was wearing a red suit, and at first, I thought He was Santa; but then I saw the tail and the unkosher hoof emerging from a puff of black smoke. I watched transfixed and unable to move, full of dread and fear, as He removed His sunglasses and I looked into His green plaid eyes. "You rang?" He asked, in a low register not unlike Lurch on *The Addams Family*. "Yes, sir," I whispered. I remember even now the strong odor of fart that filled my room.

"Let Me pose a question then," He said. "Why have you conjured Me to help you get famous and rich? Why didn't you ask God to help you do it? You have the special Jew hookup, you know."

"I just sort of knew that God would rather I lead a kosher life and become a rabbi's wife someday. Instead, I want to have an exciting life—marry a non-Jew or two, tell dirty jokes, smoke, drink, and eat ham. The excitement seems to be in Your realm, where commercials for television get made. God's realm has no timeline whatsoever. I have been praying to Her to get me a commercial of my own for six years, but it just hasn't happened, and I am running out of time! I can't stand seeing my cousin Debbie rewarded constantly for being light-skinned and thin, while possessing less talent than me." I could not stand to think that being a fat, ugly, dark girl with no ass doomed me to a lifetime of anonymity, when I can dance like I dance, sing like I sing, and act as well as any of the actors I idolized.

I unburdened myself before Him. "I want justice for my talent!" God seemed too busy to care about fairness in my world (or so it seemed at the time). People who did not pray for hours a day like I did, even people who didn't worship at all, didn't seem to be suffering like me! Everyone else had a boyfriend, too, as I sat alone in my room reading, missing every party and all the excitement that lay behind the bright lights of Salt Lake City, with its vast temptations and pleasures. I wanted to be out there in the thick of things, where the money and fame was! So I made my desires known to Satan.

He asked if I was of sound mind. I assured Him that I was, as I stared straight into the plaid eyeballs of damnation. He presented me with the agreement; I signed in my own hand—in my own blood—and grasped the brass ring like it was a warm yeast donut. Thereafter, my life changed completely.

Whereas before I spent most of my days trying to escape the unmerciful teasing and mistreatment by the Mormon children and the weirdoes in my own family by reading Torah all day, I now began spending all of my days escaping the same things by reading about the occult interpretations of the Torah. The difference was very subtle to the unschooled eye. I began to write songs and skits and to try out for the talent assemblies at my school, as I knew that I must develop some kind of talent, no matter how finite, if I were to star in commercials and become famous and rich, like the Osmond family had done.

At first I had no more trust in Satan than I had in God, as I was turned down for the talent shows twice. But, as they say, *the third time is the charm.* I was chosen to perform in the third talent show that I auditioned for, and, of course, I peed my pants onstage out of fright, as I always did once I got up there in front of my unsocial peers. Of course, I do not have to tell you that things worked out well for me—very, very well, as a matter of fact. So well that I was soon swept away by millions of fans and millions of dollars, and actually forgot about the contract with Satan until much, much later.

Chapter 7

On Writing My Book

If I ever finish, this will be the third book I have written. Ever since I was a girl, I have written about one to five pages every day—on napkins, on scrap paper, in notebooks and tablets, on the walls in my room as a teenager, and in orange paint on the cheap white plastic blinds in my room. In recent years, I have written on the computer every day—on my blog, in Microsoft Word, on email—for hours, sometimes all night long. That is the norm for me. What's weird about it is that every single page is filled with another attempt to write the perfect opening paragraph to a book. I have about fifty thousand opening paragraphs and I never seem to get beyond that part of writing the book.

I read *A Tale of Two Cities* a few times, and the opening sentence, "It was the best of times, it was the worst of times . . ." remains the most precise sentence I have ever read. It remains my favorite book, too. I find the writing so moving, and the story is so perfectly told. When I first read it, I saw all the way to my grave in the character of Madame de Farge, the old biddy who silently weaves the code of revolution into the blankets she crochets. *Roseannearchy* is my attempt to weave my own revolutionary code into the pages of this book.

To say that I have an undisciplined mind would not be incorrect overall, but it's a little off the mark because I have great discipline when I write—but only for about ten minutes. Then I get mad and kick something or drink something, and then I begin to blame and curse, which is the mind-set I prefer to access before I pick up the phone and call someone to tell them what I think their big problem in life really is. Right after they hang up on me, I write another opening paragraph, get turned off, do some carb-loading, get energized, blog about meditation and how it helps keep one centered, so that one (not me, obviously) can stay focused when writing, then I lose interest in that and check my Facebook page. (My kids signed me up so that I could see how fun the site is, and it is the worst addiction of all addictions for which I have ever killed.)

I actually regard Facebook as a huge bore, but I cannot refrain from participating in it. I guess I crave the feeling of hope it gives me to think that today will be different from yesterday, that I will find an interesting comment or poke or video, and on the extremely rare occasion when that happens, I am just thrilled. I like snooping through other people's comment pages and viewing their pictures and profiles and reading their blogs sometimes. But Facebook is largely just a boring bunch of unemployed and unsatisfied, middle-aged, mostly Jewish people pretending that they are not just gossiping and bitching about their lives but launching social groups and networks about feeding the homeless or the children of Malawi, or protesting global warming—when, in fact, many times these groups are just a bait-and-switch-type trick for selling açaí berry juice.

As a Jewish person, I can say that I think Jewish people are addicted to excitement in an unexciting world. We goose up more drama than we need in order to combat the creeping fear that the true answer to the world's problems might just be to stay inside and mind our own goddamn business. Jewish people take too much responsibility for the world, and that should stop for the good of mankind for a year or two.

Jews: Leave stuff alone in the world; stay home and just "chillax," as my son Buck says. I swear that's a great thing to do and makes everything easier. I know this goes against the modern idea that Jewish Baby Boomers' survivor's guilt over World War II, if harnessed, could usher in Utopian fullness, but that thinking is actually just a result of all the drugs we took in the '60s. Baby Boomers (gentile ones, too) need do nothing more on behalf of the planet, the species, or peace in the Middle East, and everything will just work itself out nicely.

If these words I write are incorrect or untrue, then please explain to me why God, in all of Her brilliance and talent and intelligent design, would have chosen this time to bring forth the pinnacle of female power and sinister wisdom, the solution to telecommunicable disease, the oracle, Nancy Grace. Her bewitching hold over the minds of the peri- and postmenopausal female is a phenomenon largely unexplored by others, but not yours truly—I'm right there with her.

Nancy sees through the layers of jurisprudence, all the way past the song and dance of lawyers, to the core of the seed wherein resides the voice of the voiceless victim of crime. Nancy embodies that voice and leverages it like David against Goliath. She is always defending the child who has been wronged, whether she is a teenage Natalee Holloway or a two-year-old Caylee Anthony, or Haleigh Cummings. Day after day, Nancy interprets criminal law for the underserved public, who unconsciously knows that one day soon it may be representing itself in a court of law, stripped as it is of the cash needed to defend itself against the myriad charges of lawsuit-happy lawyers, who wrote the Patriot Act, which says no American has the right *not* to be charged with a crime.

Someday soon, every American will be on trial for something, or working on an appeal to get out of jail or prison, or suing someone in some grievance or another, or being sued themselves. When the lawyers in Congress passed the Patriot Act (which is where you *act* like you are patriotic), they succeeded in completely remaking the law, so that every American now has the right to be assumed guilty until proven innocent beyond a shadow of a doubt.

What a smart bunch lawyers are! Now they have ensured their own survival for decades to come. Who would have thought that you would one day need a lawyer in order to defend yourself against the very laws that were designed to protect your inalienable rights? Nancy never seems to mention this fact, though. I guess she feels it is not as important a legal point as whether or not Lee Anthony is the father of his sister's murdered baby.

Yes, this is the perfect time for a fifty-two-year-old mother of two-year-old test-tube twins with gargoylelike eyes and pursed lips to rise up on behalf of the aging female demographic that views cable news shows and buys the products sold on cable TV—Snuggies, mood-altering drugs, and Nutrisystem diets.

The Age of the Female is dawning all around us, and it seems I am the only one who sees it in all of its manifest glory! I have always known that the female is the stronger of the sexes, that she is the one who gets things going and makes things happen. Growing up in a Jewish matriarchal world inside the patriarchal paradise of Salt Lake City, Utah, gave me increased perspective on gender issues, as it also did my gay brother and my lesbian sister. Our younger sister is the perfect Jewish-American wife and mother, and is fiercely proud of that fact. I am the most unconventional one in my family, as all of my siblings have been in relationships of twenty or more years with the same person. My brother is a grandfather two times over and still in college, becoming a doctor in his fiftieth year; my sister married her best friend from preteen Zionist camp, and they have eleven-year-old twin Zionist daughters. My big, fat Jewish family has always been in the eye of the storm, as the winds howl around us and we duck down to protect ourselves and one another from the flying debris and the damage that nature naturally inflicts on all living things—the smarter the creature, the better the target.

Nature is a bitch, and so am I. A big, fat, loudmouthed, pushy, Jewish bitch, as I have been lovingly called by admirers all of my life. I am, indeed, all of those things—and proud of it, too. I have always tried to live up to that role, as I find that it truly suits and defines me.

People sometimes think my being a loudmouthed, pushy, fat Jew bitch means that I don't care. But I do care—probably too much! I care about "not caring" more than I care about anything else! I simply do "not care" to remain silent and docile and passive when it comes to the way women, children, and the poor are treated on this planet, no matter whom that offends, no matter what crimp that puts in my money hose, and no matter whose "God" doesn't like it. I am free to take action and speak out whenever I see fit. Speaking out against what one considers wrong is the very definition of freedom. Democracy is based on female freedom! Silencing old, loudmouthed, pushy women is the first thing a smart despot tries to do.

As an aging female member of the Love Generation of the '60s, I have always enjoyed giving my opinion honestly when asked. I have been lucky enough, since the age of thirty-three, not to have to give a fucking rat's ass what anyone thinks of it. Fame and wealth have been very, very good to me. The best part of all of it is being able to avoid people I don't like.

Your Domestic Goddess may very well be the last hedge against Totalitarian One World Rule, people! The following is a list of Domestic Goddess decrees:

- Triple teachers' and policemen's pay and raise the bar accordingly.
- Establish a union of the working poor with the Attorney General as their lawyer.
- Replace organized religion with strict observance and enforcement of the Golden Rule.
- Foreign policy statement: "Hey, how's it going? We're your global neighbors. Here's our number if you need something."
- Back our currency with yummy baked goods.
- Abolish the IRS.
- Put birth control in the water supply for the next five years.
- All sewer and septic tank maintenance will be performed by convicted corporate criminals.
- All medical testing will be performed on child molesters and animal abusers.
- Minimum weight for supermodels: 140 pounds.

Righting the ills of the world on a global scale begins at home—in our own country, in our own homes, and within ourselves. Like Nancy Grace, we must take a hard look at injustice and fight for what is right, beginning with our own families. With that, I leave you with my

Recipe for Peace and Democracy in the Home

**Children are allowed a vote—*
a say in the world in which they live from day one.
Without democracy in our homes,
we will never have it in the world.

*However, during the teenage years, when they have become a severe nuisance to the general public, they must enter a time of service to the community in which they live. They must be paid fairly and taxed for hanging around in malls. At this time, they are not to be around too many people their own age, unless under the constant supervision of a grandmother figure. Teenagers need their grandparents more than they need their parents at this age, when they compose their own sense of style. The grandparent is able to help balance and correct teenage whims and dreams. That is because grandparents are secretly having a good-natured and loving laugh at the utter ridiculous futility of a teenager's dreams behind their back, and thinking of ways to help cushion reality's blows. It is definitely one of life's great pleasures.

Chapter 8

What Is a Jew?

My family spent their lives in fear of pissing off God and gentiles, and they split their time in each pursuit about fifty-fifty. But to my mind there was no contest at all. The Jewish God could destroy your entire clan in a second if you used a meat fork to sneak a scoop of cottage cheese out of the container in the fridge, according to my Orthodox grandmother. No fricking contest there for me!

I should be committed (again) over my commitment to God at age three. I promised that I would talk about the Torah all the time, no matter how much it made everyone else uncomfortable, bored, and convinced that I was crazy. To this day, I am still terrified to break that commitment, and probably never will have the guts to do so.

The cult programming that goes into shaping a child's mind in order to create a "believer" is pervasive and all encompassing, like *The Matrix*. I have made a point of noticing the delicate balance needed between self-loathing and regarding oneself as "chosen" that comprised my particular bipolar gestalt. There are so many bipolar paradigms to choose from in order to almost appear interesting to people who share your cultural neuroses—a veritable yin-yang of choices, in fact. The Catholics, Mormons, Muslims, Protestants, and even Buddhists to me are just assorted tribes within Judaism and the dualistic thinking that it spawns, bouncing back and forth between sacred and profane, chosen and humbled, manic and depressed.

That is why you always hear Jewish people say they are atheists but still Jews!

Rabbis and Nazis everywhere agree on the importance of the question "Who and/or what is a Jew?" So I humbly offer my definition:

1. A Jew is a person who thinks they know what everyone else thinks, and that it is different from what they themselves think.
2. A Jew is one who also believes that all those other Jews are wrong.

Now there need no longer be any question about the definition! A Jew fears no living human as much as he fears the God he doesn't believe in.

Recipe for Female Peace of Mind

One ounce of dark chocolate
One half of a banana (for potassium)
One large glass of water

While eating and drinking these things, breathe slowly and deeply, eyes closed. Suspend self-judgment, feel only mercy.

Chapter 9

JILFs

Despite a lifetime of battling bipolar depression, PTSD, and all the other mental illnesses, compulsions, bad habits, and superstitions that one can only hope to have in one lifetime, I am actually kind of okay all the time now, with no haunting depression or negative thoughts of suicide or self-harm clouding my brain any longer. I seem to have found that old Jewish woman's sweet spot, and I've got it goin' on. I am an old Jewish woman from the '60s, soon to be a hot sixty-year-old, just a year or so ahead of Madonna. You have your MILFs, and you have your G-MILFs, these being: mothers I would love to fuck—and grandmothers—so plentiful in today's Internet porn. A JILF (Jew I'd Like to F**k), if you can find one, is the top rung of the ladder of females! We JILFs are worth our vast weight in gold indeed!

JILFs like me learned to claw our way to the top using only our wits and our nasty imaginations, dragging our fat asses and crooked noses all the way uphill behind us. Fat, middle-aged JILFs are the hottest of the hot. We had to learn to dance without any lessons! We taught ourselves to move to the familiar beat heard in our own neighborhoods and to the unfamiliar beats of foreign climes. We danced with fat women of other nations, and left having showed them a thing or two. I have made it a point to dance on tabletops on Friday nights at finer saloons *and* synagogues all across this great country as well as around the world. "Doin' table work," as Alexis Arquette, a friend, once remarked.

The other set familiar with doin' table work are the gays and the trannies, who are largely cool, but a lot of them are whiny little shits, so it's just a goddamn good thing that they know how to dance so damned well! The gays always clamor to dance with me at parties, and who am I to deny them the pleasure? They know that fat girls are always the best dancers, and they are always very appreciative of large opinionated ladies—kudos, boys and bulls! Those gays certainly have rhythm, in their own Ellen DeGeneres way, so they make good dance partners. Not to toot my own horn too loudly, but everyone on earth loves my dancing and wants to dance with me, once they witness the full-throttle "Shirley Temple with gray hair" experience of it all—be they so blessed.

I like most to dance at kabbalistic weddings because women only dance with the bride, and I love dancing with women. It really does set some part of my female energies right. I have danced the hula with hula girls and their grandmothers, and I have belly danced with actual Persian, Egyptian, and African women. For years, I have studied the art of sacred dance. And whenever I dance with women, my dormant goddess energy is ignited. Both sexes are left stunned, amazed, and longing for democracy and freedom!

I know now that I was given a great gift as a child. Although I was denied the dance lessons I desperately wanted, learning firsthand what it means to be *on the outside looking in,* I did not let that stop me. I learned to dance with no lessons, no instructions, and no limits. I was never tamed into doing that predictable, robotic, cornball, hackneyed shit that anybody with a big ass can do. Rather, I dance like someone who has never been infected with the limited thoughts of others—raw and naked on top of the music, leading it along behind me, as I tease it into submission with an extra beat or two here and there.

I had many a conversation with Frank Zappa about this same thing. Václav Havel had invited Frank to come to the Czech revolution to claim credit for it and be honored. I asked Frank why he thought the Slavickly inclined regarded him so highly, and he said they liked his music because it didn't follow rules, and that they understood that freedom never does follow rules—once tasted, freedom eclipses bullshit, crumbling all the rules that confine it.

I know that my dancing does that for women. I am not and will never be ladylike or behave myself. I know that behind the veil, when women are only around women and feeling safe, that freedom just happens. I have seen it and I have danced it, too. I have never gone to Iran or Saudi Arabia or Afghanistan to dance for those gals yet, but one day I will. By the time Granny starts jumping off tables and dancing on chairs in old Persia, all patriarchal governments will fall, so I am pacing myself. I'm saving that for my sixties. Yee-haw! The time is nigh, ladies. Hold on to your head scarves because this JILF is about to give new meaning to the words *hot flash.*

Chapter 10

Left of Center in Denver

"It was the last of the best of times."

In the mid to late 1970s, my two sisters, Pearlie and Geraldine, came to live with my husband, Bill, and me and our three kids. They didn't want to live in Salt Lake City any longer, and I sure couldn't blame them. Now that I had help with child care and housework, I was able to get a job—first as a window dresser for a fashionable women's clothing store and then as a cocktail waitress, which worked out well for me because I was thin by then and pocketed big tips (mostly because I never gave anyone back their change once they got drunk). Soon, one of my customers, who thought I was funny, suggested I try my hand at comedy at the club that had just opened downtown. As soon as I heard that there was a comedy club in Denver, a lightbulb went off over my head—I knew that I would go there and become a stand-up comic. Newly thin and seeking an audience, I started to write a five-minute act.

My sister Geraldine and my husband, Bill, accompanied me to the Comedy Shoppe, where I signed up for open-mic night and did my five minutes. I killed the first time, which was good, because I might not have had the guts to come back a second time if that hadn't gone so well. I liked that the men in the audience looked at me like a bunch of bums eyeing a bologna sandwich, as their dates and fat wives refused to laugh at my jokes. Of course, as always happens in my life, a great high (of doing well the first time onstage) was followed by dying a dog's death the second time. The perfect bipolar experience.

The men who ran the comedy club advised me to get more experience before I returned to perform. Apparently, my feminist jokes and too-tight pants did not go over as well as the jokes about blow jobs and masturbation told by the more experienced and successful male comics. So Geraldine suggested that I come to the Woman to Woman Book Center on lower Colfax Avenue in Denver, where she had started to hang out. She thought those women would love my act, since they were all feminists and well-read. They did love my act, as it turned out—they laughed and yelled out, "Right on!" and other supportive things like that—and they also encouraged me to go further with it. I loved it and started to volunteer in the bookstore as a receptionist two days a month. I also got to perform at the many coffeehouses, organized by members of the collective, in bookstores and open-mic nights all over the city of Denver in order to work on my act.

I got more confident in my comedy because of them, but the trauma of not being able to substitute seeking the attention of men for my eating disorder caused me to begin slowly adding sausage, cheese, and chocolate to my diet. Then I would sneak-eat some more before taking laxatives, as well as upchuck like a mofo, and then start smoking even more cigarettes, so that I would eat less, and then smoke pot to quit smoking cigarettes, which just made me hungry. Being a housewife, mother, member of a lesbian collective, stand-up comic, big sister/surrogate mother, and cocktail waitress meant I was living too many lives at once, and something had to give. That something was my waistline, and therefore my job as a cocktail waitress. Ironically, my getting fat again made it easier for people to laugh at my jokes.

Best of all, volunteering at Woman to Woman allowed me to read great books that changed me in so many ways. The books of Professor Mary Daly affected me more than any others, with the exception of Matilda Joslyn Gage's *Woman, Church and State,* which I, almost single-handedly kept in print. The greatest thing I learned working in a bookstore was that you can help keep great words and great ideas alive and in print simply by ordering two hundred copies of a particular book from the publishers. I over-ordered all of Mary Daly's books, and Matilda Joslyn Gage's, too.

Dr. Daly wrote about God as a female intelligence, and that was the great capper to a lifetime of reading about God from a male point of view for me. Dr. Daly became one of the first women to receive a doctorate in Latin, and went on to teach about theology and the "Reversal of Gender" by the Vatican, by simply declassifying the Vatican's own records!

Mary and I ultimately became the closest of friends until her death on January 3, 2010. I was out on my Kawasaki Mule in the fields on my Hawaiian nut farm when I saw her apparition standing between the trees and waving good-bye to me. Not until the next day did I receive the email that told me that she had died at the exact moment I had a vision of her the day before. Spooky, spooky things are always happening if you know where to look and how to look for them.

In 1980, ours was a multiracial, multiclass, multi-sexual-preference conglomeration of activists and intellectuals. We operated a women's referral hotline that had been in existence since the year of our Lord Bobby Kennedy, 1962. We called ourselves "feminists," and everyone else called us "women's libbers." It was all so quaint!

At the Woman to Woman Book Center, we carried books written by women authors, telling of their real lives under the various world governments, none of which wished to understand or consider the ideas of women. Women were, of course, a threat to all of those governments and religions and theories, and I think I know why. It's because women seek solutions to problems that actually work and are in the best interest of the most people in their circles. Solutions are the enemy of patriarchy, which is in a total state of unending war. The stock market itself is based on the sale of weapons and WMD! If that patriarchal threat were to be removed, many people would not have jobs. No more than that needs to be said, really.

Our collective valued solutions; we had discussion groups, consciousness-raising groups, our own production company, called Black Orchid Productions, our own feminist newspaper, called *Big Mama Rag* (yes, we did have those back then!), as well as grievance groups, who would approach the collective and seek spiritual and social redress. We were geographically and psychically at the center of the Western American women's movement for the Equal Rights Amendment, called the ERA. We were also a nonprofit organization that could provide funding for programs that benefited women.

The movement toward democracy for all citizens was getting too close to being real for a lot of rich people. The effective opposition to that ideal was embodied in a man named Ronald Reagan, working for those who paid him to act the part of "President of the United States," and pass laws to help them "privatize" (steal) Social Security money, and pocket it themselves, instead of using it for the people it was created to serve. They were called Republicans.

Reagan Republicans were different from what Republicans had ever been before. They wanted to undo the social safety net that allowed the American way of life because they felt people who work for a living are paid too much, whereas people who do not work for a living (like the idle rich and what Bush called the "investing classes") are not paid enough.

In the early 1980s came the Reagan landslide, the cornerstone of which was the threatened patriarchal family, one that was headed by a proper (white), Christ-loving, strong male provider, a proper (white) Christian wife under his loving dominance, and two or three properly behaved offspring, who were not homosexual. That sanctified unit was free to overconsume to their hearts' delight, oblivious to the destruction of the planet, subsequently buried under the garbage they created.

For them, the times were just right for man-hating women's libbers (feminazis) to ruin God's plan, so that proper social order could be overturned and women could be tricked into thinking that being equal with their male counterparts under the law was a good idea! Saving the family from its own women was no small task for Republicans. Restoring proper family values was then and is now crucial to white Republicans, who oppose everything that does not go out of its way to favor those who are at the very top of the Ponzi scheme that's turning out to be our economy.

When the women's libbers were not off gallivanting braless, or having needless abortions just for fun, they were coming up with ways to blur the gender lines, such as dreaming up the ERA. Getting rid of gender altogether is what the libbers wanted to do most of all, because in addition to being man-haters, they all had penis envy and wanted to be allowed to violate the sanctity of men's private clubs (the Congress and the Senate). As if that were not misguided enough, the sluts also purposely failed to honestly inform American women that equality really meant that men could not be prevented from entering ladies' bathrooms, where ladies would no longer be safe to do the things that ladies do privately in bathrooms.

The Big Lie sure did work, like it always does. Sarah Palin is the modern-day version of Phyllis Schlaffly, who authored all of the anti-ERA rhetoric. Palin's commentary on death panels and health care uses that same dumbass doublespeak that works so well on the drugged illiterates who are her followers. "Are you going to let some big, bloated socialist government tell you that you should be able to afford health care? Say it ain't so, Joe!"

It's that old knee-jerk "Women better get other women in line before there is trouble for every woman" threat. Like hens who peck a "defective" chick to death, right-wing women react out of fear to anything that seems different from the sanctioned model of perfection and are very good at herding other women back under the big umbrella of shame. "What about the children?" they always moan, bleat, and cry, when in fact, the last thing on earth they care about is "the children." If we cared so much for children there would be seat belts in school buses, and we'd cut the military budget before we cut school budgets. Many women lost custody of their children in the '70s because they took jobs, and right-wing judges (activist judges) thought that was terrible. Republicans did not consider it ladylike to accept money for work. It was downright rude!

By late 1981, the various services and programs to which we had referred the widows, the orphans, and the needy through our work at the collective had been "unfunded" by the Reaganites, whose sole purpose was to begin the dismantling of the middle class, and to divide and conquer the American Woman's Movement for Equality and Parity. The first step in this class warfare, waged to dismantle the New Deal (specifically Social Security, so that it could be put into private hands), was to flood the streets with mental patients who should never have been released from hospitals. Their benefits were cut, and as they began to roam the streets, they gravitated toward the mom-and-pop stores that flanked the Woman to Woman Book Center—sitting outside, begging, peeing, and putting undue burden on those small business owners, who began to close their shops and vacate Colfax Avenue in disturbing numbers almost immediately. I guess this was what Reagan Republicans had in mind when they called themselves the "party of small business." In Reagan Republispeak that meant *destroy* small businesses so that the moneyed classes could later move in and pick up some choice real estate bargains. I never understood how they got away with calling themselves "the party of small business." *What sheer balls!*

I saw my first glimpse of the frightening future when an older woman, well-known to all on middle Colfax Avenue, was taken down by two uniformed police officers, one of whom held her head to the pavement with his black boot. I ran outside, yelling, "Officer, what are you doing?" I had never seen the likes of it. What did she do, pull her fork on him? I wondered.

"Get back in your shop!" he yelled. But I, indignant and suburban, crossed the street anyway and said, "I want your badge number! I am reporting you to your sergeant!"

Two large, black lesbian collective members, who were there long before my sister Geraldine and I had joined in on the fight against "patriarchy," grabbed me by the arms and told me to get back in the shop and to shut up. I was immediately thereafter schooled by Latina, Indian, and African-American women about what America had always been like underneath the thinly lacquered veneer of equality.

The bookstore's collective began to faction in opinion as to what should be done to counter all the disappearing resources. It got pretty heavy, and one of us wrote an article in *Big Mama Rag* that called for full-on revolution against the government. This upset a lot of our constituents and collective members and readers, who said we would probably get audited and lose our nonprofit status now that we had opened that huge can of worms inside of Pandora's box.

The Left's MO invariably seems to devolve into dogma wars about terminology and theory. This gives birth to more factions and petty politics while everyone does less and less to solve the real problems. That is why it was possible for the Republicans to prevail; they have shown us what they really meant by "free markets": slave wages and substandard conditions. Even their talent for doublespeak can't completely hide their two-fisted greed for more: more money, land, power, military supremacy, and compliant women.

By early 1983, I was the last of the straight women at the bookstore. Most of them said that they felt they had been run out of there by the lesbian separatists, who thought that if you shaved your legs you were a gross, disgusting pig and a traitor, and they wanted no hairless-legged women in the collective. They continually voiced the idea that straight women were the actual oppressors of lesbians. That really pissed me off. I used to say, "You are driving out the middle! No revolutions happen without the middle! Let's organize welfare mothers and waitresses!" Everyone snickered at me.

I got to stay because everyone loved my sister, and I loved her lover, as one loves one's in-laws. The lesbians used to call me all kinds of names, from "dikey-likey" to "closet case," and I would good-naturedly tell them to go fuck a man just once before they swore off it. They would giggle like schoolgirls, gagging and screaming, "Yuck!"

We kidded one another, and sometimes things got unmercifully tense as a result. Mostly, we saw one another as compatriots for correctly choosing to stay in the collective at Woman to Woman and insisting on taking a multicultural, multiracial position in the movement toward international feminism. Women Workers of the World United (WWWU) was what we decided our name should be, and then that was changed to Women Workers of the World United with Men Workers of the World, or WWWUWMWW. We wanted to show that we were feminist but inclusive. Later we called it Multi-Cultural Women for Pay Equity, or MCWPE, to show that we were diverse, feminist, and working class.

We couldn't get too many people interested in joining up with us, though, printed flyers or not. Later we changed our name to WAP, Women Against Pornography, which used a traveling slide show to raise funds to help smash patriarchy. We desperately needed to raise some funds to replace the funding that had been cut. We were seeing dozens of homeless women outside our shop now, and we figured that we could hold benefits to raise funds in order to help them.

We were hired to go to Wyoming to present the slide show, but when we got there, we found out there were a bunch of men in the audience. Chi, who had the most seniority of anyone in the collective, said, "This slide show is not for men; it titillates them, and that is not what we want to do with it. We want to radicalize women by letting them look at the way women's bodies are exploited so that they will join our struggle." Sadly, Wyoming's women weren't that interested in getting radicalized by the porn slide show, and even if they were, they never had any real funds to give us in our struggle to make all that sex and porn profitable. That's f**king patriarchy for ya! We knew we needed some profit if we were to operate a nonprofit organization and get anything done at all in this lousy world.

Another thing was that we were all "self-identified." That term became the IN term, the buzzword, and everyone said it as a prefix. I actually said, "I am a self-identified straight woman" as kind of a joke, but no one got it at all. Soon enough, a few staunch ladyfellers came in and called themselves self-identified lesbian sadomasochists. We thought it was weird that a white woman came in to plead the S-M case for inclusion in our multicultural center with her "slave," who was a black woman. I thought that white woman would not get out of that meeting alive. White women think they can say anything at all to black people. It is astounding!

There was a lot of discussion and fighting over whether lesbians who like other lesbians to slap them around was politically correct, until the black woman told the collective's black women that she was getting all the sexual servicing she really craved, and was, in fact, the one in control of the relationship, as the bottoms always are. She explained how it should actually be called "Masosadism." Well, I never!

I had the last word, which kept them out: "You can't whip a black woman, even if she says she wants you to, 'cause it just ain't right." Some black woman S and M-er out there right now might be thinking of taking off my head for saying that, weird as those S and M-ers are. She might think what I just wrote was akin to slinging the N-word around. That black lady masochist would probably vote for Sarah Palin, too, were she a black lady masochist Evangelical. Everyone lost their damn minds when Reagan became president.

Separate from the slapping lesbians, a battle began to rage between the lesbians who were pagans versus the lesbians who were Christians, and then the lesbians who wanted to have "baster babies" factioned off, too. That was a huge impasse, I remember, that ended with two women crying and screaming, "We are women, too, and we want babies, too!" and other women crying and screaming back at them, "They want us all to be brood sows—come on, wake up! Don't go all breeder! The continual celebration of spitting out more children has been forced on women in the glorified 'pedophilia-without-sex' cult called Motherhood!" Thirty years later, the "gaybies" (what the good-humored offspring of baster-wielding lesbians and gays call themselves) are all grown up, and are as huge a pain in the ass as the young adult offspring the rest of us had naturally.

Then, always bubbling under the surface, the Jews' infighting began to go public, as Zionists and Jewish Socialists destroyed each other and the Jewish presence at Woman to Woman itself—except for me and Sis. Then the Transgendered versus the Butch Dyke wars started—to see two of those folks fighting about being female was quite an eye-opener for me. You haven't lived until you have seen a huge guy with boobs talking about female hormones and deciding to keep his penis, and how that was a feminist issue.

Back in the mid-'70s in Denver, Jewish and black and Latino and Native American and white women used to sit around and hash out what to call themselves and then what to call one another, as they attempted to envision a more just world. Shortly after that, of course, they started fighting about whose group was the most racist and whose group suffered the most. We threw all the old racial charges back and forth, and it involved some pain and some blood, too.

I remember big, dark women crying and screaming at me about Jews involved in the slave trade and pulling books off shelves everywhere to prove it, as they attacked me for not questioning my white-skin privileges. I would not back down, though, and I let them have it. I initially thought the Jews had it the worst for sure, because of the whole gas chamber thing, but the black women ultimately aced me when they reminded me that slavery had lasted four hundred years. Nobody can really argue with the four hundred years point; at least I don't think so. By the time we found agreement, every white, lesbian, and middle-class woman had left the collective and come together to build a gay and lesbian community center down the street instead.

They were more comfortable joining ranks with white gay men than with black women and Jewish women, who were obsessed with leveling charges of racism and anti-Semitism. The Latina women got sick of hearing about how Catholicism was a Jew-hating religion and started their own group, La Raza Unida.

My sister and I stayed and were two of the four white women who chose "international feminism" over class, race, and religion. Many of the books in our library said this same thing had happened before, back when feminists and abolitionists were trying to force woman suffrage and put an end to slavery. Some of the white women thought some of the more radical black women were off-putting to the mainstream racists and excluded them, thereby greatly weakening their own movement. For her troubles (exiling Ida B. Wells), Miss Susan B. Anthony's image was put on silver dollars.

Sis and I flung back our charges of anti-Semitism, yelled about Zionism, cried and argued, admitted our racism, let go of it, and cried and argued some more about heterosexism and oppressive political correctness. I kept saying that we were going to lose the women in the middle, the housewives of America, with all of this extremism. I was, of course, right about all of it.

Then the worst happened: The Jewish women left to join either Zionist groups or anti-Zionist groups of their own, and then the sad day came when the black women with white women lovers left us, too. Now it was just me and Sis and Chi, Heloise, Patti, and Dree, who had been adopted as a baby by black parents who told her that her real mother was a Jew and that was why she had big boobs and a big nose.

Dree couldn't decide which side to take sometimes, and she

would just sit and cry till we all shut up and went to the IHOP next door to drown our sorrows in pancakes. (I heartily recommend eating pancakes for peace—it always works!) Dree and pancakes at IHOP were the twin pillars that bridged the gap among us.

Black, biracial, or white/Jewish, we all agreed that feminism, "Womanism," was the thing that mattered most, after years of inner and outer struggle. Now that we had all of that straight, finally, the six of us could begin to build an international movement. It was to be based on diversity.

I said, "Let's go check out that women's group by the Terminal Annex and see if they want to join up with us." Chi and I went into their bookstore, which was all about candle spells and witchcraft.

Chi said, "Yeah, maybe this women's movement could use some goddess energy."

Before, we had always argued to keep Wiccans out, mostly because we felt that they were counterrevolutionary, in that they settled for personal politics and sexual power games over radical feminist analysis of socialism. Also, the Wiccans were still largely heterosexual and were fighting with their own lesbian faction over the issue of males leading their worship circles; the straight women preferred their husbands to lesbian Priestesses, whom they said were "too male." Chi and Dree used to make fun of the Wiccans by prancing in circles, waving old scarves around, and singing in falsetto voices about how they were magic wood nymphs who were trying to teach "Negroes" how to worship a *white female* as God.

We were desperate for more members in our collective, though. And even though we snickered behind their magical backs, we admired the Wiccans somewhat for at least being out of the cultural box enough to recognize female divinity. It was all fun and games until someone got hurt, and someone did. The Wiccans opened their faux castle doors one day to find it smeared in chicken blood. They called it "being blooded" and immediately closed down their witchy storefront and disappeared. We heard that some Latina lesbian Wiccans "blooded" them in reaction to their having a white male transsexual leading their woodsy ceremonies. See what I mean about factioning?

About this time, Sis came up with the idea of "reaching out" to the women at the university in Boulder, Colorado. The women's studies group there was busy trying to prevent the black history curriculum from being dismantled. There was no groundswell to protest that development, due to the fact that white students were starting to claim that black students were getting preferential treatment on campus. The rich were victims now, and as a result of that conservative "grassroots" movement on campuses, groups that had anything to do with racial or gender parity were becoming obsolete and disappearing—all within a year or so of the triumphant Reagan Revolution.

By 1983, everything that took root in the '60s was dead. That year, our shaggy collective was approached by a woman named Cynthia Raging Thunder. She said she was going to be arrested soon for smuggling guns from Central America through Mexico to go to the Indian encampment at Wounded Knee. She came to us to ask if we could help her pay for attorney fees and help her fight the charges.

I asked her where she got the weapons to sell, and she said she had been a member of the armed services when she smuggled those weapons. "Why are you trying to overthrow the country that you are serving in the army to protect?" was what I asked her. She said she knew many other soldiers who were becoming rogue arms dealers, too. I remember thinking, I wonder if that Ronald Reagan knows that when you make everything for sale, someday it will get sold out from under you.

That meeting with Cynthia Raging Thunder might have been a setup, some said, but it proved to be one of the final nails in the coffin of Denver's feminism. That nail followed a spike through the heart, when our sister collective, which published *Big Mama Rag*, lost its tax-exempt status because the IRS deemed it an advocacy group and not an "educational institution." Although *Big Mama Rag* challenged the decision, it took appeals all the way to the D.C. Federal Court of Appeals before the IRS decision was struck down. The ordeal was a blow to our cause. We started closing down the bookstore, donating and shipping the books to other women's nonprofit bookstores in other countries, as the American ones were all closing down. We sent books out of America to international women's parity groups in the hopes that our multicultural authors would be read and studied everywhere, but mostly in the places they actually lived (which is almost never the case with most women's political writing) now that no multicultural feminist groups existed in Denver anymore.

The books at the new gay and lesbian center were all about sex and "gayety." There was no politics, no socialism, no feminist analysis. Those books had been removed, and the switch to Log Cabin Republican money worship was encouraged among the business-friendly white gays and lesbians there. In California, some twenty-five years after this, the same business-friendly GLBT organizations felt betrayed by black, working-class Christians in Oakland, whose vote against marriage equality passed Prop 8. I thought, This is like Denver factioning all over again! If official gay and lesbian organizations had not stopped supporting class struggles, Prop 8 would have easily been defeated. The divide-and-conquer tactic always works, and always cuts both ways, too. I am happy to see lots of GLBT centers now supporting single-payer and pro-labor issues. I always say, the minute that everyone who *isn't* right wing teams up, everything will change.

We all complained to the gay bookstores that there were no more lesbian feminist books in their stores, and then more and more Wiccan books started showing up where feminist intellectual books had been, as well as more and more books on exercising and dressing for success. The new gay bookstore had a lesbian shelf in the back that was marked FEMINISM, but had no books at all about feminism or working women, just several copies of *Our Bodies Ourselves* and lesbian erotica, which I admit I read. By the time they get to the licking, it's page 190, and the preceding pages are all about how to enact a rape fantasy while still "feeling safe."

Christ, same old shit for us gals.

The Reagan Revolution (same shit, different century) worked perfectly for the minority it was created to serve: the Palins who go around encouraging the chickens to vote for Colonel Sanders. The thing that is so intriguing to me still is that the whole heap of shit is strung together with only words; and I keep plugging away at writing the right ones that, hopefully, honestly define the crazy times in which we live.

Whenever I hear of some women's group rising up in some repressive country, I think perhaps that the voices in those books are still blowing minds, like they blew mine. When I guest-edited the women's edition of *The New Yorker,* I insisted that Professor Mary Daly, my favorite author and expert on Latin and theology, be included. Tina Brown did in fact keep her promise to me and made that happen despite the hit she took for inviting me to guest-edit the first and only women's edition. The fact that Mary's words made it into the intellectual mainstream meant more to me than any award or accolade I have ever been given, including the Peabody and the Eleanor Roosevelt Freedom of Speech awards.

Feminist intellectualism has largely been erased since the Reagan Revolution, as seems to happen in every revolution. Still, after only a few decades, the same old voices return in new ways.

Every so often, one of those voices employs the right words that tell the actual truth and not the "derivative" truth funneled through nature-hating religions or female-hating philosophies.

That voice is coming; it's bubbling up now.

It gives me pleasure to know that we hippies and lefties were right about everything, and when I am in Hawaii, I find that there are many, many men's groups that now talk about their "inner female" and getting in touch with it. I love men who know that embracing the female is the way for them to become real men! Any man who has a brain in his head has already figured out that he will attract a higher vibration of female devotion on this earth by doing that! Unfortunately, a lot of men are homogodly, and are only able to love the male energy of God, which is, ironically, the one that women need to stop prostrating themselves before if they want to implement solutions for this world!

I also love that the pendulum is swinging back to self-sufficiency and perma-culture. It's good that we are coming back down to earth; things are getting way real again. We simply have no other choice now. So, in a weird way, I say, viva the Reagan Revolution; it's what brought us here, now, to 2011. For the first time in history, America's workforce is 53 percent female. The future is indeed female! Without our influence, there will never be solutions or peace, which we must have to survive what is coming.

We must see clearly what lies before us this time. Reduced to our most basic needs, we will be forced to figure out how we are going to get food to the hungry with the least amount of waste. That is true feminist spirituality, I think, after all these years.

Cold hard reality will be good for us, after we all start to understand the debt we got tricked into, as the schools, hospitals, and police protection we used to get for our taxes disappear everywhere around us. Soon, the words *community* and *communal,* and even the word *socialist,* will not be able to be demonized by fat cats anymore. More and more people will change their obsolete definitions and create new systems that work for *most* people, not the *fewest* people anymore. It's evolution in the making, I think, as fundamentalist religious opposition to equality and justice will go the way of other dinosaurs.

I did my part—and continue doing my part—by voicing these truths at top volume. In fact, the words I said in 1986 on *The Tonight Show* got a powerful woman in television, Marcy Carsey, interested in selling a show for me. I made my debut into impolite society on a television comedy that told the story I wanted to tell, about a woman who lost her union job at a plastics factory, took a series of minimum-wage jobs, opened and lost two businesses, and her husband. At her lowest point, she begins to write about a woman who wins the lottery and buys the town's plastics factory and gives it to the townspeople.

Does life imitate art? I sure hope so!

Chapter 11

Rants for a New Century

Now that the big SIX-O isn't too far off, I still can't hardly believe it, as we say in Utah. At fifty, I got really depressed, but then, one day, after staying inside and drinking alone for three months, I realized, Hey! I've survived fifty years of shit, and that's half a century that I don't have to do again. I'm kinda baaadd!

Then I started getting defensive (my greatest talent in the world), and I thought, Hey, I'm fifty, and fifty means: Fuck it! Fuck it all! Fuck everybody and fuck everything they think I should do, think, or say! It's time to tell everybody what I think, and then tell them to kiss my fat ass! 'Cause I'm fifty, and that's what fifty earns you the right to do!

Here's some of what I want to say: Forget dieting. It's a useless waste of time perpetrated by woman-hating, heroin-addicted clothing designers and pill-pushing doctors and greedy little shits. The world is blowing up, okay? We must stop dieting, and we must stop paying attention to dieting experts, who run a bazillion-dollar-a-year industry and have no idea what they are talking about, telling us things are safe and then two years later confessing that they aren't.

I *am* the diet expert. After all, in my life I've lost a thousand pounds, and gained back twelve hundred. Diets are a temporary solution to a permanent problem. They only put you in that loop of obsessive-compulsive disorders: Yes, no, yes, no, yes, no—starving, hoarding, binging, purging. They just don't work.

The reason people are fat is because it's genetic. If you are a great big old pie wagon, you probably come from a long, long line of great big pie wagons. You are going to have to move around if you are going to eat, and that is all there is to it! I'm tired of the abuse I have had to suffer my whole entire life for being a fat person. I'm tired of all the discrimination toward fat people—and all those barnyard names, like pig, hog, heifer, cow, making us go to fat farms to lose weight. Equating people with animals is degrading—to animals, I mean.

People are afraid of fat people. They think we are going to eat them. They also think it's contagious. I can't really blame them, though, since I have a fierce eating disorder that has survived even bariatric surgery. I got even fatter after that! Hey, maybe fat people are just trying to get *closer to others,* did anybody ever think of that?!

I must say, ladies and gentlemen, I support a woman's right to chew. I also support a woman's right not to be shot up with hormones. The minute I turned fifty, doctors started hawking the premenopausal hormones right away. They're not going to stick me with any goddamned hormones! Have you seen all those horrid commercials on TV? They sell drugs like they're Skittles; it's awful.

Another side effect of menopause is that you lose your sex drive, and they try to make you think that's a bad thing. The doctors tell you to take hormones—*male* hormones (you know, testosterone)—because they say it will restore your sex drive, the elasticity of your skin, your youth, your memory, and will keep your girl chute receptive to your old man's wiener, which is all hopped up and stiffened on Viagra. Speaking of old men and their wieners: They shouldn't be fooling Mother Nature with those boner pills—she got mad enough about the margarine, remember, Boomers? The occasional organic woody is more than enough. And, trust me, gentlemen, gray hair does *not* make your gnarly knob look *distinguished.* And when it does rear its ugly head for old times' sake, you should think of that as "me time"—a chance to catch up on your hitchhikin' to heaven.

Women don't need more testosterone; men need *less*! This is the time in the world where we need cooperation and not competition. Testosterone makes people testy and competitive! Of course, the doctors tell you that fear of taking the hormones is a symptom of menopause. They got ya coming and going!

I don't need to be on male hormones. I have enough worries without having my IQ decreased by half, getting obsessed with duct taping things, watching cage fighting, and being unable to find anything when I need it. Oh yeah, I don't want to get that obsession-with-*balls* thing, either: Throwing 'em, catching 'em, hitting 'em, kicking 'em, punting 'em, slamming 'em with racquets, tossing 'em through hoops, running with the egg-shaped ones through crowds of attackers to the end zone, bouncing 'em, batting 'em, or scratching 'em—balls, balls, balls! But enough ball-bashing. As I have joked for years, men do some things better, like reading maps, because only the male mind can conceive of one inch equaling one hundred miles.

Fuck hormones, fuck doctors, and fuck all these pharmaceutical companies! I'm not taking hormones or anything like it that comes from a drug company, 'cause that's another bazillion-dollar-a-year industry that experiments on us like lab rats, telling us things are safe and then reversing their position two years later. I have no trust whatsoever in the drug companies after what they did to me with phen-fen. How can I trust them? They said it was safe, then three-quarters of the fat people in America died. But it was government approved, and I think that's scary—the government approving drugs that elevate your mood on the one hand while fighting a war on drugs on the other. They're fucking with our heads. The war on drugs is a war against poor people on street drugs waged by rich people on prescription drugs. Trying to drug us all is the goal of the hyenas who control things these days. I believe in self-medication as much as the next guy, but we don't need chemical mood elevators. That's what carbohydrates are for!

So, fuck dieting and fuck aging! And fuck sex, too!

Some things are just supposed to end. Now, with Viagra and those kinds of drugs, men are more out of control than ever before. It's mainly old men who are taking the Viagra, and let's be honest, nobody really wants to fuck an old man. Let alone for *four hours*! Who the hell wants to do it for longer than you did when you liked each other? All these old men are running around with their old boners, on their fifth set of children, who are all hopped up on Ritalin to slow them down so the old man can play ball with them.

Since this menopause shit kicked in, I now hate sex. And I'm so glad. I feel liberated. Sex was never good for me for anything besides having kids and keeping the gardeners happy. Now I am much more spiritually centered and have more time to plot revenge—a much more satisfying pursuit, I assure one and all.

Sex is the worst drug of all; that's my opinion. When I think of all the horrible things I've done, the people I've betrayed just to have sex, I become almost too nauseated to eat. (I said *almost.*) I believe that the government—and by *government* I don't mean the U.S. government, but the satanic world government—is drugging us all on testosterone-laced Starbucks coffee so we can be led by Satan's disciples through the use of computers, including the chips we have in our heads that are constantly recharged by cell phones, to continually have our lower chakras overstimulated so we become lazy and unaware of everything that is actually going on in the world and only worry about things that don't matter—like sharing our own germ-infested sex fluids with other members of the human race. Yes, that government is afraid that someone like me, a menopausal woman whose vision isn't clouded with perverted, sickening thoughts, might actually stumble across the truth.

I'd love to share this truth with you, but I can tell you're all just a bunch of horny apes and it won't do me any good. You'll simply report me to the government, and they'll send someone after me with a hypodermic needle full of male hormones, like the WHO flu shot! Women will be forced to take the male hormones or be shut away in FEMA camps until they start becoming part of the whole oversexualizing and duping of society.

Now, I might get into some serious trouble on this next subject, like maybe I won't ever be able to be in a Mike Myers movie, but what the hell, Grandma's going for it. Fuck all the greedy corporations, like McDonald's, Burger King, and all those responsible for the destruction of the rain forest. I read in *Time* magazine that these corporations are destroying one hundred thousand acres of rain forest per day. At first I didn't care. I thought, Who gives a damn about parrots and monkeys and slugs? They ain't even good eatin'. But do you know what else comes from rain forests? The cacao tree, where chocolate comes from! Holy God Almighty, is there no end to the greed of the fast-food nation? Goddammit, STOP THE MADNESS!

The next subject on my "fuck you" list is a little closer to home. I have five kids, four of 'em grown, with their own lives, and to those four I say, "Get a job! You ungrateful little bastards!" These kids, after all we've done for them!

Remember the times your mom lost it on you? Not the everyday losing it, but the kind that always seems to happen in parking lots? The kind when you'd see that terrifying look on her face just before giving you five on the butt in front of everyone in the world? "I TOLD YOU TO GET IN THE CAR NOW!" And you think, When I'm grown, I am going to get even with her by screaming at my own kids! Which you do, and then when they are grown, they try to get even with you. First, by saying everything you do is hypocritical and stupid, and then by yelling at your own precious grandchildren simply because they like you better than their own parents. They want to punish you for that and for everything else you have ever done.

I remember my daughter saying, "God, Mother, you are such a fucking hypocrite!"

I, of course, retorted, "Did you just say the F-word? Did you just fucking come in here and use the fucking F-word in front of your fucking mother?"

Or how about the first time you realize your kid is on drugs?

"Are you on drugs?"

"No, I'm not, you old bag!"

"Yes, you are, I can tell."

"No, I'm not on drugs, Mother. Gawd."

"Then why are you slurring your words and sweating?"

"Um, am I slurring my words and sweating?"

The tip-off! If they weren't on drugs, they would have said, "I'm not slurring my words. Nor am I sweating. You're just a blowhard old bag!" Or something smart-assed like that. But a show of instant self-doubt gives them away every goddamn time!

"So where did you get these drugs that you are on?"

"Out of your bedroom drawer, the one with the big rubber penis thing!"

Ungrateful little bastards. They have no appreciation for the amount of drugs their parents have had to do in order to buy them the things they wanted. I told my kids: "C'mere, you. Listen very carefully. Mommy is an adult who pays the bills around here, and as long as you are living under Mommy's roof, you will respect Mommy's right to drink or take drugs or stand on one foot naked in the middle of the living room. And you are to be drug- and alcohol-free, bring home good grades, and do whatever Mommy asks you to do with a smile on your face! Understand? Mommy is old and has earned the right to be drunk or on crack or whatever she wants!"

Do you think I *should* take the hormones?

I'm actually on this new experimental drug for menopause. The FDA hasn't approved it yet. It's an extract from the flower of this one herb that gives off this chemical called THC. . . .

Everybody is on marijuana. I am under a doctor's care and she has prescribed medical marijuana as the treatment for my obsessive-compulsive disorder, which causes me to smoke too much marijuana, brought about by years of smoking too much marijuana. Haile Selassie is the Lion of Judah! I saw a sign on the side of a bus in Beverly Hills that said, "Talk to your kids about pot." So I went home and said: "Kids, do you know where I can get some weed?" Because that's the only drug that should be legal. In fact, it should be mandatory.

Women, wake up! Get off your diets and your hormones. We now possess the technology to biologically reengineer the male gender to be more docile and to have uniform penis size, thereby negating the need for wars.

Hence my plan to harness the powers of genetic engineering and reshape, restore, and reinvigorate every penis on earth. This alone could bring peace and stability to our planet. Don't you think that every government on the planet is controlled by a guy with a wiener identity issue? And who is telling women that we can't get fat? Men who feel uncomfortable about their penises, that's who! It's Psychology 101, really. They call it projection—that's when you project your problems onto another person. In this case, the men with penile issues are projecting their insecurities onto us, the women of the world. They don't want us to get fat because their penises can't get fat. Skinny dicks, skinny chicks. That's how they want it.

But it doesn't have to be that way. Not anymore. I have the solution. We must begin immediate funding for mandatory penile normalization surgery, until there is just one size fits all and no more reason for conflict. "But where's the money going to come from?" you ask. It doesn't matter. Take it from anywhere. Because once every man in this world has had his penis normalized, we'll have more money to burn. Take the military budget, for example. We won't be needing that anymore. There won't be any more wars. All the men will be too busy standing in front of the mirror admiring their new penises to fight a war. And even if you could somehow pry them away from the mirror, they still wouldn't do it. Too dangerous. After all, they might hurt their penises. Once this happens, we can get as fat as we want. And no one will care. Women will finally be happy. We'll be able to eat what we want whenever we want. And if for some reason we find ourselves in the position of having sex with a man, as with everything else, the job gets done quicker and more efficiently when you use the proper tool!

The Bible claims that only two people can be trusted at the End of Days: the drunkard and the insane. Lucky for you, dear readers, I'm both. I hope that I've helped.

Let's recap:

1. No more dieting
2. No more hormones

3. No more sex
4. More laughing, more drinking, more singing
5. More getting right with God

Even God gets on my nerves sometimes. You know when you are all alone in your room, talking to God, and you're getting answers that kinda piss you off? Like when you ask, "Why? Why do I have to be fat? Why?"

And God answers: "Umm, because you eat hundreds of donuts a day."

Or you ask, "Why is yet another man leaving me? Why?"

And thus speaks the Lord: "Because you treat them like crap."

And then you have to clarify just who is really telling you these heretical things, so you ask, "WHO THE HELL IS THIS?" and the conversation goes like this:

God: "Let's just say I'm your conscience."

You: "Well, where the hell have you been hiding?"

God: "You just stopped listening."

You: "No, if you remember correctly, I told you that I would not bother you and you should not bother me. I was being nice and thoughtful of all the hard work you do."

God: "No, you were being a slave to your lower chakras. You get what you give. Don't you get that yet? You ungrateful little bastard!"

You: "Don't you have war or starvation to attend to?"

I want to remind everybody that even though we are living in scary times, we don't need to be scared because God is smarter than all of us put together. I think I need to repeat that. God really doesn't need our help, and I wish people would stop bringing God into their own heap of personal shit. She doesn't care what we believe. She doesn't care what we think. She only cares what we do. For centuries we've been killing each other over religion, over the holy books. Hmmm. Here's a thought. I wonder what the Holy Book says about that? Let's see, there's nothing about waging endless war just because you don't like the way the other guy wears his beard; there's just lots of stuff about love and forgiveness. So much for centuries of theoretical moral questions bantered about by sages, professors, existentialists, and other assholes.

Now, I know what you're thinking. You're thinking, Isn't the Bible full of fighting, arguing, and acts of random bitterness? Well, yeah, it is. But if you read the *preface* to the Bible, the preface that has been hidden away all these years by those who seek to hide the truth, it all makes sense. And, as it just so happens, I have a copy of the preface right here.

It says: "Note of caution. Please be advised, the following references to fighting and other aggressive acts refer to the internal battle with one's own self. These metaphors are not to be taken literally. They are a *code.* Signed, God."

Got it?

God, in Her infinite wisdom and mercy, thinks of us as precious little retards. And She's not going to rush in after we've fucked everything up and save us. She really isn't, because She's not codependent. We need to get out of God's way. It's people who fuck everything up—people and their goddamned justifications to try to control everything, to try to make it better than it already is.

Take mad cow disease, for example. Cows were fed other dead, sick, crushed-up cows—that's how they got it, in the feed. Cows are not meat eaters, they're not cannibals, and when they ate their own kind, it blew all their circuits. Now we have to deal with an awful, incurable, fatal disease that was not even in existence until some idiot tried to cut corners! And what are the scientists doing to rectify the disease that they created? They are trying to clone a cow that is immune to mad cow disease. Hey, idiot, just don't feed the cow any more rotting cows. It's very simple. It's very simple because God meant for it to be simple, without us getting in the way and messing everything up.

It's the same with war. I think all the scientists who figured out how to split the atom should have a great big meeting and figure out how to put the atom back together, and then leave it the fuck alone! This is the kind of thing that happens when you put all your faith and trust into the hands of a few so-called "leaders." These guys don't give a damn about us. They're all in it for themselves. And these days, there is no such thing as a "surgical strike." If anyone goes up in a blaze, we are all going with them.

We need to stop the fighting. We need to make war illegal. We need to get over these ancient rules of tribalism. We need to evolve. We need to *will* evolution. And I know how. I have the *evolution solution.*

It's a computer chip to be implanted in all those who are willing to receive it. I call it the evolution chip, but you can call it the Holy Grail. This chip will wipe out primitive, instinctual behavior that is no longer relevant in the twenty-first century. It will block the urges toward tribal violence. It will eradicate stupid, selfish thoughts and replace them with altruistic ones. It will open our eyes, and make us see that *we* are the problem. Not everyone else. *Us.* And it will give us the desire to improve ourselves, and will make us really good gardeners. Because we need to grow more things—things like marijuana. Every day there is less green and more sand than there was the day before. And once all the green has been replaced by sand, the battle will be over. And we will have lost.

So, heed my advice. I beg of you. Or don't. I mean, it's not like I'm saying this for personal gain. What could I possibly get out of it? I'm already rich, gorgeous, funny, and impossibly stylish. What else is there?

No. I'm saying this for you. And your children. And your children's children. I tell you these things because I must. As the People's Queen, the Domestic Goddess, I have no other choice. So you people had better start listening to me. I'm fifty-eight years old now, so everyone had better listen to me because I have all the answers!

You know that play *The Vagina Monologues*? The one where everyone's talking about their vaginas and whatnot? I was in that play once in L.A. I wanted to add some of my own words to the piece, and I got permission from the writer, Eve Ensler, to do so. She claims to have been inspired by me. One of the many.

My monologue was titled "What My Vagina Smells Like." And I decided to close the piece by adding, "My vagina smells like my husband's face." Apt, succinct, and to the point, don't you think? Of course, the rest of the play was the regular propaganda regarding modern-day womanhood—you know, my vagina, boo-hoo, boo-hoo, blah, blah, blah.

And that's when I realized something. That's when it all crystallized. I wouldn't have called it *The Vagina Monologues.* I would have called it *The Clitoral Monologues.* After all, the clitoris *is* the sweet spot of the entire female apparatus. The jewel of the Nile! So threatening is the mighty clitoris that it must be relegated to a backseat to the vagina in a play that has to do with female parts! The vagina is nothing more than a baby-making tube that has nothing to do with real sexual pleasure in a woman! Even thinking women like Eve Ensler come up with new ways of denying that fact!

Do you see what I mean? These are the things that are in my head. These are the things I ask you to examine closely.

So if you are going through "the change of life," remember that it's really the second female metamorphosis. The first one was at about age twelve, right? Do you remember the horror of going through that one? It was like a horror movie for me. I was an outcast. People shunned me. And then, at the prom, all those buckets of blood—it was horrible. Wait a minute. That wasn't me. That was *Carrie.* Sometimes I get confused. It was still pretty bad, though.

In middle school the school nurse took all the girls to the auditorium, taped up the windows so the boys couldn't see in, and then the horror movie of all horror movies began: "Girls, today we will be talking about changes in your bodies. Something that happens to all girls—something beyond your control. BWAH-HAH-HAH! Watch as the body you trusted begins the transformation. Watch as innocent young girls are turned into raving shrews! Coming to a theater near you, every twenty-eight days."

As if it wasn't bad enough that I was fat and Jewish in Utah, now I had monthly hemorrhaging to deal with. And to add insult to injury, I still had to go to gym class. I think gym should be illegal. It is child abuse of the worst order, waged by awful perverts called gym teachers—mine was named Ms. MacNeeley. She was obsessed with making us shower. I did not want to shower with other people. I did not want to look at other people's bodies, or have them look at mine. The terror of that prospect made me go into the obsessive-compulsive suffering mode that fat girls do so well.

I had a lot of problems with body image, besides the fact that I was fat. I have no butt, and that takes a toll on a girl because everywhere you look people have butts, and you're like, what's wrong with me? I have no butt at all; it's just like this hump with a crack in it—a crack in my back and a source of embarrassment.

I wore my gym uniform under my clothes so I wouldn't have to get naked in front of all these naked, thin, perfect, Mormon blond girls. The only way to get out of showering at the end of class was to say you were menstruating. Then you got to keep your shorts on, cover yourself with a towel, and dab under your arms instead of having to shower. Eventually, Ms. MacNeeley, that sadistic bitch, called me into her office and said, "Roseanne, you need to bring a note from your doctor—you've been menstruating for fifty-eight days." I begged my mom to intervene, but she said, "Stop being such a baby—get into that shower with all the other girls!"

I remember that day like it was yesterday. Disrobing in front of all those people and marching into the shower, no longer having any control of my body or my life, I could hear all the girls behind me: "Look at her, she has no butt at all—just a crack in her back is what it's like!"

This single event caused me to hate my school, my mom, society, myself, and all those girls who were thinner, lighter, fatter, and darker than I, plus the Serbs, Croatians, Basques, gentiles, Jews, French, Germans, Russians, Asians, Africans, Pygmies, American Indians, Europeans, Semites, Mexicans, Spanish, Italians, Dutch, Arabs, Siberians, those from warmer southern climes, inhabitants of all seven continents, nonbelievers, true believers, and anyone athletically inclined—as a result of that OLD GYM HAG, may she rot in GYM HELL! Gym class made me a hater, as I am convinced it does to everyone who is forced to endure it.

Vegetarians say that eating meat makes people mean and hateful, and maybe there is some truth to that. I am close to vegetarian now because my daughter is, and she always has to ruin everything by reminding me that you are eating babies when you eat veal and how the poor calf has been kept penned up, fed butter, and not been allowed to move around at all for a whole year. Christ, I wish I could become veal myself! The butter and not-moving part would be like heaven to me. If someone kills me and eats me after that, I probably wouldn't even mind.

I wouldn't really mind being a goose, either. The same vegetarian daughter tried to dissuade me from eating pâté by telling me how they nail the goose's feet to the floor and pour tons of vodka down it's throat until its liver swells up. Damn, that doesn't sound half-bad of a lifestyle to me, either.

Actually, I have been laying off eating dead animals for a while now, and I feel like I've at least taken a step back from that whole "Cowshwitz" cruelty machine. It's probably the only real sin—cruelty, I mean. Like another great prophet and avatar of my age, Elvis, put it brilliantly: "Don't Be Cruel." Those are words to live by. I'm trying, but, oh man, sometimes the whole enchilada gets on my big nerve. Did I say enchilada? I'm outta here. See you in the next chapter!

Recipe for Change

Do something unexpected and new.
Stop doing something old and rehearsed at the same time.
Repeat!

Chapter 12

S-E-X, Do We HAVE to Talk About It?

I'm going to make a lot of people mad with this chapter. I'm certain of it. The bitchy little troll in my head who likes to shock the prim-and-proper witch-burner wannabes among us is wringing her chubby hands and drooling in anticipation. There's nothing she loves more than watching people squirm. And there's no better way than talking about S-E-X.

We really labor under some myths about sex and we need to get over it. That's why I've always liked Woody Allen's answer to the question: Is sex dirty? I don't know if *Woody* (get your mind out of the gutter) was the first to say it, but his answer was: "It is if you do it right." I've always thought that just about the lamest thing you can call sexual activity is "making love." Give me a break. Two horny, slobbering, thrashing humans rolling around on top of each other are not "making love."

There are more euphemisms for sex than there are Eskimo words for snow, and every single one of them is more honest and descriptive than that treacly, telltale expression of repression.

Some of you may squirm a little when the less poetic souls among us call it "slamming the ham," "packin' pork," "harpoonin' the poon," "riding the baloney pony," or just plain old "screwing." The truth hurts, especially people who seem to be allergic to it. But trust me. The sooner you stop making love and start fucking, the better your sex life will be.

Now and then, while surfing around on the tube, I've paused to watch some lily white TV evangelist, who looks like either a closet case or a hypocrite who sneaks off to the Dominican Republic with somebody else's Viagra prescription to get with slave-wage prostitutes—oh, wait, no, that's Rush Limbaugh. Anyway, one of these inbred hillbilly Talibangelists is always happy to proselytize about sexual "union" or "congress" or something else that sounds suitably *not* like what sex really *is.*

You know the spiel: "Sexual union is a sacred sacrament that God has given to those who are united in the bond of holy matrimony by which they can express their sanctified love for each other and by which they may be blessed with children." That's what they preach just before they get caught with their pants down in a public bathroom and right *after* they publicly repent and start slinging the "sacred sexual sacrament of marriage" shit again. Sacred sacrament, huh? Really? Well, what is it that the rest of us have been doing this whole time? You know, those of us who weren't virgins when we got married (if we got married) and who have actually had sex with more than one person? I guess that's a sin, because it sure as hell isn't anything like the bleached-out, sanctified, Sunday school stuff that Right Reverend Billy Bob is prissily preaching.

Lest you think that I'm going to piss off only the repressed people with my views on sex, I should mention that I'm also turned off and grossed out by people at the other end of the spectrum: people who constantly stick sex right in our faces, people who never tire of using cornball innuendo or other lame attempts to convince us that they're major studs or studettes just waiting to happen. Please! Strut your skanky stuff somewhere else—somewhere I'm not!

I'm not even going to go into this "cougar" bullshit; I'm going to be eating later. As much as I should be grateful for an appetite suppressant, I can't hack it in the form of a slutty-looking, liver-spotted granny with rodeo clown makeup, an Ace bandage bulge under the knee of her spandex pants, and cleavage that looks like it's been prepped for bypass surgery.

And don't even get me started on the men—crispy old geezers with their belts cinched just under their nipples, steel-wool hairballs the size of baby squirrels growing out of their ears, and hairpieces from the irregulars bin at Toupees-R-Us, bragging about all the "banging" they're doing again. Wow, *Dead Man Humping,* what a turn-on—NOT! It is men like this who make you long for kinder, gentler times, when Grandpa might suffer the hardening of the wrong artery every Memorial Day or so, drag himself somewhere in the vicinity of napping Grandma, hump on her arthritic hip for a moment or two, and then say, "Well, it ain't what it used to be, but you get the idea."

All this emphasis on miracle drugs from hell is fueling this repulsive wave of geriatric rutting. And for some reason, those unavoidable, satanic boner pill ads have a way of coming on when you're watching TV with family or somebody else you really don't want to be sitting around with in front of a boner pill ad. Always—without fail. You know the ones I'm talking about—those smarmy, airbrushed scenarios that discreetly hint at sex, and have clearly been slapped together by some frustrated fruitcake producer who wishes he were producing smarmy, airbrushed movies instead.

I have a couple of problems with these ads. *Número uno:* The people are too old to be having sex. Now, before you get your Depends in a twist, hear me out. I can't imagine that the irresistible desire or even feasible opportunity for geriatric intercourse arises often enough to merit all of these commercials. But for the sake of argument, let's say that you're old and you just *have* to have sex. You know, like if it's your insignificant other's birthday and you lost the coin toss, or it's Cinco de Mayo and you forgot how much of a wallop a couple of tequila sunrises can pack, and your old man (who's had three) is suddenly prying you out of your Spanx, even though your arms are too numb from the elbows down to give you enough strength to push him away. I'm sure you've experienced something like this, right? It can happen to senior citizens—although just saying the words "senior citizen" should be enough to dampen what should already be pretty soggy ardor by now. But if you find yourself still doing it, somehow, for God's sake, don't talk about it or even think about bringing it up. The mere thought of old people humping makes me vomit in my mouth a little bit. Where's my wine?

And the people in those ads—I mean, I know they have bills to pay and acting work is scarce and all of the rest, but let them hold on to their dignity—at least until the incontinence sets in. The deep, loving, slightly suggestive looks those poor old bastards are giving each other not only induce nausea, they're probably part of the reason that antidepressant sales are up; they're all made by the same companies, you know.

And last but not least: Get rid of the side-by-side matching bathtubs in these commercials. What in the hell is *that* twisted "Freud goes to Madison Avenue" symbolism all about? Precoital baths in the wilderness—*this* is what we have to look forward to? Leave it to some marketing major from the University of Bullshit to drag a couple of bathtubs to the beach or to a lake in the mountains to induce Baby Boomer boinking. Just imagining two blissed-out octogenarians soaking their wrinkled flesh in a tub of soapy water makes me pray for the nurse to come sponge them down quick before they shrivel into walnuts and drown.

Despite my hatred of the pill-pushing pimps behind these sad-vertisements, I sort of like that Enzyte Bob guy who does those male enhancement ads. He's kind of cute with that stupid, crazed grin and his infectious enthusiasm for life inside a TV commercial. They never come right out and define male enhancement in clinical terms exactly, which is sensitive and tasteful of them—not to mention good business sense, by conveniently allowing them to avoid fraud charges. But in Bob's world, where his golf putter is always pointing skyward, and the line on his graph at the *staff* meeting just keeps climbing up, up, and up, it's *hard* to miss the *thrust* of Bob's message. (Sorry, they had a sale down at Trite Sexual Innuendo Mart.)

I kid about my platonic fondness for Bob (he actually looks a little more Gay Mormon than I prefer); truthfully, I watch for the women. They don't just look admiringly and hopefully at Bob, as if he were the proverbial warden in a women's prison with his hand full of pardons. No, there's also the glazed, joyous, grateful gaze that comes from knowing that he's always generously ready, willing, and able to summon up a hefty, can-do, top-shelf erection that won't quit till they say "Uncle!" Ah, we've come such a long way since the bra-burning, consciousness-raising days of my youth, when we had to make do with Mr. Whipple. (Excuse me while I grab a tissue and try not to weep, deeply and openly.)

Seriously, sex is weird. Watching my youngest son turn fourteen, shed some baby fat, get a girlfriend, and begin snickering over objects that are longer than they are wide or words like *wiener* and *beaver* is weird, too. But seeing him turning into a young man and a *sexual being* is—YECCHHH!—really a gross-out! OMG, did I just say that? What I meant to say was that it's a real opportunity for growth on both of our parts, as well as a chance for me to reflect on the role that healthy human sexuality has played in my life, and how I can help encourage and foster that attitude in my children and grandchildren. Oh, who am I shitting? Sex is weird and there's probably a good reason why we, and our kids, cringe when we're forced to confront it in each other's company. Come on, we just do!

And now that my son is becoming a full-on teenager, it's a little extra weird. I want him to enjoy life in every aspect, but I'm his mother and I want to protect him, too. That sounds a little too pat, now that I just said it. You always hear dads talk about it in those terms, mostly when their daughters are involved. But I have mixed feelings for my kid; there's some dread—actually a lot of dread—and a touch of horror, too.

There are all kinds of feelings and emotions and neuroses and murky depths to puberty. I mean, hard as I've tried to block it out, I still remember being fourteen. I remember the planning and the manipulation and the plethora of ways devised to "trap" a man that I, and all my young teenage girlfriends, spent hours and hours discussing.

When I look back over my life, particularly my life as a female, wow, have we all gone through some changes. The difference between sexual attitudes from my mom's day and mine were huge. Back then, men really did expect to marry a virgin (poor bastards—and I say that with empathy for the men, too). A lot of weight was given to a girl's reputation, which meant one thing: her sexual history as recorded and blabbed by the neighbors. Before I start to sound like I'm calling all that "morality" hopelessly quaint and old-fashioned, let's remember that those were the days before the Pill. They knew what they were talking about when they warned that "A few moments of pleasure could turn into a lifetime of responsibility."

My mom was a very pretty girl and men have always been attracted to her. But my dad was the love of her life. They married young, and my mom says that there's satisfaction in not having been someone who slept around and took sex lightly. I wouldn't know about that. I grew up in the '60s and '70s, and we know what that time was like. I have to say that the hippies were right about some things. No disrespect to the hundreds of generations that came before the Pill, but our ideas about sex and morality really needed a little loosening up—and I was just the girl to do some loosening. I sure as hell wasn't alone, though let's just say I was a product of my times and then some.

With all the talk about the Sexual Revolution in the '60s and '70s, there was something about it that was a lot less tawdry and disrespectful to women than the times we've been living through in the last few years. It's not so much about freedom nowadays as it is pride in sluttery (I think I just made up that word). It's like slutwear is America's burka. I mean, the day after a raunchy sex tape shows up on the Internet, the *leading lady* makes it a career move, issuing a public statement about how it was meant to be a private memento of the passion that she and the guy she's now suing shared during the night they hung out together. Then she's off to the next meaningless appearance, or rehab, or wherever she's going.

But what really gets me is the way so many girls seem to be content to just be meat, to be portrayed as meat, treated like meat, and for me that's a turnoff. We should be treated as sex goddesses if we're bestowing our gifts on lucky men, not as grateful playthings for "players" who are up the street doing it to our sisters the next day, or the next hour, for that matter. This new devalued-and-fine-with-it approach may seem cool, or stylish, or modern, or whatever for a while, but time passes and there's not much future in just being a party girl.

More than ever, we are awash in commercialized, trashy, irresponsible sex that doesn't seem all that good-natured and fun for everyone involved. And somehow we're predisposed to think that anybody who has a lot less sex than us is a repressed prude, and anybody who has a lot more is a big ho-bag. Fair enough? But the fact remains that sexual energy is the bottom line of biology in that it keeps the race replenishing itself (too much, if you ask me). *That's* not going away.

I spent some serious time at the mercy of my hormones—and other people's, I guess. I am not a prude or anything. In fact, I have charmed more than a few snakes in my day, and done most everything there is to do except for getting paid to strip. I never publicly removed my clothing completely ever, since I was usually pretty fat, and the few times I got thin, I got saggy, and therefore had more of what needed to be left to the male imagination than most other gals. Keeping the male imagination stimulated is quite a task for a fat girl. But trust me, it can be done, and to your delight, it can be pretty wild once you get it revved up and going. Most of the time, though, keeping the male imagination actively engaged after a brief soiree or two, before the terrible boredom comes home, like a cock, to roost, is nearly impossible, as most guys have very limited imaginations when all is said and done.

The big difference between then and now is that back then I actually experienced sexual urges, but now, at age fifty-eight, I am completely free of all sexual thoughts and feelings and completely happy about this development. I firmly refuse to gulp down the estrogen pills that other sex-obsessed women my age are gobbling. They call themselves cougars, but I think they are more like coyotes and hyenas, all Botoxed and fixated on men, hungrily eyeing them like candy bars or donuts all the time. I guess I am a "badger." I hide in the dark and try to fall asleep before any attempt at sex can be sent in my general direction. I am over it—perhaps because the last time I visited my doctor for antibiotics due to yet another urinary tract infection, and listened to her tell me that when you are postmenopausal, your vaginal tissue loses its tone and gets paper thin and tears easily during sexual activity, and that in order to partake in the old in-and-out safely I should take male hormones, estrogen, and lube up my parts in excess and use condoms. I am allergic to latex, and, of course, we all know that using nonlatex condoms feels kind of like having sex with a balloon animal.

My boyfriend, Johnny, who is also old, has his own issues, the kind that lots of sixty-year-old men have with their (snicker, snicker) "wieners." I just had to eventually put it all behind me (snicker, snicker). But one of the few advantages of getting older is that sex is so much less of a drive and a distraction.

Sex is such a bore to talk about nowadays. Everyone and their brother yaps about it constantly, as if it is not something any common idiot, person, or goat can also do. I recently tried to have the birds-and-bees talk with my son on the way to pick up the girl he had invited to the homecoming dance. I said, "Hey, don't have sex or you are grounded, okay?" He said, "I have already fucked three or four chicks, Mom." I replied, "You better be kidding or you are going to lose your cell phone." He said that he was kidding and has only kissed a couple of chicks. I said, "Kissing is fine, but leave it at that, and wear a rubber when you do." Then we just laughed.

My son really likes this girl, though. And this was the first one of his dates I was allowed to meet. I insisted that he bring her a nice wrist corsage. We got it very late in the day because my son kept saying, "No one gets corsages for people anymore. This isn't the 1850s, Ma!" However, I still insisted that he do what my boyfriend, Johnny, said guys were supposed to do. I wouldn't know about homecoming dances, because I dropped out of school right after completing the ninth grade and was never invited to one.

But the girl actually wore it to the dance, as her Japanese mother insisted she do.

Shortly after dropping the kids off at school, my neighbor Lisa, who knows everything about everyone and everything in general, forwarded me an email from one of her outraged Republican pals from church, saying that kids are participating in sex acts at school dances these days, and included a link to an article in the *Orange County Register* about some private-school kids who were caught having sex at their homecoming dance. I always pay attention to these kinds of emails because the senders are conservative Christian Republicans who are often real pervs, so they know firsthand what goes on. I find them to be reliable sources of information because they are in the know about tons of the sin stuff—since it is the same sin stuff that they themselves are doing and feeling bad about yet *still doing* and kind of hoping to get caught doing, and then repeating after getting caught, and apologizing for in the public exhibitions for which they are so famous. Every Republican story, without exception, since the beginning of time until now, ends the same way. Period.

The article from the *Register* said that the boys at the dance were taking their wieners (snicker, snicker) out of their pants, wearing rubbers—another sign of how far we've come (snicker, snicker)—and the girls were getting down on their knees and giving out free blow jobs or butt sex or what have you. Those Orange County rich kids should be suspended forever! I guess their permissive, conservative, Christian, Republican parents have been too busy trying to prevent gay marriage over the last few years to notice how badly their own kids were out of control. Some of these girls today have gone wild and need to be tagged and caged.

The day after the dance, I asked Buck if there had been any inappropriate activity at his school dance, and he said that if there was, he didn't see any of it. I told him what Lisa's email said, and he said, "Christ, Mom, I go to public school, and that stuff only happens in private schools!" I am choosing to believe he is right about that.

My son will find out someday, after age thirty, ideally, that sex is a big, weird-ass, magnetic, repulsive, natural, alien, fun, embarrassing mystery that we just have to learn about and experience for ourselves, with all the attendant awkwardness, slobbery urgency, goose bumps, anticipation, disappointment, gross-outs, remorse, wicked self-satisfaction at getting away with something and the alternating fear of not getting away with anything, and then just STOP doing at some point! I only hope that I have instilled a healthy, heterosexual balance of fear and respect for women in him. If he were gay, I really wouldn't care, though, since gays seem to stop having sex far earlier than straight people do. Sometimes I wish he would be gay, or become a priest, or be both at the same time, like most priests are—as long as he was able to develop some interests and entertain himself with things other than his wiener (snicker, snicker). Like a mature person does!

Chapter 13

Looking Back at the '90s

The '90s was the decade that really changed my life. I went from being a working-class woman in the late eighties to being a multimillionaire who *played* a working-class woman on TV. Half the year I'd be quarantined in a windowless world where it was all about the Connor family, while outside the real world seemed like it was getting whipped around in a blender. I was like Rip Van Winkle waking up to the new decade after each season of my sitcom, and it was like that for me for years.

Computers and cell phones and beepers and fax machines were invading people's daily lives, but I lagged seriously behind in all of that. Suddenly, people had three phone numbers but never answered their phones. I thought computers were for nerds till I found out I was the nerd and had some serious catching up to do. The '90s brought us technology whether we wanted it or not.

Politically, the decade started with President Bush the Elder, but it quickly became the Clinton era. "The man from Hope" seemed kind of folksy in a younger, hipper way, what with the Fleetwood Mac theme song and his "white trash to Rhodes scholar" backstory. But Clinton was basically a company man in Democrat's clothing. He convinced people who were getting the short end of the stick that he "felt their pain," but slowly and steadily we got used to words like "downsizing" and "outsourcing" and "corporate raiding" and "globalization" and all those other words that meant that lots more people would be getting the short end of the stick before it was all over.

There was plenty of talk about "dot-com millionaires" and everybody seemed to be in a hurry to "have it all," but working people were slowly losing ground. I guess the upside (for me) to the ugly mess at the end of the Clinton era was that the leader of the free world risked it all to have some nasty diversion with a fat Jewish girl. Speaking of *nasty* . . . Ken Starr and his typically American sex-obsessed, puritanical torch-and-pitchfork army of self-righteous zealots took a gross minichapter in our history and turned it into a somehow *more* embarrassing pulp *novel.* Their exaggerated outrage and endless parading of the sordid details was off the sleazometer.

The '90s was a wake-up call for Americans in more ways than one. The horror at Columbine (I lived in Colorado for years before I made it big; my kids went to school there) drove home the fact that high school was hell for most kids, and that lots of parents who thought they were doing well were strangers to their own children. I guess I wasn't immune, either.

In my TV family, the Connor kids went through some tough life passages, but the family was tight in its own way and they muddled through. In real life, my marriage finally came apart for good and I wound up sticking my own kids in some of those bootcamp-type schools. They all like me now, so I guess things worked out, but as anyone who read the tabloids knew, the Roseanne on TV wasn't exactly the same me who was leading my private life, or should I say being led by it.

I felt grateful and privileged to be rich and famous; I was, after all, an attention-craving kid from Utah. But I felt victimized by the spotlight, too. Some of my worst behavior and lapses in judgment (as I affectionately refer to big chunks of my private/public life, like my second marriage, among other things) were blown up on the front pages of the gossip rags. But I quit feeling sorry for myself and for my lack of privacy when the tragedy of Princess Diana took over the headlines, Superman fell off his horse and was paralyzed, and Mother Teresa died. I had my physical health, but my *mental* health was almost totally wrecked.

Speaking of health, the '90s were a super-health-conscious decade. Even *I* lost weight thanks to what I call the *surgery diet.* Exercising like crazy was hugely popular, but for me, being Jewish and all, *that* was never really an option. Lots of Baby Boomers were fortyish and wanted to hang on to what was left of their youth and vitality. Some of my generation decided to hang on to somebody *else's* youth and vitality. I, for example, dumped my younger husband for a *much* younger husband. I'm a feminist; I wasn't about to let men be the only ones allowed to trade in their ultimately insignificant others for a newer model.

The '90s were a little like the '60s upside down. There wasn't really a counterculture to speak of, unless you want to call the growing rabid right-wing hordes, who thought Rush Limbaugh knew what he was talking about, a counterculture. The left had been bought out, discredited, blamed for everything from crack cocaine to AIDS. *Liberal* was a word that was hissed at people. Slowly but surely, the advances made by working people were being eliminated for the purpose of lowering the cost of doing business and competing with those who could always find a Third World workforce that saw working for pennies as a step up.

Yes, the word *liberal* was demonized. The few people who openly spoke up about the environment were called "tree huggers" by the right-wing nuts, and the few women who still spoke up about equal pay for equal work were branded "feminazis." Unfortunately, that brand of BS sold like shares of Microsoft and we're paying the price—but, hey, I'm supposed to stick to the '90s here.

Anyway, for those who thought that Rush Limbaugh and G. Gordon Liddy were practically hippies, there were right-wing militias. They were an especially interesting phenomenon. These were groups of men who played army in the woods in preparation for what they figured was the coming war with (take your pick): an intrusive government (quaint), liberals, blacks, gays, people who had or might have an abortion, Mexicans, tree huggers, feminazis, or some or all of the above. A lot of the wind went out of their sails when the horror of the Oklahoma City bombing temporarily shocked us all into a stunned realization of how wrong such things can go.

The pop and rock music of the era was all over the map. Rap was gaining momentum; Tipper Gore wanted to label lyrics that seemed beyond X-rated. I was divided there. The artist in me rebelled at the idea of censorship, as my friend Frank Zappa did. But the mom in me was turned off by what I saw as misogyny and glorification of violence and pimp culture. We still wrestle with it. Grunge came shuffling out of the Pacific Northwest. Some say they dressed like the people on the *Roseanne* show did and made that look really hip, bringing back long hair and thrift store fashion with its surly, introspective, hard-rocking themes of alienation and rejection of the stale hype over what some were now seeing as a discredited American dream.

A big movie at the time was *Pretty Woman,* which I thought was a minor insult to prostitution and a waste of a good Roy Orbison song, but an even bigger movie was *Titanic.* As far as movies about sinking ships are concerned, though, you can't top *The Poseidon Adventure* because Shelley Winters was in it. Shelley played my grandma on *Roseanne* and what a great old broad she was! She represented a colorful, more golden age of Hollywood for me—one where it was still *women* who sometimes slept their way to the top but brought their talent and brains with them.

My favorite Shelley Winters story (that I can tell in print) was the time Shelley started to act out her Oscar-winning scene from *Lilies of the Field* on set, and scream out the N-word over and over as a way of showing both of our cameramen, both black men, how enamored she was of the civil rights movement. It was classic Hollywood to me. Shelley had, in fact, been a major player in the group of Hollywood stars who walked with or supported Dr. Martin Luther King Jr. Both camera guys just stood there staring at her for a couple of minutes before they burst out laughing and had to take a break back at the craft service tables, where I, too, ran for cover.

Shelley was yelling, "What's so funny? That is what America was like back then!" I told her they were laughing because they were uncomfortable hearing a white woman yell that word at them. She got mad and said, "I didn't call them the N-word. I said *nigger* because it was in the movie! I would never use the N-word myself!" Which just made it even more cringingly hilarious.

She tortured everyone all the time. If she had only a line in the show, she would end up acting out an entire scene from an old classic she had been in, or else she would start telling sex stories of Hollywood, or else she would tell us secrets about Marilyn Monroe and the Kennedys, as she had been Marilyn's roommate for a number of years. She did everything like that for hours. The only thing she didn't do is ever once say her line right. I loved that part. It was hilarious to me, and I enjoyed her so much. A scene with her, Estelle Parsons, and Laurie Metcalf was absolute heaven for me to watch. The wonderful part of that is that I got to think up situations in which to put three of the world's greatest actresses. What a rush to be involved with that.

Another rush for me was just hanging out with Sara Gilbert, who is a remarkably deep human being and a talented actor and comic. I think one day we will all be watching something she writes and directs herself. She is a big talent in many ways. She has two kids of her own now, whom I hope I get to see more of soon.

Michael Fishman has two kids and a wonderful wife; he also has a unique and funny personality, and a lot of talent and potential that I hope he continues to bring forth. Lecy Goranson, who played Becky, is also one of the more interesting actors I have ever worked with. She has more potential than almost every other young woman actor out there right now. Sarah Chalke is a great person, a funny and darling girl who is having great success on her own. I am proud of her down-home Canadian country girl, rock-solid green values that she never lost touch with.

We all miss Glenn Quinn, taken by the hard drugs, like so many good, young, sensitive artists.

Sandra Bernhard was the first actor ever who was gay and who played gay, years and years ahead of Ellen and Rosie (who should thank her someday), and I still tell her no one has ever been that brave since. She stands alone in honest vulnerability, and all of that shows in her acting. John Goodman is one of the greats. Even when he would piss me off a lot by acting bothered by having to do the show after he got involved in the movies (again, I hate anything to do with the movies and movie people), I always reminded myself to just shut my trap, walk away, and be grateful that I got to work with such a great actor. John and I would stand in anticipation of the way Laurie would play a scene, and Laurie and I would be lying on the floor laughing at John. It was a great, great show that we all made together.

I had a lot of great friends around me on *Roseanne;* some I see a lot and some I see hardly at all, but I always think of them and remember it all with lots of happiness. Most of all, though, I remember the fun I used to have with my prop crew and my wardrobe women. They made me laugh every day; they brought me flowers when they knew I was down; their wives sent me home-baked cookies and hand-crocheted baby booties for Buck; and they brought their families to meet me; and they were always so nice to me and loved working on my show. The wardrobe women, Erin and Mary Quigley, kept me in stitches, and sane and safe through a terrible personal time. They, along with Laurie Metcalf, gave me the kind of loyalty that is really beyond what any boss can ever hope for from dedicated people who care for her. It was just great fun drinking with my crew on many Friday nights after taping.

George Clooney was the most fun person on earth to get drunk with. His practical jokes are still legendary. The great writers whom I pushed and pushed to get better ideas out of and who now hate my guts, as they sit in their million-dollar homes where they would never be without my show, can consider themselves thanked here and then go and fuck themselves. LOL.

Television was going through its changes at the time. I liked and respected Bill Cosby, but business is business, and my ring-around-the-blue-collar family knocked his show out of the top ratings spot with a thud heard around the world of showbiz. Bill did his best to honestly represent the kind of black family that lots of white families wished there were more of, but a big chunk of the America of the '90s was ready for the Connor family. Dan and Roseanne didn't have much money, but in spite of that they managed to be fat and stay out of foreclosure. They didn't kiss up to the establishment; in fact, they smirked in its face when it deserved it and they got through somehow, and so did their kids. They weren't all airbrushed and squeaky clean, but they were likable, somehow, and even though it usually wasn't pretty, they got through the day and somehow hung on to some real core values that made their underdog story one that people could relate to in crazy, changing times.

Crazy, changing times—that was the '90s; although they can look almost tame in light of some of what's come since then. I'll never be the same and neither will the world. That's why I say we should all party like it's 1999!

I hear they are making a porn version of the *Roseanne* show (as if the original with me parading my svelte two-hundred-and-thirty-pound love goddess bod hither and yon wasn't sexy enough), and that prompts my hastened retirement from show business.

I hope they do something to try to stop the porning of everything. I don't like it! I guess if people feel the need to sexualize their fat neighbors, though, who am I to stop them? It's an idea whose time has come. Fat women are the hottest of the hot, after all. You know you won't get hungry with a fat girl around! The gal playing me in the porn version is Asian, of course. It's no accident. I am thrilled for the Jewish people that many of us can pass for Asian, especially in our old age. All old Jewish women look just like Mao Tse Dung, I've noticed.

Speaking of Jews, one night, my sister and I met up with Sammy Davis Jr. at Patsy's restaurant in New York City. Mr. Davis was entertaining his family in an elegant manner in a private room upstairs, and they were gracious enough to excuse him for a moment to come out and greet the likes of yours truly. He said the most awesome words to me—words that I would be embarrassed to print here for fear that prying, inquiring minds might suggest that I am immodest in my old age. It simply isn't true, assholes! But Sammy and I and my sister got into some kind of a Hebraic contest of who could be the most gracious of all Jews, which is a thing all Jews like to do when meeting other Jews. It's in the Talmud; look it up sometime!

Here's what happened: After Sammy said the most flattering things in honor of the message I was bringing to mankind, Sis piped up with "Excuse me one moment, sister dear, if you will. Did I just hear Mr. Jewish Chocolate God of awesome unparalleled genius and talent, such as has never graced our people, the Jews, before in its international scope of brotherhood and justice, say to my own sister, that he, as a man, indeed understands that the Power of the Mother is the Power of *Hashem*? I must say that now that I have heard Mr. Sammy Davis Jr. say these things, I am even more in awe of this great and wonderful man, which is you, sir!"

So I had to top that, and top it I did, folks. I said, "For Mr. Sammy Davis Jr., the man who birthed the civil rights movement almost single-handedly, to call me a true original, is to me the greatest moment in my life as a Jew. I want to say, God bless you, sir, Mr. Sammy Davis Jr. You are a song-and-dance man, a comedian, an actor, and are, therefore, a quadruple threat to agents and producers and talent everywhere! Yet you, my most humble Jewish brother, are also a shining light, an avatar, a bodhisattva, and a messenger of peace! I am beyond honored, sir," and then I kissed his ring.

But Sammy wasn't finished yet. He then said, "Before I return to my wonderful family in the other room, I must also say that the two of you, sisters who love and care about each other, are wonderful representatives for the strength and the love of family. May your lives be long and happy. To joy!" And with that, he took a drink from his glass and went back to join his family. That was the pinnacle of all my childhood show business dreams!

I still think fondly of all of it—meeting Johnny Carson and Rodney Dangerfield, drinking with Phyllis Diller and Bob Hope, speaking to Carol Burnett and Joan Rivers and Virginia Graham and so many others. God, it was fun! The most unforgettable woman I ever met, besides all the other amazing women I have met—Madonna, Hillary Clinton, and so on—was this Chinese fortune-teller in L.A.'s Chinatown. This is what she very loudly told me, after I handed her twenty bucks: "YOOO TOOO TELPICH! YOU DO WHUT YOU HUBBAND TAY! HE NO GOA DO WHUT YOOO TAY!" And then she laughed like a hyena. I asked her to repeat her words, and she repeated them verbatim, only much louder. I gave her some extra money and asked her to repeat them for a third time, and she did. I understood her the last time, too—"You are too selfish. You should do what your husband says for you to do. He is *not* going to do what you say to do."

I said, "Lady, that's why I don't have a fucking husband and why I don't want another one ever again!" Then *I* laughed *my* ass off.

Recipe for Laughter

One part unconscious,
Two parts logic.
Strain through smooth cheesecloth,
Then take the strained extract,
Add wry and spread thin on
Those who have thick bread.
Comedy changes rich people, I have found,
And it saves the poor.

Chapter 14

Marriage, Cheatin', and Dirty Dogs—This Ain't a Country Song

Famous serial adulterers just keep climbing out of the clown car that is our "culture" and onto the tabloid covers and our TV screens. From presidential candidate to late-night talk show host, from world-class athlete to husband of America's Sweetheart (I thought *I* was America's Sweetheart!), the only thing they have in common is their well-known names (or those of their wives) and the fact that you'd think they'd all have known better. Not necessarily should they have known better than to cheat, but to think they'd keep it a secret in this scandal-driven, gossip-hungry world—I mean, come on, guys!

Before I just go and unload on these dirty dogs, I have to represent like the modern woman I am and say a few things that might *not* sound like something worthy of an American sweetheart, but who knows: Maybe some men, at least (and cheating women), might like me more after this. I'm not one for making excuses for people who break serious promises, especially the kind that bring the emotional and other consequences (gunplay) that come in the wake of cheating on a spouse or committed partner. What I am saying, though, is maybe it's time to poke around in the embers of the Sexual Revolution and see if any of them throw a little light on the causes of all this betrayal and heartbreak and condemnation and all the rest of that painful crap.

I've thought for a long time that there are probably a whole lot of people who shouldn't be married or even in any kind of monogamaniacal relationship. Making grand pronouncements about never sleeping with another human being besides the one you're locking things in with on your wedding day may have been a great idea back in the day, but lots of people used to die of old age in their forties, too, and lots of people never ventured beyond their little villages. I mean, aside from marriage, how many other important aspects of our lives do we try to live in accordance with arrangements that were invented thousands of years ago? Maybe by now you're thinking: What the hell? Roseanne, a woman who liked marriage so much that she did it three times by the time she was in her forties, is now talking it down? Very funny, reader whose mind I'm reading!

Seriously, though, maybe it's time to just let relationships be what they are as they unfold and as they're agreed upon by the couple, after some superserious, realistic considerations. Maybe asking everybody to relate to the opposite sex in exactly the same way might be an idea that has since expired. I know I won't make any friends among those who have a stake in what I call "The Wedding Industrial Complex," but I have to be honest. I'm not looking to take jobs from people who make wedding gowns for a living, and I don't want to close down factories that produce those lovely garters that brides toss over their shoulders, or even reduce the workload of divorce lawyers, but come on, people! I mean, when something fails more than it succeeds, it's time to at least reconsider the institution of marriage, don't you think?

More than half of all marriages fail; you've heard the statistics.

When we hear that lovely sentiment from young marriage-minded women that goes, "I just want to have that ONE special day when it's all about me," somebody should tell them, "Honey, chances are you're going to have a couple of those. You may wish you'd saved some money and energy for a second or third 'one special day.'"

And before anyone asks the magic question "Roseanne, you insane, blasphemous lunatic, what about THE CHILDREN? THE CHI-HIL-DREN?" I ask, "Well, what about them?" I just quoted the statistic; if more than half of marriages end in divorce, then guess what? Half the kids are living with divorced parents. My kids were children of divorce and they've turned out great! Okay, well, maybe my kids aren't the best example. I'm kidding, of course; they're kind, decent people. Sure, they still have festering resentment for me because I left their dad, and they've carried it around and nurtured it for close to two decades. But they take it less personally since I've dumped two more husbands since then. They've matured, and they know, deep down in their hearts, that if they want to stay in the will, they need to forgive, accept, and move on.

The psychic in me hears you saying something else now: "When are we going to get to the good, scandalous, gossipy part, where we rag on the dirty, cheating men-dogs?" Well, you know I love a good gossip session as much as the next three people combined, but I've had to reconsider a few things as the wisdom of age comes over me, along with the thought of how much money and perfectly good booze I wasted on weddings with the wrong husbands.

Okay, back to the dirty sex part. Now, I'm sure as hell not going to excuse or condone dishonesty; if you're in a monotonous—I mean, monogamous—relationship, you need to honor the promise you've made to be faithful, and that's that. None of this "I'm mostly monogamous" crap I've heard people say. I'd like to see their face when they find out that their temporary love interest is *mostly pregnant.*

Inevitably, people look at whoever is the Cheating Dog of the Week in the scandal rags or on the tabloid shows, and ask, "Why in the world do those awful men, those dogs, cheat when they have a perfectly lovely wife (girlfriend, fiancée) whom they should be showering with that physical attention?" Men do it for the same reasons that dogs do it—because they're drawn to the sheer pleasure and excitement that makes sex as fun as it was when they first got with the significant other they're cheating on. And, staying with the dog comparison for a minute, let's remember the "hard" fact that dogs do it when there are *females in heat* around. Sometimes their bitches are not so readily available, and the horny doggy "suitor" has to climb a fence with a few strands of barbed wire strung across the top at great risk to his pesky 'nads, or swim through a flaming oil slick out at sea, but his targeted, temporary lady love is always putting out a biosignal that turns him into a furry heat-seeking lust missile.

For every dirty, cheating, heterosexual man there's not just a betrayed woman left in his wake, but one or more women who are his partner(s) in crime! The tired old idea that they only stray when they're not getting what they want at home is bullshit, at least in a whole lot of cases. There are plenty of red-blooded women who are more than willing to go for just about anything that their guy can dream up (if it doesn't hurt too bad, leave a scar, or burn the house down), not that I'd know from experience (wink!).

The question shouldn't be: Why do people want to have sex with somebody besides their sanctioned partner after a certain amount of time? For some people, the "certain amount of time" probably begins on day one. Rather, I think the question should be: Why not put off getting married unless you are absolutely sure you'll never yield to the temptation to stray if and when the opportunity arises? People who aren't man or woman enough to face that question and give an honest answer probably shouldn't be getting married or making a serious pronouncement about the future of their urges and what they're going to *not do* about them. They sure as hell better be sure before they ask me to change *my* plans, show up for their wedding, and bring a present. Now that's something *I'm* sure about!

So why do people screw up (pun alert) one of the biggest commitments in life? Why do people get married who shouldn't? There are a few reasons why even people with lots of options decide to limit them—people like rich celebrities, for example. Even though they may have tons of money and willing sex partners, they still may not be happy (poor babies!).

Truthfully, being happy may qualify as a sign of mental illness, I've decided. I mean, if you're spending lots of time skipping around, clicking your heels, and smiling till your face hurts (or thinking you should be), you're not paying attention to the real world. I'm not suggesting you should be bummed out constantly, but get real. Unfortunately, getting real is the last thing that a world that runs on advertising wants you to do, and marriage is sort of like a product—a megaproduct, in fact. That's why it gets "bought" when a single celebrity, or any wealthy, privileged person, male or female, eventually comes to the logical conclusion that money and the things it can buy, and even the fawning attention of the opposite sex, doesn't make them "happy" around the clock. What else is left for them to try once they've gone down the hedonist highway as far as it takes them?

The answer, usually, is the marriage-and-family myth—you know, the sugary, oversold one that we hear from cradle to grave. Sure, you're loaded and you get all the attention you can handle, but as the story goes, there's nothing like the wondrous thrill of finding that one magical someone who will "complete you" (or some other mostly nonsensical notion like that) and with whom you can raise a happy little family—happy, happy, happy—happily ever after. I'm not saying that it never happens, but people shouldn't try to use it to cure their lack of appreciation for what they already have, or to fill some sense of lack that they shouldn't expect another human being to completely fix for them. It won't be cured by entering into the most serious and complex relationship you can opt into, dude! It works just fine for some people, but some people win the lottery, too; that doesn't mean you should count on winning the lottery to pay your bills.

I'm not saying that marriage isn't an awesome thing for lots of people, all things considered. It's just that a lot of people don't consider it carefully enough. Finding out, after you're married, that having your freedom—socially, sexually, however you want to put it—wasn't so bad after all makes you wonder why you gave it up in the first place.

I really didn't start this little part of the book with the desire to bad-mouth monogamy. I've practiced it for most of my adult life. I'm choosing my words carefully: I didn't say all my adult life or even all my married life; I did some straying. It started out as revenge for being cheated on, but turned into something like a "calling" for a while. You can read about it in my second book—it's old news. But in the face of all the scandalous headlines that are considered news today, remember to think twice before you do anything you might wish you hadn't. Take it from me—I know what I'm talking about.

Recipe for Disaster

For every part True Believer,
Mix in two parts
Appetite for Destruction.
Add beer and wedding rings.

Chapter 15

Love and Marriage

This year will mark the eighth wedding that I have planned, executed, and paid for in my lifetime. My own weddings are so far in the dim mists of the past that they seem like they almost never happened—and oh, were that only true, most of my life would have gone along much better for me.

I organized and paid for my kids' dad's second wedding. He got married on my now defunct talk show; I forced my third husband to marry me on my show, too, but basically did it for the ratings. Forcing my then-husband to marry me on my show for ratings basically destroyed that marriage, but I count that wedding even though it seems a little off. Anytime I get to dress up in a wedding gown or bridal outfit counts, since that is the whole reason to have a wedding at all. It's each girl's show business moment, and she gets a whole year to act out all the fantasies of her childhood and make her mother go into hock in order for her to do it. It's a young girl's perfect revenge on her mother. As a mature woman, once you see how smitten your daughter is with the man she is marrying and all that happy horseshit about living together in perfect harmony, your septic tank of toxic dysfunctional memories may be full and ready to spew.

I want to start having big wedding gown balls, where all the little girls get to show up and wear one, be walked down the aisle by a handsome male escort, and have a blast without having to actually live with the asshole afterward. That's the part that is just too, too horrible even to think about. I will forever be haunted by the faces my exes made when they orgasmed, and knowing that they saw my face during that unfortunate time is enough to make me want to gouge out my own eyes with a rusty spoon. Ugh! I wish I could say that I faked them all, but alas, shit just happens sometimes, usually with the wrong people around you.

The last of my daughters to marry, as we old Jewish ladies say, was my middle daughter, Jessica, who got married on June 13, 2008. To say that I breathed a sigh of relief once she got a man to take her off of my tired hands would be an understatement. Now she would have a man to blame everything on instead of me; I rejoiced.

I must admit that I married men just to have someone to blame for everything that went wrong in my life, as a lot of Jewish gals do. Sometimes you feel so sorry for that man, knowing that the way his wife treats him is not the poor dear's fault at all. However, that wasn't the case with my second husband. I could prove that everything was indeed his fault, and that he still feels no shame at all about the cheating and lying and the actual harm he caused me. But the frightening thought that I had done the whole thing to myself by choosing unsuitable partners (talk about towing the line on the gag order!) overtakes my desire to blame others. I would fall in love with the first guy who ever looked at me twice. I never shopped around; I just settled and made do. The first time I married a guy it was because he had no cats.

The first wedding other than my own that I planned was my

youngest daughter's, Jenny. She was the first to marry (I sound like Tevya in *Fiddler on the Roof* with this, don't I?), and she married her little brother's best buddy from high school in a Las Vegas ceremony on December 20, 1998. My son-in-law, now *he's* a delight. I shouldn't even call him a son-in-law; I think of him just like a son—another unemployed, hostile, disrespectful son. He and I get along pretty well most of the time. He'd been hanging out at my house since he was fourteen years old, so he was used to the way I run things.

I must say I was shocked when he went for my daughter and vice versa. It was a little too European shtetl for my liking, like marrying your cousin or something, as every one of my overly hairy relatives indeed did. My mother's aunt was married to her own uncle (and by the way, I'm my own grandpa!). Two of my sisters are married to a brother and sister, and both of my sisters' last names are Epstein-Barr. You can't make this shit up, folks!

I was just so happy that my son-in-law took my fat daughter off my hands, and that he finds her so incredibly hot that he cannot take the time to put on a rubber before having sex with her, thus giving me four gorgeous grandsons who are the funnest people I have ever met. These grandsons know what's funny. In fact, I would say that I have never personally appeared before a better crowd in my life! Lifting your leg and farting makes them howl for hours! Even the little one is amused when I do that tongue-thrusting, eye-rolling thing. I know how to entertain an audience. So don't tell me that Roseanne Barr isn't funny anymore, network executives. You guys can kiss my ass. You guys are complete fucking idiots, and I am writing this here because I know people of your ilk never read books. You read scripts and there is a fucking difference, okay? God, you people couldn't tell the difference between a book and a good shit if people like Oprah weren't telling you what to read.

Hey, Oprah, tell your fans to read *Das Kapital* by Karl Marx. Talk about a good, relevant read! Oprah has never done one show on economics or capitalism and that pisses me off. Not one show on how television advertising, which made Oprah a billionaire, makes money by keeping people in front of their TV sets while the guys at the top rob them blind! Are we supposed to ignore the elephant in the room? That YES, WE NEED MORE SOCIALISM AND LESS BANKSTERISM HERE IN AMERICA!

"Socialist" is what they called Dr. King and all the other activists. "Socialist" is what they always call me, too, erroneously—I am more of an antisocialist. I am completely antisocial and prefer my own company to any human contact that does not involve me standing in front of a happy, laughing crowd of respectable and intelligent bon vivants (or drunks who read literature).

But back to my family and weddings. Jenny, my big-legged daughter, was quite a handful as a child. She could not sit still, would tear things up, and she'd scream a lot, too. I, of course, am known for having an irritating voice, and she had a voice that made her mother proud. As soon as she started screaming in restaurants, people would get up from their tables and rush out to get their tubes tied. What a thrill it is for me to see that all three of Jenny's sons (not counting the newborn alien, named Buster Lyle) are the dramatic types themselves. Sitting in a restaurant with little four-year-old Cosmo Dexter, watching him get irate at the waiter for not asking him if he would like a cocktail, too, I said, "Hey, dude, don't act like your mother, okay?" Just seeing his mouth pop open as he laughs secretly with me behind his mother's back is a gift of *nachas* (Jewish for "joy") from God Herself!

My daughter still has quite the hot temper, as do I. But luckily for us our fat asses keep us grounded; we cannot physically lash out in anger at anyone, as it would require getting off the couch, and not just to go eat! Jenny claims I made her fat by always trying to force her to diet. It is true that her father and I put a padlock on the fridge once. There was nothing in there but pickles at the time, but she got in somehow and drank the pickle water—damn, girl, that's h-u-n-g-r-y!

My daughter is too smart for me, though. She once blackmailed her babysitter to sneak her out to Del Taco after school. The babysitter, getting chummy with my kids after working for me for about a month, told my preteen daughter that she smoked PCP on the weekend but made it a point never to smoke it during the workweek. She smoked only pot during work hours. Jenny, who is conniving and evil, then said, "My mom would fire you in a minute if she knew you had told us these things. I am not going to tell my mom what you said as long as you go to the store and buy me two large cans of sauerkraut that I can keep in my bottom dresser drawer and run me to Del Taco whenever I want." The babysitter was high on pot and understood about breaking rules, so she was cooking the diet meals for my daughter and moonlighting as a snack ho.

Jenny is quite a painter and artist and poet herself, but because I encouraged her to go to art school instead of getting married and having children, she chose instead to marry her brother's odd yet handsome friend and have a baby every single God-blessed year. Clearly, she inherited her rebelliousness and her weight problem from me. She is the most wonderful mother I have ever seen, though. I did not want my daughter to suffer from being a fat girl like I had been, and I guess I went overboard. But I was just trying to help her, and I hope that someday she will understand that.

It is not easy to be the fat mother of a fat daughter in this society! If you and your kids are fat, you can never go to another all-you-can-eat buffet for as long as you live unless you want to be shamed by everyone around you who, as they eye you and your little ones, say things like "You'd better take your kids to a gym and not a buffet, lady!" I would walk right up to them and that shocked them—I guess they thought that a fat person would rather cower behind a buffet than be confrontational about their rudeness. I would say, "Don't talk about my kids, pal, and don't talk about their mama!" Of course, the smart fat family learns that Tuesday night is the night that all the real, real fat families can shamelessly go to the buffet and not be alone because it's Taco Night (this is a fat mom top-secret alert—after reading this page, tear it up and eat it) and we can all smile at one another instead of looking down at the ground to avoid judgmental eye contact from the furiously fit.

The second daughter to marry was my oldest daughter, Brandi, whom I did not raise. She was married in May 2003 in Manitou Springs, Colorado, and her wedding day was overwhelming in so many ways. It was the first time that I had met her adoptive mother's family and the first time that my mother met "My Baby Mama."

My daughter's other mother, Gail (Brandi was given up for adoption by me at birth, and then reabsorbed into my crazy family twenty years ago), is a wonderful person. I could not have hoped for a better woman to be "My Baby Mama," as I call her. I love Gail. We are girlfriends who have worked it all out. Gail divorced Brandi's adoptive dad when Brandi was younger, and he has since married a woman who, though not Jewish, controls his every waking act quite nicely.

Our daughter Brandi married a Jewish fellow from Saint Petersburg, Russia, who looks exactly like Putin, and whom she met on JDate. Russian Jewish males are incredibly intriguing people, I have found. They are left wing in a crazy right-wing way. I used to write letters to the Soviet government when I was part of the Committee of Concern for Soviet Jewry, asking them to let my people go. The USSR was no match for the thousands of Jewish American women who wrote and sent those letters, and soon they gave up and allowed all the Jews who wanted to leave Russia to go. (A word of advice: Do not get Jewish women started if you do not want to stir up trouble for yourself. Just do what they tell you and do it quickly, and everything will be okay.) We all know what happened after that—their economy collapsed and so did their central government.

The collapse of their economy frightened the Russian people so badly that they actually allowed the Jews who stayed in their country better comforts than they had allowed them before, which is good for civil rights of minorities, something Russians are no better at ensuring than Americans. I am all for civil rights, and I love minorities because I am part of several minority groups myself, from the female to the Jew to the fat to the lefty to the feminist. Being rich is another one of my favorite minority groups, though, I must say. And still, within that infinitesimally small segment of the population, I have found that being a rich person who gives 20 percent of her money to charity annually makes me a member of a minority group of fewer than ten people! There are almost no others like me!

Governments are run by the smallest minority in the entire world—the rich or the royal 1 percent. And since I am part of a group of fewer than ten people—a fraction of that 1 percent, which is the world's smallest economic group—I must claim some land of my own somewhere and become its benevolent ruler. My son-in-law Vladmir and my daughter are in real estate sales, which means they like capitalism. I do not like capitalism at all, and consider it a Ponzi scheme that the entire Western world is at the mercy of. In my utopian fantasy there would be no money system at all, just drinking and singing and partying, bartering goods, growing gardens, and making art.

Needless to say, the Russian son-in-law and I find each other peculiar. He thinks I am a loudmouthed, disillusioned female who is intent on defying patriarchal order—and of course, he is right, on paper. I think that he is confusing me somewhat with his own mother, who took him to Denver, Colorado, when he was ten years old so that he would not be forced to serve in the Russian army. Of course, I had always heard from my own grandmothers about how their Russian mothers and grandmothers attempted to put a firewall between their own sons and the Russian army in creative ways for generations, but I had never met one of them in person. (What's the difference between an immigrant, Russian Jewish mother and a pit bull? The overly dark lip liner and the lipstick, though they both have the loud and terrifying snarl.) My daughter's mother-in-law and I have physically fought over who hogs our grandson the most. Can you imagine a crazed Russian woman acting like that? Me neither, and that is why I punched her fucking lights out!

On the night before our kids' wedding, I made a joke to my daughter about how happy she would be once the wedding was over and she could start regaining all of the weight she had lost to fit into her wedding gown. The Russian, Vladmir, got a little too upset by that small joke, I thought, and he said, "I thought about what they say about how in twenty years your wife will look just like her mother. But I figured out that you did not really raise her, and her adoptive mother is very thin, so I took that into account and I will marry her anyway."

I was completely floored that the Russky had the balls! I threw back my shot of wodka, and in no uncertain terms told the *boy* that his wife shares my genes and would one day be fat just like me, so he better get used to the idea. He looked me in the eye and said, "I will not allow her to get fat." I said, "You won't be able to stop her." He said, "I *will* stop her or we will get divorced."

It was the way he said it that sent shock waves through my body. There was no fear in his eyes at all! He knew of my volatility, and yet he dared to challenge me in spite of it. His eyes flickered and his back straightened, as if he were bracing himself for battle. I had not seen a man stand up to me and get in my face like that since the time my first husband told me that he was not the marrying kind, and that I should stop bugging him about it. Of course, I cheerfully made him rue the day he was foolish enough to make that claim by employing various types of emotional blackmail and torment that eventually led to our beautiful and meaningful wedding at the courthouse in Golden, Colorado, in 1972.

I was about to haul off and give my daughter's intended a piece of my mind, and start toying with him rather like a cat does a bird she is stalking, when my daughter began yelling at us both to stop drinking wodka and arguing with each other or she would get pissed and leave the dinner table. Things calmed down for some time after the nuptials. But later on I told him that I expected him to bring my daughter and grandson Ari out to visit me on the nut farm in Hawaii for Thanksgiving. He informed me that he would get back to me. The nerve!

He went on to say that his family would do as he wished them to, and not as I wished them to, since he is the papa and I am only the grandma, and that I should learn how the world really works in that regard. I became enraged and said to him, "It might work like that over in Russia, where people have to line up for bread every day instead of just baking a variety of useful preservatives into it so that it will last for several weeks. But here in America, you might want to look into how things really work in the real world of Jewry's matriarchs, son!" He said, "No, it is yourself who is in for quite a rude awakening in this world. No woman, old nor young, will tell me what to do."

I just had to shut my mouth. Never before in my life had I allowed a man to make me back down. I am a strong, Jewish woman from Utah, but I had to admit that I was no match for the fucking

Russian, or any grown man who has the power to keep my grandsons away from me. This shocking problem is a very, very common one for the women of my generation, who have learned to be bossy alpha bitches who, after driving all male partners and suitors away, then attempt to control the only men left in their lives—their sons. We are simply no match for the men in our daughters' lives, let alone the men in our grandsons' lives. Sad, really.

Oh, I suppose that I am not an easy person to have for a mother-in-law. No, really! I don't like my kids all that much, and I have also learned to soundly doubt their judgment, since anything I ever tell them to do causes them to roll their eyes, cluck their tongues, and say, "Oh, really, Mother? Well, why should I take *your* advice, after the way you . . ." Blah, blah, blah.

Also, I am not easy to get along with because I don't like to listen much to others' likes or beliefs because it bores me, and I don't have a lot of patience with people who disagree with the things I say. And I can be hard to make plans with, as I never know what whim might strike me or when I might run off on some tangent. Still, I cannot understand why any man would not want to make it his life's purpose to do as I decree he do to keep me happy at any and all costs, since it will ultimately just make it easier on him if he insists on continuing to be a player on my life's stage. Disagreeing with me makes no sense to any rational human being.

Anyway, my middle daughter, Jessica, who is actually the oldest daughter in my first marriage, married a Mexican named Christian, whose Hebrew name is Yacov, according to the Las Vegas rabbi who married them. Despite his name, I am thrilled with him, as he has raised a gorgeous little shiatsu named Kobe, who is cuter than any other dog that has ever lived on this earth.

As you may have guessed, I don't really care much for dogs or other living things that didn't come, at least indirectly, out of my own vagina. But this dog, this precious little dog, is to be the crowning glory in my postmenopausal incarnation. My son-in-law Christian has consented to letting me dress the dog up in little outfits and cart it around town with me! My own Barbie dog! Is that crazy or what? I mean, in this crazy life that makes less sense to me every day. Thank God for a lighthouse of sanity and a safe port in an endless hurricane of horror—I now have a little dog I can dress in a matching ballet outfit at my parties and receptions! These are the blessings that save my sanity. What's left of it, that is. Well, that and the transfats and the Headline News channel (HLN) with Miss Jane Velez-Mitchell and the Oracle of Crime, Nancy Grace!

I also really love and adore Christian because being around him makes my daughter strangely calm and almost rational! I told Jessica in her earlier years, after she had wrongly accused me of racial prejudice because I was not thrilled with her choice of Mexican-American dating partners, that it was actually not because they were Mexican Americans that I did not like them, it was because they were unemployed Mexican Americans who smoked crack all the time.

This is an important distinction. There is real ethnic prejudice, and of that I am not guilty. I am, however, completely guilty of not being thrilled by unemployed crackheads who just happen to be Mexican Americans dating my daughter. I explained the difference to Jessica after her many irrational accusations regarding my racial insensitivity, but she wasn't having any of it.

She also accuses me of being prejudiced because I do not like pit bulls, which are quite a popular pet choice for Spanish speakers. They are all the same and could snap at any moment for whatever reason—pit bulls, I mean, not the Spanish speakers—and therefore they are not suitable family pets. I refused to allow my daughter's pit bull, Rufus, to ever come into my home. He had to be tethered in the backyard or garage when she came to visit (to ask me for money). Of course, I was right. One day, Rufus escaped and ran to the park, where he started trying to bite men on bikes and was arrested by the dog police, put on trial, and given the death penalty. I know a thug when I see one.

Now, I like tattoos, as everyone who knows me knows—I have several of them on various parts of my body. I can, however, spot a jailhouse or prison tattoo at five thousand paces, and I was not all that thrilled about seeing my daughter with a guy sporting a teardrop on his cheek and a spiderweb on his elbow. But again, there are various distinctions to consider in that subgroup as well—someone with a teardrop and a cobweb who has gone to AA meetings for forty years is better than someone sporting the drop and the web who smokes crack, is unemployed, and wants to hang around my kid. I tried to be as clear with my daughter as I could be. I told her she should go on JDate, like her older sister had, and meet a nice Jewish boy, too. I explained that because she was half Scots-Irish, she could now return to the Jewish gene pool safely, with little chance of producing nerdlike offspring, and that I had decided that sharing a common cultural identity based on the genital mutilation of sons was a good way to go.

She said, "Mother, you are the last person on earth whose advice I would ever seek on matters of matrimony or relationships of any sort!" and then laughed with that snorting noise she always makes. But she ultimately signed up for JDate, and who responded but a man born in Mexico City named Christian, who always felt that his birth parents had been Jewish! Some things are just karmic.

Christian actually takes my advice, and tells my daughter to do so as well. And that coupled with the fact that he has raised the most perfect little dog that ever lived makes him a fantastic choice in a son-in-law. They have promised to have a little brown granddaughter for me, but I think they should just stick to dogs. I tell Jessica just to travel and party because having children will ruin her life forever. I say, "Trust me, I know what I am talking about." And I do.

If you are a writer, which she is though she denies it, you can actually lose your mind if you are unable to write every day. And screaming brats put quite a damper on your writing time, thereby inducing insanity in you. My daughter has written some of the best pieces I have ever read, and because I encourage her to develop her great talent, she now says she is "over the whole writing thing."

To have daughters is to truly know heartbreak. You envision having a relationship with your daughter that allows you to talk to each other as two women friends who let each other be, in peace. But that scenario often doesn't materialize until you're both much older. I have had a lot of those kinds of conversations with my mom these days now that she's in her seventies. The mother-daughter talks we have are soul-satisfying and healing, though I must admit, I always try to hang up right before the subject changes and she starts recounting which of her friends has the lupus now.

My oldest son, Jake, thirty-one, got married on September 12, 2009, two months after his sister. He married a woman who is Native American and Filipino. My younger son, Buck, is going for the darker type as well—he likes the Asian girls. I always thought that both of my boys would marry someone of the Asian persuasion, on account of our Filipino nanny, Linda, who is like a second mom to them, and me. I adore the way Linda says "feanut butter sandaweech." It reminds me of my *bubbes'* immigrant accents in many ways.

Plus, Buck's dad has married or lived with a couple of Filipino women since our divorce. I have come to see that the Filipino woman is exactly like the Jewish woman in every way, only even more controlling, which is truly a marvel to behold! She seems so nice at first, and then, before he knows it, the man is owned, totally. However, like the Jewish woman, the Filipino woman has the makings of a fantastic mother.

I hope my daughter-in-law and I will get along. She does remind me of me in many ways—she is tall, thin, and has lovely hair and good style. But unlike me, she is a tad bossy and controlling. Hopefully, she will learn to be more gracious after some of my tutelage rubs off on her over time.

In planning the wedding, she and her mother set about creating little corsages for each chair to match colors and plates and did the seating arrangements and invitations and everything else all by themselves, and just sent me a check for half of it. I was pleased to see that my daughter-in-law would be a perfect homemaker—marrying her was one of the few good choices my son has ever made.

I have always thought that having an Asian granddaughter would be quite fun, as we can use the ethnic thing as a wonderful way to excuse our shopping trips to Malaysia and China and Vietnam, the Philippines, and all those wonderful Asian places. Although I do not want to go to any of those places where they skin snakes alive and eat live fish eyes—after all, I am a Jewish woman and I have my limits. My limits are usually anything that requires me to touch an animal (except for Kobe, and a horse I used to have named Buddy) or sweat.

My middle daughter and my oldest daughter have sons. As of 2009, I have five grandsons. I love them very much, but would love to have even just one granddaughter so that I can get the matching ballet outfits made. That has always been a dream of mine, to dress like twins with my granddaughter. It's very, very Utah, but what am I going to do about it—I am from Utah, after all! Neither Bubbe Mary nor Bubbe Fanny would ever dress as twins with me. I remember those girls from my childhood who used to wear the matching outfits with their grandmas. White gloves always topped off the ensemble. They were all really pale, blond, and blue-eyed. I was jealous of the way they looked, especially at Easter, in their twin outfits with their grandmothers out in the yard having their pictures taken and smiling. But I knew I was smarter than they were, and I knew that I was braver and would live a more interesting life than they would, despite having no waist and a flat ass. The shape of my ass is something I could write whole chapters on—what it was like to have fat everywhere on my body except the one place where it is adored. I was assless in an ass-based economy. That has made me a very angry female indeed!

Anyway, the daughter who ruined every holiday and birthday I have ever had, as well as every vacation, with her drama married a Mexican American who has a job and is a talented graphic artist, who has contributed to my happiness by bringing Kobe over to my house after his grooming sessions, and that is, I have decided, good enough for me. Anyone who pleases me in any way is on my good side. Anyone who displeases me excites me, too, in a way, because nothing is more pleasurable to me than a real good fight where the system of jurisprudence will be invoked.

For Jessica and Christian we had a big fat Greek shower and another Vegas wedding! We decided that weddings are all about the gown and everything else is secondary. My daughter's gown cost $6,000, and she had to smoke and go on the cookie diet for a full two months to fit into it. I went on the *real* cookie diet in order to look right at the wedding, too—I gained twenty-five pounds and looked like a fat Latino mother of the bride, and that actually made my daughter very happy. She feared that any female in our clan might look thinner than she on her wedding day, and so the extra weight was my gift to her. (Plus the price tag, which was ridiculous!) Weddings are a Ponzi scheme. If they get divorced, I want my money back!

I beg my daughter Jessica, the writer, not to have children. She is simply not cut out for the job, I can tell. I realized too late that it was not something I was cut out for, either, and I was not really that good at. I would rather drink and party, honestly, if I had it all to do over again. The bitching and the blaming and the abuse I have had to suffer from my kids isn't really worth the three or four minutes of pleasure they have provided me since they have been able to think for themselves. Now I wish they could use that brain to figure out how to provide for themselves and stop driving up here like I am a human ATM machine.

I like it when very little children think for themselves, because they do not have access to car keys or credit cards or crack pipes, but they have some really funny lines. That is why I love my little grandsons. I tell them all the time, you have to grow up and get a job. I also try to convince them that they should not get married and have children when they are older, because all of that just ruins your life forever. I offer to buy them really cool cars for high school if they will have vasectomies first. I know that these days you can freeze your sperm if you want to, for use later in pies or what have you. I do not want any more little children to have to come to this shithole planet that is run by fucking idiots. But that is just me!

Our family celebrations are the best, though. Bar mitzvahs, wedding receptions, and Passover are a hoot—we always end up getting drunker than your regular college professor's wife. And it is traditional that our nanny, Linda, and I end up dancing on top of tables, while my boyfriend, Johnny, plays rock-and-roll piano and the little ones do their very special break-dancing hip-hop thing that they do. They are very nimble for Jewish children. And like all Jewish children, pretending to be African-American gangstas is what they like most.

Chapter 16

My Shameless Showbiz Name-dropping

The end of the *Roseanne* show was really rough. It provided the most sanity and stability I had ever had in my life, and I wanted to keep working. With no job on which to focus my racing thoughts, I was afraid for myself. I got angry at ABC, the network where I worked for more than nine years, for telling me that I could have a tenth year but that I would have to take a pay cut to continue the show. I had gotten used to being paid $1,000,000 per show, and I didn't see how I could live on half that amount. I had five kids, for God's sake! How was I supposed to make do on that pittance? (The air is thin when you're up that high.)

Oddly enough, in the midst of negotiations with ABC, my then-manager, Jeff Wald (Helen Reddy's ex), who also managed George Foreman and therefore had a hand in the sport of boxing and knew Don King, received a call from Mike Tyson—yes, that Mike Tyson. Jeff said that Mike wanted me to interview him because I was the only person in Hollywood he felt he could talk to now that he was out of prison for rape.

I just knew that interviewing interesting people was the next step for me in my career, so Jeff set it all up for me. I would be given my own special hour on ABC to interview The Champ, Mike Tyson. I was the loudest feminist (pre–Joy Behar) on television at the time, and Mike was a convicted rapist, so it would make for good TV. Ted Harbert was the president of the network, and he liked me a lot. The deal was done, and it seemed the die was cast for my next career move. That is, until the news division got wind of it. The network canceled the interview after the late great Roone Arledge, ABC News president and Barbara Walters's boss, called to say that any interview with Mike Tyson on ABC was "news," not "entertainment," and all news interviews were to be conducted by Ms. Barbara Walters, who had successfully interviewed Mike before and had a relationship with him. Get your mind out of the gutter; it wasn't *that* kind of relationship, although Barbara did fess up to having had a relationship many years prior with a handsome, successful black man who happened to be married. His name escapes me, but I think it might have been George Washington Carver.

I have nothing but a grudging respect for Ms. Walters, as she has done what almost no other woman in show business has done, and that is, of course, outlived the competition. Most women in showbiz die by the time they are fifty-five, due to either the drinking, the drugs, or the payback of one criminal or another, who was stepped on and screwed on the way to the top of the middle.

I had already grown a bit leery and distrusting of Walters since, when in my home, interviewing me for the second time around, she and her producer asked to take a picture of my baby, Buck, and I said no, that I wasn't comfortable with that. My baby nurse came in, interrupted the interview, and said, "Mrs., can I talk with you?" I excused myself and was led into the nursery, where I caught one of her producers directing a camera at my newborn son against my wishes and behind my back. I shooed him out and stationed my huge bodyguard husband at the nursery door.

Barbara sees what she wants to see, and hears what she wants to hear. Meeting her in an elevator haphazardly, as I did one fine morning at the Four Seasons, where I had taken my son and grandson to swim in the pool for a few days and shop around Beverly Hills for the darling little-boy outfits that Jewish grandmothers are always on the lookout for, I could see she was surprised to see me, and she asked, "What are you up to?"

I answered, "I am spending the weekend with these little guys. This is my son and my grand—" She cut me off, completely uninterested, and said, "No, I mean careerwise." The fact that she missed saying hello to my godlike offspring and the godlike offspring of my godlike daughter, was shocking to me at first—the callousness of it—but later, when I thought about all the pins that have been stuck into that poor woman's voodoo effigy by every young female journalist who wants her job, I felt empathy for her struggles and triumphs.

She is not like the rest of us. She created television's first smart and sexy Jewish woman. She interviewed Anwar Sadat at one time, which was flawless. She showed the world that a woman can go toe-to-toe with a powerful man and ruin his image and get him assassinated by his own people, who were mad that he talked to not only a cursed woman but a Jewish one at that.

When Mike Tyson caught wind of ABC's decision to give the interview to Barbara, he stuck with me instead, and Jeff Wald got King World to underwrite our interview and commit to airing it on one of King World's syndicated news programs. The King brothers and Jeff promised me that I could have a blank check to do exactly what I wanted to do for the interview. Elated, I flew to Las Vegas to talk to Mike.

I fell in love with him immediately upon listening to him talk about Hannibal, as man and metaphor, while we sat poolside next to a too-small statue of the man in his backyard. Mike is so sweet that he kept the statue, imperfect as it was, and didn't make a stink about it's size, because he didn't want to hurt the sculptor's feelings.

Mike is a king for sure. We taped for five or six solid hours, and talked about everything: Islam, Judaism, Mohammed, Mohammed Ali, racism, mental illness, prison, Allah, mortal and moral strength, the nature of love, black history, white tigers, child abuse, heartbreak, interior decorating. We did not talk about Don King, who took us to lunch at the Forum Shops at Caesars and shouted to everyone in there shopping: "Ladies and gentlemen, Roseanne Barr, Mike Tyson—let them hear it! Please give it up for two American legends, and move out of the way so they can shop at Versace!" The entire crowd parted, as I followed Mike into the store and watched him buy $25,000 worth of towels and bracelets. I wished that I was young and had a big butt so that Mike would want to marry me, but I was already married, I reminded myself, and snapped out of it. It was the wildest and most exciting of all previously exciting days I had ever spent.

Standing just behind Mike, I got to see the faces on the kids who looked up to him. I was pretty famous, but Mike was an idol, like Elvis. Somehow, being seen or acknowledged by your idol can change your life forever. I saw people who looked like they had received the answers to heartfelt prayers approach him, breathless, and say, "I love you, Mike!" And Mike would reply, "God bless you, sister. I love you, too, and Allah is love!" Mike was a regular Mahatma Gandhi, I thought. He seriously means that much to a lot of people. He is nice, and conflicted, and I bet I could write a nice part for him in a movie if I ever finish this fucking book.

The most amazing thing about the interview was that as we

were sitting in his bedroom, Mike told me that the judge said his sentence would be suspended if he would admit that he raped that girl. Mike even showed me the transcripts from the trial to verify it. But he chose to go to jail instead because he would not admit to something he did not do—not to a white judge in Indiana, the birthplace of the KKK. I was stunned since I had never heard this before.

The interview aired, and we were both very happy with it. It caused a lot of controversy in feminist circles and in African-American circles, too. Mike has had a lot of problems in his life—with women, with circumstances, and with the bad people around him who stole every dime he had—and I have a soft spot in my heart and soul for him, and always will. I told him that I saw him someday gathering all the children who grew up like he did, helping them figure out a better way to make things right for themselves and the world. I see Mike as having that power in him still.

I was there the night he bit off Holyfield's ear. It was right after the interview aired, and when they introduced me from the audience on the Jumbotron, I was soundly booed by the entire audience. I was already used to being booed by large crowds, due to my musical rendition of some song I sang once, but I was pissed at them for booing me for liking Mike when they were all there because of him. I was so worked up by the time Mike went in for the bite that I was screaming, "Kill him, Mike! Get him, Mike!" when my then-husband, Ben Thomas, put his hand over my mouth and escorted me out of the auditorium, as the crowd poured out all around me. I hadn't noticed that they were running for their lives at all, because I was too upset that Holyfield had gotten away with head-butting my buddy!

I was also there the night another buddy of mine, Tupac, was shot and killed after the fights. Tupac Shakur and Ice-T once sang a duet on my late-night Fox show, *Saturday Night Special,* where

Kathy Griffin made her television debut. (The Fox network did not want her on the show because they thought she wasn't "pretty" enough—as if that has anything at all to do with comedy—ugh. I made that point, and offered myself and my looks as proof.) Tupac thanked me for putting him on the show, as he, too, had just gotten out of prison for sexual assault that week. He said, "It was very brave of you to put me on, and my mom is really happy to be able to see me on your show." I have no idea whether he was actually guilty or not, but like Mike, he was charming and sweet to me, and had survived the mean streets and the prison-industrial complex of America, where they train the guards for Blackwater.

Anyway, because of Mike, I got offered my own talk show for King World, Oprah Winfrey's distributors. I figured I would be making Oprah money, so I told ABC to F off—another of my genius moves! Even though Oprah has never been married, has no kids, and is a billionaire, she has made a career of giving advice to the average woman and still manages to make women cheer for her and to feel that her success is their success, too, by placing toasters under her audience's chairs during sweeps. I was a guest on Oprah's show nine times and was graciously invited back all the time—until I pissed her off, which was bound to happen someday. She was also gracious enough (after faxing a fifty-page document telling my producers what could be asked of her and what was taboo) to consent to an interview with me as a guest on *The Roseanne Show.* And she did tell me that my interview of her was *the* best one she had ever given. We talked about how we hate to look at ourselves in profile in the mirror, and Oprah good-naturedly admitted to having peed in a swimming pool at least once.

However, at the end of the hour, she and I arm-wrestled for a million dollars to go to the charity of our choice. Oprah cheated! It is right there on the tape. You must keep your elbows on the table, as everyone knows, but she stood up to get more leverage, and that is not allowed. After she declared herself the winner, I demanded a rematch, refusing to give her the million bucks for her angel network until she capitulated. But she wasn't having it. I called Roger King personally to complain, asking him to talk to her about a fair rematch. But he told me to drop it, noting that Oprah had flown from Chicago to guest on my show and was not amused by my insistence that she cheated (even though she did), and that I should focus on figuring out how to get some higher ratings instead. I told him there was no better way to get higher ratings than to accuse Oprah of cheating, show the tape, and get her back on again. But he was done with the whole million-dollar bet.

Roger had already offered $1,000,000 to Monica Lewinsky to be interviewed on my talk show, yet she chose to go on Barbara Walters's show for free. (I am sure Barbara's evil minions pulled their evil strings to get that one away from me, too, and I will bet my hat Monica wishes she had that million bucks now.) Unlike old Babs, who is well over one hundred years of age now, at least I knew what a blow job was, and had some common ground with Miss Lewinsky on that topic, as well as on being a fat, Jewish girl who knows how to rock a beret. (I used to be known for my berets back in the day.) I was over the moon that Bill Clinton went for a fat, Jewish chick; it really, really helped my self-esteem, I am not ashamed to admit!

I got to have dinner with Bill at a Barbara Boxer benefit right after the whole Monica thing went down. (Man, the scams these politicians run could fill volumes.) With the scratches still across his cheek, where Hillary tore a piece out of his ass for all the world to see, Bill got up and said, "Good evening. Thank you for coming tonight. Hillary, my wife, is the smartest woman I have ever met in my life, and she said . . ." Blah, blah, something, something. . . . He had me, though. I mean, I liked him before and wanted to like him now more than ever, that red-hot devil, that Bill uh-huh Clinton. I got to take a picture with him 'cause I paid the twenty-five grand. I wish he had turned to me and said, "Hey, Roseanne, thank you so much for getting me elected. That one episode where Roseanne Connor tells the audience that it is time for a 'change' in the White House—I really believe you helped get me elected and I owe you big-time. If there is any way I can ever repay you, you let me know, sugar, 'cause I will so be there. Here's my number. Wear a beret."

But no, he didn't, because he is too damn dumb. Oh well. Bill, call me! Fart! I mean, wink! ("Old age has you farting when you want to be winking." —Roseanne Barr, 2009. I am putting my name on that, trademarking it forever. I do not put my name on everything, but now I wish that I had, so I could sue every motherfucking thief I have ever met in Hollywood. DO NOT even get me started bitching at Rosie O'Donnell about trying to trademark the name Rosie.)

Despite my admiration for Bill and my affinity with Monica, I didn't get to interview her. And the King World and network powers-that-be were not happy with my talk show rating, which was 3.2, so they replaced my show with programs that never got more than a score of 0.1. Go figure.

I was depressed about it and still am, honestly. It was so much fun to get into trouble every day. The memory of the Seattle and Mississippi affiliates refusing to run the show one day because I came to work wearing a teddy in protest of all the women on TV who were half-naked all the time still cracks me up. Even though it was extremely difficult to do a serious talk show when the studio audience was being bussed in from suburban mental hospitals and rehab centers, or paid fifteen dollars a day to leave their sidewalk perches as homeless people and feign amusement in a show where young actresses talked about the pressure they felt to stay thin so they could make millions of dollars wearing teddies on TV's prime time, I still loved it.

Right after that, I got cut from a David Spade movie. I know what you're thinking: How does one get cut from a David Spade movie? You either suck worse than anyone can mortally imagine or you were actually funny or something.

I'd gotten the part after running into Adam Sandler at the Four Seasons one night. He came over to my table to say hi, and then he said, "I really want to say thank you for helping me out when you hosted *SNL* and telling Lorne that you thought I was really funny." I said, "Thanks for telling me that—and, hey, why don't you write me a part in one of your movies sometime?" He said he would, and within about six weeks a script came. It was for me to play the part of David Spade's mom in the triumphant film *Joe Dirt*. Basically, it was exactly like every other disappointing role that anyone from *SNL*, including Lorne Michaels, ever came up with for me to play. They have all pitched me the idea of playing some variety of a slovenly and desperately repulsive slut, which, as actors say, is too close to home for me to have the emotional distance that an actor requires in creating a character. (Actors talk endlessly about this and it's complete bullshit. Acting is pretending and lying convincingly, which are both things that actors in real life are extremely good at doing.)

The only person I ever met in Hollywood who could sit and jaw with me about what complete bullshit acting and actors are, and make me laugh, was Heath Ledger. I enjoyed an evening drinking with him on a veranda at a Hollywood party one night. We sat and talked for a couple of hours about how acting is just pretending, like a kid playing dress-up. We talked about how we thought it was coolest of all to act like you aren't acting, and to leave in all the mistakes to make it look real. We talked at length about how phony everyone acts around you when you are famous. We impersonated assholes at the party and made fun of them. We talked about how everything sucked in Hollywood, except the performing part.

He was delightful and soulful and had lots of interesting things to say, and he became my favorite young actor. I was more surprised by his acting talent in each movie he made. His Joker in *Batman* was the best acting I have ever seen; the details he added to that character were just stupendous. (I really identify with his Joker character, too. Comics, or jokers, can be dark forces that expose the supposed good guy's evil underbelly—at least the good ones do.)

Having the opportunity to shoot the breeze with people you admire is one of the perks of showbiz. I used to meet a lot of stars—I once met Gregory Peck at a 7-Eleven and we traded autographs; another time, I met Barbra Streisand, and I have never recovered from the awesome majesty of that encounter. But the one who really blew my mind was Bob Dylan. I got to talk to him about the number five for a long time—he has the five thing, too! We also talked about Joe Hill, a union organizer killed in my hometown.

Once, I met Harry Belafonte, whom my mother had been madly in love with, and that was a thrill. Now I am madly in love with him, too. He really is gorgeous. But he made me mad when he refused to be on my Hanukkah special for *The Roseanne Show.* I literally could not find one Jewish person in Hollywood to be on it. Every Jew said no, except for Neil Diamond, and he said he would only come on if he could sing a Christmas song about Jesus. I did like the idea, but, Christ, come on! It was a Hanukkah special, for chrissakes! I found out that a lot of people in Hollywood liked me when they thought that I was interested in hearing their tired old stories and coming to their tired old parties to hear the tired old stories of other tired old stars. Of course, I was not in the least bit interested in any of it, as I only want to be surrounded by fawning sycophants—let's get that straight.

Anyway, I called Adam Sandler about the part he had written for me, wanting to say, "I wanted to be in one of your movies, not fucking Spade's," but Adam was producing Spade's movie and that seemed rude. So I asked if I could get a rewrite on the part, and he said, "Of course, just talk to the writer." The writer I had to talk to was named Fred, and I not only gave him his first job as a television writer, I personally went to Lorne Michaels and recommended him for *SNL,* so I figured he would be only too happy to help me out with a nice rewrite.

I was quite wrong about that. The rewrite came and it was worse than the first version, a tactic I found common to almost all male writers whose genius I had the audacity to second-guess. It was as if they wanted to punish me for not falling over in praise of the self-abasement they wanted me to portray as their muse, or something.

The writers I have met in TV are very juvenile, and they all hate women. The only women they can bear to write into their shitty little scripts are vacuous models, whom they hope to bed in their sad, still adolescent, sexual fantasies, but never really do—unless they become directors, that is. But I kid the writers! I hired a couple of them for one of their first show business jobs; they were quite good and have gone on to be very successful. The two who come to mind are Judd Apatow and Joss Whedon.

After I discussed the revised script for *Joe Dirt* with the female director, she assured me that she would get a rewrite from Fred, that she knew how to handle male writers and so on. When Fred refused to change the script to accommodate me, or even to allow me to rewrite it, the director said that I could ad-lib some lines that were not as sexually debasing as what was on the page in a scene with the actor who was portraying my husband, the amazing Mr. Gary Busey. Gary, thinking he was free of the confines of the script, did not really understand what "ad-lib some character lines" meant, and in every take he portrayed a different character altogether, including a six-year-old child.

I wanted to walk off the set and just quit, but feeling I owed more to Adam and to David, just out of mutual respect for being comics and casual friends, I pulled David Spade aside to tell him how difficult things were for me. He put on that actor face that actors use when they pretend they know how to summon "The Method" and "embody their character," as if to say, "If only you would stop your constant whining, which is preventing great art from being created around you."

Shortly thereafter, the director called to apologize for having to cut me out of the movie.

I never got the chance to thank Adam for his gracious repayment of a favor. That experience made me decide never to get involved with movies or movie actors or movie producers or publicists again, no matter how much I wanted to act.

Buck liked *Joe Dirt,* though, and repeated lines from it for a while. He thought I was a large loser for not being featured in the total entertainment experience that was David Spade's last movie. And I hated myself for being depressed over the whole thing. Personally, I think David Spade is a leading man, and that he could oust George Clooney. I should get busy and write him a part someday!

The best comic from *SNL,* the one I loved best, was Chris Farley, who was the greatest thing to happen to that show and to David Spade. My husband and I tried all we could to help him get sober and take care of himself. My son Jake was Buck's age when Chris used to come over and be entertaining and hilarious. My son Jake is hilarious, too, and was profoundly influenced by Chris's genius. Chris was even more obsessive-compulsive about food and germs than I was. He demonstrated for me once how he had to touch his tongue to every piece of furniture in the room before he could go on stage to perform. I loved that; it made me feel completely normal and calm.

When we saw that Chris could not stay sober, I asked Lorne Michaels to kick him off the show, because I knew that *SNL* was the only thing he really cared about and that losing it would make him take inventory and seriously get off dope. I knew from my own experience with others close to me that coming down hard on addicts can help them, and I felt that tough love would also work for Chris—and I loved Chris. Lorne refused to use him for a couple of weeks, and when it looked like Chris had sobered up, he let him come back. I wish the banishment had gone on a little longer, but maybe even that wouldn't have worked.

Performers are selfish, lying babies who must be appeased at every turn. When they are really, really good at what they do, they get away with murder, and then they murder themselves.

The time did indeed arrive when I had to deal with my addiction to marijuana. And I dealt with it by getting a legal prescription for cannabis that helps me deal with that addiction, which is a medical condition. Oh, and yes, I am my own grandma.

Thanks to the "rehab" treatment for my addiction, and also to the money I made from doing the *Roseanne* show, I can now blissfully retire from giving a shit about showbiz or anything else anymore—except my family, writing jokes, planting more snacks on my Hawaiian nut farm, and, of course, waging my psychic war on the pigs there.

Chapter 17

Pig Politics

When I was a little girl I had a collection of pigs that I added to whenever I could. I was always trying to make friends with the whole notion of pigs, since my Orthodox Jewish grandmother said they were cursed, and also because I was called a fat pig frequently at school by those who saw little fat girls as targets on which to project their well-deserved lack of self-esteem. But I thought pigs were kind of cute! At one point, I had about a hundred little piggy knickknacks and dolls. When I became a huge international sex symbol, many of my adoring fans sent me a ton of little piggy favors that they had either hand made or bought for me.

After a while, I felt buried alive in all of those pigs, so I stopped collecting them and started collecting thimbles, teacups, dolls, antique fire hats, and alcohol-advertising posters and buttons instead. Buried alive in those collections, I bought the house next door to mine and started to collect other things, like spoons, crystal vases, glass fruit, cupboards, paperweights, and silver picture frames. By the time that house was full, I was old and moved to a macadamia nut farm in Hawaii.

The first thing I noticed the day I got the keys and drove up to my new little cottage on the Big Island was a bunch of big fat pigs standing around in my yard, looking straight at me. They continued to look at me as they went about having sex in full view of me, my boyfriend, Johnny, and their own little piglets.

I was completely offended by the repeat display that took place right in front of my window, and ran outside and screamed, "Get out!" I watched them scatter only to return later on to continue rutting in my yard. At this time, I forgot to mention, I was somewhat "Kabbalah crazy," as we in the spiritual survivor trade like to call it. It's when you first realize that you can think your way to happiness, health, and wealth, and it works for a while. Unfortunately, what follows is bankruptcy and divorce, because there is always a backswing to everything. Every so often, the high comes back around, but you eventually have to learn to weave your way through the highs *and* the lows by staying in the *middle,* where it's safest for old women and religious hysterics to stay.

Anyway, with all my mystical knowledge, I thought I would try to communicate honestly and directly with a real live pig, as I had always heard they were as intelligent as dogs. I could communicate with dogs in a rudimentary fashion, but I bonded big-time with a horse named Buddy once in Iowa, and it was pretty spiritual and otherworldly. Buddy would patiently parade my ass around, but when he was done, he was *done,* and we were going home, back to the barn, and with no arguments! Once, to show that he did not agree with my attempt to prevent his return to his stall in the cozy barn, he walked over to a pool of mud, slowly lowered us into it, and then rolled onto his side and made horse-shaped mud angels, as I slithered out from under him, caked with wet, dirty mud myself. I respected Buddy and never tried to pull rank or do him wrong again. I simply gave in to his will and we got along famously after that.

Also, I hate cats, and whenever I see one, I have to use my mental telepathy to tell it to stay the hell away from me. They always try to get next to me, too. They are attracted to fear. They like to mock it, too. I have found that the best way to keep cats away from me is to pretend that I am overly interested in them, and then they will flee.

So I figured that I had enough of an animal mind-reading résumé to let the pigs know that I was equal to the task of being their worthy opponent, their landlord, and their ultimate queen. It made sense to me that pigs were my karma and dharma.

Drinking a lot, and planting and picking and thinking a lot, too, Johnny and I came to a nonviolent solution to the "pig problem." We fenced the forty-eight acres, and graciously left a few choice nut-tree-filled acres on the other side of the fence for their perusal and pleasure. Indeed, I also left the rest of the entire island of Hawaii for pigs to roam at their whim. I figured that if I left them enough room on their side, they would leave me alone on my side. I thought I had found the perfect, nature-based metaphysical formula for preferential pig–human relations. But no! After two years, I realized that they were only pretending to peacefully coexist with me. They resumed digging under the fence just when I thought we had reached a two-state solution. I mended the holes, refilled the dirt, cut up fallen trees, and plugged them in there only to find that the pigs would begin a new terrorist campaign two or three feet from the last repaired part of the fence. They wanted me to see that they had less than no desire to recognize my right to exist as a sovereign entity.

Increasingly frustrated, I took my little grandsons to the fence and told them to pee on top of the logs and around the perimeter. Then Johnny and I got drunk and peed on the places where my little grandsons had previously marked their territory, and then we sprayed ammonia on top of all of that, too. The pigs refused to stop coming for my nuts! I had hexed and peed to the extent of my powers to try to get the message through to them that they have *enough* on their own side. Yet they remained blissfully unaware of how nature worked. They had unmitigated gall and no sense whatsoever of other beings' boundaries! They overran my orchard, rooted out my lawn, and rubbed mud holes into my garden. One of the bastards took a dump right on my front porch!

That's when it hit me: They are Repiglicans! The flaw in their intelligent design is that they *never learn their lesson,* ever, and they breed like crazy, having their babies about every four months. The babies can get through any fence at all, I noticed. If nature is so smart, then why don't Repiglican mothers know when their piggery is putting their young at risk? Why don't they stop breeding for lack of food and water? Their inability to control their seed is vexing to me. Don't they have a desire to survive? Why do they have such elemental cognitive errors in their instinctive senses?

I realized that I was going to have to accept and initiate the "final solution" and execute some of these elitist swine. Granny—thinking, Don't tread on me!—went to the police station and registered for a rifle so as to engage in battle with these disrespectful pigfolk! I was proud to live in a country where I can bear arms against intruders who never get enough of anything and shoot them right between their little raisin eyes. But I told some Hawaiians of my plans to do so, and they got all upset with me. The Hawaiians think it is impossibly haole to use firearms against pigs, and insisted that their ways were The Way of doing things. So I relented and agreed to let them do what they have done for eons.

The Hawaiians arrived in their pickup trucks with their "pig dogs" in the back. The pig dogs have the hugest heads of any dog on earth, their tongues flapping around in their huge jaws like those giant flags at car dealerships. I went into the house because they scared me, while Johnny went outside with the men. The pig dogs were sent out on recon and soon were barking up a storm. Johnny yelled for me to come out and see what was going on. You have not lived inside of nature properly until you have seen snarling pig dogs corner a huge, terrified mother pig the size of a small Volkswagen.

The Hawaiian men must step up to the pig and stab her through the heart with a great big spear to end her life with one thrust or they are thought to be less manly than the ideal. (After all, the Hawaiian warriors were the fiercest of all the warrior nations that American interests decimated and usurped so that they could build KFC franchises outside the American mainland.) The dogs are given a taste of the pig's blood and they go wild from it, running and howling. I felt like I was going to vomit, pee, shit, go blind, *and* faint; I wanted to run around barking at things myself when I saw the dogs' bloodlust, and the eye of the dead pig, not raisinlike at all, but deep and large, staring into eternity. It looked like the eye over the pyramid on the dollar bill, kind of a symbol of infinite consciousness, or some other symbol of symbolism.

Then the hunters all stood around the carcass and quietly began to talk about nature and cycles, and the end of life, as they waited for the dogs to calm down again. I was thrilled that all of this led to a discussion about the Goddess Pele. They are the only men with whom I have ever had the pleasure of discussing Pele and nature, and it was deeply mystical, I thought. Every life that ends takes something with it and leaves something behind, it seems. Moving out of physical existence into memory takes no time at all. I saw two little pigs peeking out from behind the tall grass, and the men said those were her babies. "Why," I asked them, "if nature is so intelligent and so perfect in design, as all the religious nuts claim God made it, why can't a pig sense when it's unwanted and why does it go to the most dangerous place it can go, after being repeatedly run off?"

They aptly answered, "So they can be caught and eaten. We will bring you some of the sausage we make."

"Uh, no, I am a vegetarian," I lied, and then almost immediately became one.

Then they packed the dogs and hauled the pig carcass off to their homes to be made into sausages. "Gotta serve somebody," as Dylan says.

Johnny said, "Let's take a meat break for a while. Ingesting all of that cruelty is kind of gross." We have not eaten meat since then, now about one year later. The mother pig's orphans, after a brief and suitable period of pigly mourning, began rooting and digging in my yard again, ignoring the other forty-seven acres where there are even more nuts, taller grass, and no humans.

I have a new concept for dealing with this generation of interlopers. I read a study in the *New York Times* that described pigs as highly intelligent as well as vain. The study said that pigs enjoy looking at themselves in mirrors. I decided to install big round mirrors at a low level around the fence, so that when the pigs approached they would be too caught up in checking themselves out to dig under the fence. I will let you know how that turns out. I will not accept that I have been outsmarted or outdone by any pig, ever! You would think that if we can send a man to the moon, and destroy an entire city's humanity with one of our bombs, leaving only buildings standing (for new KFC franchises?), we could invent birth control pellets for pigs!

These Repiglicans should start evolving a new system of behavior that leaves a smaller carbon imprint if they are to survive Granny's new world order!

Chapter 18

The D-word and All That

Let's face it: Some days we don't need to be reminded of our mortality because it's damn near impossible to forget. At times like that, it's not the elephant in the room; it's more like the room in the elephant. I have the worst fears about how I am going to die. I would never want to be discovered naked, even while alive, but especially after I am no longer.

Don't think I'm being morbid and please don't tune me out. But if there's one thing that lots of Baby Boomers don't like, it's the idea that we're getting closer to the end of the line with each tick of the clock. I'm determined, though, to have *fun* with that. Honest! Well, if not *fun,* exactly, something like a good-natured response to the thought of kicking the breathing habit one day. When people say that life is too short, I say it's not that life's too short; it's that we're dead for so long! If that doesn't get them to at least consider the potential absurdity of it all, I try something else. Like: Maybe we should shed that Baby Boomer handle and start calling ourselves something that still has a youngish feel but doesn't kid itself, like, for example, *Casket Patch Kids.*

"Fifty-seven isn't *old,* Roseanne. It's just middle-aged!" No it isn't. Nobody lives to be a hundred and fourteen. And if you do, your payoff is sitting in your wheelchair faintly hearing Willard Scott (in that charming, shall we say, *drunken* way of his) wishing you a happy birthday from the TV room at the nursing home. As I like to say, "Thank God for *Depends*!" And yes, I *do* want some free Depends, thank you very much! You have to laugh to keep from crying, they tell me, and that's partly why I'm a comic. Well, that and the free Depends.

I just found out that one of the warning signs of a fatal heart attack is . . . *NOTHING!* You heard me. Great, so now feeling perfectly fine is a damn red flag. Oh, well, what are you going to do? Even if you try to be careful and play by the rules, you can still fall prey to any number of things that can take you down. But there's no sense in whining about it. God knows I tried that for years and found out the hard way that it doesn't help and nobody wants to hear it. I like what old Hugh Hefner said about it when they asked him how he felt about aging: "Getting old? It's *way* better than *not* getting old!" (By the way, no matter what it says on his birth certificate, isn't it weird to say "*old* Hugh Hefner?")

I have a line that I think says a lot—it's a play on another old one and it's not as dark as it sounds at first: "Remember, today is the first day of *what's left of your life.*" It's not really negative. It makes me remember that the less you have of something, the more it's worth. I want to use my time here for good things and live to the fullest. But I'm not the type who says you have to rush out of bed and go bungee jumping on your way to tango lessons after you climb Pike's Peak with your hypercaffeinated lifestyle coach. Do what *you* like as much as circumstances permit. I, for example, am partial to engaging in eating cheese, drinking wine, getting lots of bed rest, reading tabloids, and hanging out with my grandkids (for brief, controlled periods).

My health is pretty good. If it ever gets terrible, I guess I'll have to deal with it. Worst case scenario: I heard that Dr. Kevorkian is out of prison and running for Congress, as if a man that age can be said to be *running* for anything. Wait a minute, what am I thinking? Does the name John McCain ring a bell—or is that my tinnitus?

Jeez, Kevorkian, Dr. Death! I can hear you guys now: "You're not going to start up about suicide or euthanasia or completely cutting out carbs, are you, Roseanne?" No, I was just thinking, I don't know what party Dr. K is representing, but I bet he's not the life of it.

Speaking of getting old, a lot is written about . . . okay, let's get it over with: sex and companionship and love and junk among old people. I know, it's part of life and all, but let's not talk about it too much, okay? I just know that lots of older women outlive their husbands, and finding new guys can be rough. I'm always amazed at how many guys in their twilight years are looking for chicks half their age. I guess a few older women are turning the tables there, but most of them just happen to be, coincidentally, *rich.* Go figure. The ones who aren't rich often say that they don't want to hook up with a guy their age or older because such guys usually need a nurse more than a "girlfriend." Lots of older women just don't want to take care of an old guy. They probably still have to do that with one or more of their "adult" children, or as I call them, *teenagers in their thirties.* Some of these really old guys' idea of fun is sitting up in their oxygen tent and pushing the nurse button all by themselves.

I laughed when I heard that they give out free Viagra to senior citizens in Mexico. That is certainly a creative way to thin the herd. At some point, someone has to bring up the fact that if Baby

Boomers would just die and get it over with, instead of getting plastic hearts and such, and going to heroic measures to stay alive, we might be able to leave our kids some of the limited resources that still exist. I say, as soon as you hit sixty-two and get sick, you should just take the Paula Abdul morphine patch and say nighty-night.

Anyway, to wrap things up: What can we do about getting really old (if we're *lucky*) except take reasonably good care of ourselves, enjoy life as best we can, make plans for dealing with our bodies when that number I mentioned is "up," and then forget about it. Try to be good to yourself and everybody else and keep on rolling! It ain't over till the fat lady sings, and I promised I wouldn't. The way I look at it is that when my death comes, I won't be there anyway, so why waste one more second thinking about it? There's an old song that was popular when my parents were young: "Enjoy Yourself (It's Later Than You Think)." Well, I say, "Express yourself—it's later than you think."

Chapter 19

Celebrities Dropping Like Flies—What I've Learned

As I get a little nearer to the end of my book, there's been an incredible wave of deaths among the famous. Ed McMahon, Farah Fawcett, Bea Arthur, Walter Cronkite, Heath Ledger, Dom DeLuise, Karl Malden, and, of course, the big shocker, Michael Jackson—it's been positively eerie. Forget about that crazy "Rule of Three" that gets tossed around, the one that says the famous tend to go out in some kind of celebrity death triangle. There hasn't been enough of a break in this grim procession to bear that old superstition out—2009 and 2010 were busy years for the Grim Reaper, and 2011 is shaping up to be the same, as the roll call continues.

Before I go any further, I have to say that I hate all those bullshit euphemisms for dying. (I don't know why I even brought up the Grim Reaper.) I mean, when I hear that so-and-so *passed*? I want to say, "Did they croak, for chrissakes, or get their driver's license?" We DIE, people. Get used to the word. There may or may not be an afterlife or whatever, but from this side of the net—we just plain DIE.

Here's what I've learned from the way we seem to react, or at least the way the media reacts, to death and how I think we should change things: We should pay more tribute to people *before* they die, while they're around to hear it. You know how people like to say, at funerals and such, that the "dearly departed" is looking down on us? I don't know if they're looking down on us or not, but I know they'd damn sure have appreciated knowing how highly we thought of them while they were still here to be appreciated. I think that's true for everybody, not just the famous among us.

Sure, people have said this before, but do we take their advice? Why do you have to die before anybody really pours out their heart and talks about all the good things you've done and how much you've meant to them? Does anybody get the kind of tribute in life that we seem so ready to pour out when they're gone? We should lay it on each other, good and thick, while we're still around to say it and hear it. I'm not just talking about celebrities; I'm not even talking about family, per se. We should tell anybody who tries to do the right thing, everybody who touches us in some way or another, that we notice them and appreciate what they do and who they are every day.

The world is getting tougher and more impersonal in so many ways. Sure, we can Facebook or Twitter, and talk about our hundreds of "friends" or whatever else we do on the Internet to feel like we're reaching out to one another, but a lot of that is shallow crap. I think it's important to look somebody in the eye and tell them that you've noticed the kindness they've shown you, or the steadfast loyalty they've exhibited in always being there for you, doing what's expected of them and then some, being one of the people in your life who you know you could call on in times of crisis. All of that needs to be said and needs to be heard.

I don't care if it sounds a little sappy. I wanted to say this because, as I've watched the people I mentioned at the beginning of this little reflection come to the end of their lives, I couldn't help but wonder if they heard, loud and clear, anything like the outpouring of appreciation and recognition and affection that was there *after* they died. The truth is, though, as celebrities, the odds are probably better that they did hear and see the love and respect people had for them, more so than many of the other good people who aren't well-known but who deserve to know that they're appreciated for just being decent people—who played a meaningful role in the lives of the people around them.

Okay, it's not the newest notion on earth, but it's one of the messages that have been coming through loud and clear to me during this rash of celebrity deaths. Starting with your family, and then working your way out from there, tell people you appreciate them, their work, their kindnesses, or anything else for which they deserve some credit and recognition. It's rougher out there than it's been in a while. Let people know they're noticed, respected, and recognized now—while they can hear it and you can express it.

Sometimes I think we do the opposite—while people are alive, we heap shit of all kinds on them with both hands, and then just to indulge our guilt after they die, we praise them and never "speak ill of them" out of "respect" for the fact that they were once living, back when we happily slung shit all over them. That's why reading obituaries is such a guilty pleasure—if that's what you call something that's not really that pleasurable. (Come on—don't pretend that you never read them.) There's always some ninety-three-year-old whose "cab came" while they were surrounded by friends and family after a long and satisfying run, mostly in the sunshine. I start to feel good when I see those high numbers because I'm only fifty-eight and don't feel a day over seventy. But *then*, there *has* to be *one* in every crowd: the fifty-eight-year-old who brings us all down with his rebellious gesture of dying while being no older than I am and having an obituary full of those disturbing terms like "taken too soon," and "suddenly," and so forth.

I know my number's coming up at some point, with the added insult of not knowing my damn number. But, hey, I don't need to read about it before I've had my coffee in the morning. Sometimes, when I'm really in touch with my *inner child,* I realize that I'm barely over the whole Santa Claus being an anti-Semite thing my dad used to tell me! I hate obituaries more and more the older I get, and I hated them when I was young. I was angry when I heard my grandfather Ben's obituary read to me at age three. It was full of lies and omissions. The guy promised me that he would always be with me, and that was never mentioned in anything anyone ever said about him, yet to me it was the most important thing of all!

Therefore, it has always been one of my fondest wishes to write my own obituary, and I began that undertaking in the first grade. I have updated it along the way, and I want it read at my funeral, if I have one. I might not, as it would truly disgust me to look down from the wave particle I will be riding and see a bunch of people who treated me like crap, or who ignored me or owed me money, unburdening their guilt about me and singing my praises. They know who they are, and unless they contact me soon, apologize, and bring me cake, they can go fuck themselves and forget about me forever!

Chapter 20

Flattery Will Get You Everywhere

Writing my own obituary has made me reflect on the beginnings of my career in entertainment and the course my personal life has taken since that very first night on stage at the Comedy Shoppe in Denver. Once I made the transition from a thin cocktail waitress with a wicked sense of humor to a fat comic with comedy chops, I began to go out on the road and work a few comedy clubs. I had been encouraged by the fact that audiences seemed to really like me, and so did other comics from Los Angeles, who told me to hone my hour and then come to L.A. to audition for Mitzi Shore at The Comedy Store, which was mecca for comics back then, before cable television.

At a club in Minnesota, I met Lizz Winstead, who later co-created *The Daily Show*. Lizz introduced me to another fat comic, named Tom Arnold. Tom and I were on the same bill that week as another really, really fat comic, Scott Hansen, who booked the club, and Louie Anderson, who was really fat, too. We all sat around and made fun of one another and told fat jokes, but Tom got the best of everybody with the best fat joke of all. He was introduced onto the stage by Scott, who weighed about six hundred and fifty pounds (give or take a hundred), and after thanking him, Tom said, "Ladies and gentlemen, Scott also works as a rodeo clown in his spare time. Now, a lot of guys will stay on the horse for ten or fifteen seconds, but Scott stays on until the vet comes." Offstage we howled, and when Tom came off, I went on. He laughed really hard at my act, and hung around till it was over. He told me he thought I did great; in fact, he acted like he was in awe of me, and his compliments and flattery went on and on and on. I loved it, of course. I had never in my life had so much positive attention paid to me from a man.

We started talking and kept talking well into the next morning. We found each other funny, and we told fat joke after fat joke, and talked seriously about how much we hated being fat. Tom and I had some pretty intense eating issues, and matching character flaws, too. He also had quite the cocaine addiction, which I didn't find out about till later.

That first night that we hung out, he talked me into trying some cocaine with him by telling me that you don't get hungry if you are on it, and that was true in a way. You would not get hungry when you were on it, but the minute it wore off you were starving like nobody's business, hungry enough to eat the lining out of a bear's ass. I did it with him about four or five times, but the pre–heart attack feeling, coupled with the après-high eating linings out of bears' asses at Denny's at 2:00 a.m., cured me of doing it more.

I had never really had a guy friend before Tom. He became my *best* friend soon enough. I listened to him confess that he cheated on all of his girlfriends, and only went out with them if they were good-looking and had a car or a nice apartment and would support him so that he could pursue comedy. He had a nice girlfriend at the time who worked as a waitress and idolized him, paying for everything. She was always warning him that she would leave him if he didn't stop doing drugs and drinking all the time, and he told me that he had quite a double life going on and that he lied to her all the time. I told him, like a regular big sister, to stop treating her badly and to sober up. She, like the girlfriend he had after her, kicked him to the curb eventually, and I rolled up to retrieve him. After he had used up every bit of the other women's time and good graces, I told him that he deserved to be treated better, and he said he would never forget my saying that to him.

Tom was the quintessential bad boy, which is very attractive to women, and to me, too, I admit now. I knew the guy was a shithead, but I thought I could save him. That's what I thought, and it's what a lot of women think. I'm sitting here right now, as I write this, watching TV, and everything on it is about Sandra Bullock's shock that her bad-boy husband, who was a biker with an attraction to Nazi memorabilia and was previously married to a porn star, *ended up* being a biker with an attraction for Nazi memorabilia who was out fucking porn stars while she went to work in la-la land. It's sad for her, but I have to laugh a little at the way a lot of us women ignore what's right in front of our eyes once we fall for the sex-and-love bullshit. We always think we can make a leopard change his spots, and when he doesn't, we blame ourselves and keep living in a big fantasy world, despite all the clues, until it all just blows up in the most humiliating way. We are allergic to reality or something!

Tom wrote some funny jokes and I bought some from him, off and on, for a few years. Later, when I got the *Roseanne* show, I encouraged him to move to L.A. and write on it. The best times I had with Tom, though, were when we went on the road together as comics, and we would go to bars to hear music. Tom would always schmooze the band's leader until he let us get up and sing

"Johnny B. Goode" together. We developed our singing routine and continually perfected it each time we met up on the road. Of course, he would end up singing louder than I did, or shove me out of his way sooner or later, but I loved singing and I loved him for taking me places where I could sing. He would always tell me I had a great rock-and-roll voice, and that is what I wanted to hear at the time more than anything else on earth. I also fell hard for him when I heard the classic Tom story that he tells on every talk show and in every interview: The one about how all Tom wants in this world is his own children. More than he wanted fame, more than money, more than publicity or anything else. This so fit my whole "I must have baby number five" thing!

My parents and siblings, not to mention my husband and kids, did not want me to divorce Bill to marry Tom. They didn't like Tom at all, so, in classic codependent style, I stopped talking to my family.

I felt that I was finally in the right mental space to show the world the full range of my talent; it was time to get out there and show people that I could sing! Now, at the top of my game, was the right time to revisit the past and put it right at last! When my aunt Sadie visited me on the set of *Roseanne* (Aunt Sadie was Cousin Debbie's aunt, too), I was sure to show her around and ask if Cousin Debbie watched my show. "Of course she watches it!" she answered. Look out, Cousin Debbie!

When my husband arranged with Tom Werner, the owner and producer of *Roseanne* and the owner of the San Diego Padres, to invite me to sing in front of thousands of people who liked me at a Padres game on Working Woman's Night at Jack Murphy Stadium in San Diego, California, I thought it was going to be the best day of my life—the culmination of my earliest childhood hopes and dreams. I practiced and practiced, I knew all the words, and I felt that I had finally conquered all my fears and was ready.

The day of the game, the Padres sent their private jet, and I took my son Jake and my daughter Jessica and my then-husband with me. On the way down, my son, who was twelve, asked me, innocently, "Mom, I'm just afraid that people might think that you are making fun of our country."

I said, "Why would they think that? I know all the words."

"But usually really great singers sing it, and not comics. I don't know . . ." said my son, shaking his head. Out of the mouths of babes! Tom, supportive as ever, said, "Jake, your mom is a terrific singer, and everyone loves her. She is going to blow their minds down there, trust me!" He really believed it, too, I think.

Unfortunately, *I* really believed that I could do no wrong.

I took the kids to the best seats in the house, and left them there while I went down to the dugout to meet the team. One of the players said to me, "Hey, why don't ya grab your crotch and spit? That would be so funny!"

"I'm singing it serious, though," I said to him.

"Oh, do you sing?" he asked.

I said, "Well, mostly I sing country music, but, yeah, I do sing." I was really feeling good now. I knew lots of people liked me, and that in and of itself was a whole new feeling for me—to be liked and accepted, and respected, too. I was like one of those kids on *American Idol,* the ones who come into the tryout room and soon expose themselves as being "all attitude" with no singing chops whatsoever. They have been told by their parents and their lying, insane families (like I had) that they sing as well as the guys on the radio and on TV. Then they have to face Simon, who plays the part of Satan himself, and who looks them in the eye and tells them the exact truth about themselves, which they hate to hear. "Your singing is hideous." Then everyone gets mad and boos Simon, because they think he is so cruel, when he is, in fact, truthful and kind, yet firm and resolved. I have a huge crush on

Simon; he is the baddest of the world's bad boys. He is such a bad boy that I want to marry him—that dirty old Simon.

My old rickety sex urges still try to register in my brain after all these years, but now, as I approach sixty, I let my laziness work *for* me. I don't bother to get up and pursue my sexual thoughts; I just keep them in my head, all cozy. Yes, mentally, I have become a dirty old woman. No more *Cherchez le Dong por moi,* as we French types say. *C'est la vie.* These days, I have a man at home who reads Kierkegaard and plays five musical instruments. We discuss the world and God every day at three o'clock sharp over wine at lunch. And that is exactly how I like it.

I now hate germs, all bodily fluids, and all human contact, anyway, really. Unless it's a fine massage at Beverly Hot Springs Spa by Deborah, the older, bowlegged Korean woman who wears a black bikini and hoses me down after she scrapes all of my skin off with a brush. Then I go into the hot mineral baths. There is nothing as wonderful as that for me to do for my body's enjoyment.

Anyway, I was completely deluding myself that I was going to sing in front of sixty thousand people and get a standing ovation for being so good at it. I remember thinking that great opportunities like this come around only once in a lifetime, and I was sure right about that. The night before I sang, I went on Johnny Carson's show and told Johnny that I was going to do it.

Johnny said, "Are you sure you want to do that? That is a very difficult song to sing. Bob Goulet took quite a hit for screwing up the words one time. Be careful, and whatever you do, don't start too high." Well, I started too high and had nowhere to go but down. I was about three notes in when I first heard the booing; I couldn't believe it! And it kept getting louder and louder until I couldn't hear at all, so I just starting screaming to try to make it look funny. I got judged by sixty thousand Simons!

My kids were traumatized and shaking as we boarded the plane and were flown back to L.A. When I got home, I received a call from the Padres saying they would shield whatever bad reaction was headed my way. It was so sweet of them to try to do that, even if they changed their minds the very next day.

After I sang, Ronald Reagan's son Michael, a small-time San Diego Rush Limbaugh wannabe, took to the radio waves to say that I had purposely disrespected our country, our God, and our flag. I wanted to apologize all over the place right away, but my advisors said they didn't think I should do that. Tom thought it would pass in a day or two, and he said that comics should never apologize, that it would totally ruin my credibility as a comedian.

And also, on TV was the president, George Bush the elder, boarding Air Force One and stopping on the stairs to call me disgraceful. Michael Reagan's ratings went through the roof, and he appeared on TV shows coast-to-coast, saying that I personally hated each and every one of our troops and that I was giving oral sex to Saddam Hussein and Fidel Castro, or some shit that ridiculous. The fucking guy wouldn't stop! Then came the death threats, which were extremely anti-Semitic, and reawakened all my childhood fears of Nazidom, and people were such rabid assholes that they also threatened my kids' lives. The armed policemen that guarded my house every night were a calming influence that helped us all to be able to sleep. I really do thank them for that, too. It was a most scary time.

Subsequent to my tragic singing accident, the fallout included getting sued by the clothing company I was in business with, losing several more lawsuits with a variety of people, the cancellation of my ABC morning cartoon, and losing my Burger King and Toys "R" Us deals. Then the Veterans of Foreign Wars called ABC and threatened to boycott the network if they didn't cancel my show. The president of the network called to tell me they might do just that, and that I would have to wait until after the summer hiatus to see if the ratings were still there or if I had lost every single last American fan that I had ever had.

In the middle of a huge manic high, I had shot myself in the foot. I knew that the subsequent depression was going to be hard to come out of, and I honestly wondered if I could. I had a nervous breakdown, and no one even noticed!

When the attacks in the press didn't pass after another few days, my husband changed his mind. He decided that he himself should do a number of television interviews on my behalf, explaining how sorry I was for singing the National Anthem so badly. He arranged for media trucks to come to our beach house, and he got ready for his close-up, telling me to just stay upstairs and he would handle everything, like he always did.

I listened to him talk to Jane Pauley with the door open, and instead of saying, "She actually sings pretty well; it's just that she panicked," which was what we agreed he was going to say, he said, "She didn't mean to sing it so badly; it's just that THAT'S HOW SHE SINGS!" To me, that comment meant that the whole basis of our relationship was suddenly a lie. He didn't think I sang well at all! It took a few moments for the whole thing to register in my mind. I stood there thinking that something was not kosher at all. In fact, it was pork stuffed with lard and cooked in milk! I asked him why he lied and said that I didn't sing well, and he said, sheepishly, "Well, you aren't the *best* singer that's out there is what I meant. I mean, yeah, you're good, for sure, but, I mean, you aren't Barbra Streisand or anything!"

I continued, "But I *am* a good singer, and you didn't say *that*! You said that I sing badly, and that is a lie!" He looked like he thought I was completely crazy, or that I couldn't tell the difference between bullshit and reality, like he wondered what fresh hell he had flattered his way into this time.

The interviews worked as planned; everybody now thought that Tom was a good guy. Of course, they all hated me more than ever but . . . they stopped calling Tom bad names and insulting him constantly after that. We retreated to Iowa, where Tom grew up and where we had a wonderful farm and two thousand acres of gorgeous farmland. For some reason, since I was a girl, I longed to be a farmer. Maybe it was because I loved the book *Rebecca of Sunnybrook Farm,* which I had read over and over. I loved nature so much—the digging in the dirt, the sun, the fields where there were no Barr family members around. Ahhh!

The summer passed like a bad flu because of the Anthem, and it was the worst of times. Yet, in another way, there in Iowa, where Tom and I dressed like twins and ate four or five meals a day, and invited all of our neighbors, including the entire town of Eldon, Iowa, over for a barbecue, it was the best of times. We had built our own barn, with a stage so that our band, the Allis Chalmers Experience (named after our tractor), could perform. We sang John and Yoko songs; I sang "Stand by Your Man" by Tammy Wynette, and all of our favorites, including, of course, "Johnny B. Goode." We gave away millions of dollars to help abused kids, too, to make ourselves feel better, and when I finally went back to work, the ratings showed that there was no slippage at all, and I learned that I could keep my job!

That's when I secretly decided that I would attempt to turn my life completely around in every way. In other words: No more Mrs. Nice Guy! I, with Tom's help, was now going to get even with everyone who had "disrespected us."

I also realized that there would be no end to the humiliation part of stardom, ever, and that I would forever be a symbol of hatred for the unenlightened out there, masturbating compulsively to pornography when not writing letters to say they'll boycott any advertiser that pays me. And because of their righteous

Christian charity, or just to show support for their fellow Jew, they promised to do it forever. I longed for what I had lost: direction and meaning and the conversations with God that I had somehow replaced with talking to shrinks, reporters, publicists, and recovering drug addicts in show business.

Chapter 21

Eat, Pray, Shit, Shower, and Shave

Shortly after the National Anthem horror, I started to feel as though I were waking up from a bad nightmare. The Prozac, Zoloft, Klonopin, and several other mood-altering drugs that had been prescribed for me by psychiatrists (whose destruction by Scientology I now welcome) for my "Multiple-Personality Bipolar Obsessive-Compulsive Disorder" were no longer doing the trick of shielding me from reality. I became even more depressed than normal, like a lot of people do after they take antidepressants.

I had stopped smoking the Herb of the Goddess that had forever kept me balanced enough to become successful and rich, in order to support my then-husband's "sobriety," and that led to massive bipolar troubles that were all capped off with tons of psychiatrists and psychiatric drugs, none of which helped with my problems at all and, in fact, made them even worse. One thing I would like to tell you folks out there who are reading this, is this: Never marry a cocaine addict in their first month of sobriety! Give them a year, as AA recommends, before they rush off to replace their appetite for drugs with something else, such as straightening out your life, your family, your fame, and your financial affairs. This is just a tip from your old pal!

The thing I really do not like about AA and 12-step programs is that they never tell you that dealing with a sober addict can be way more trying than dealing with a drugged one! Once the user stops using, his demons come out, and he has no idea how to handle them. The entire reason he takes drugs in the first place is to quiet the demons, and without drugs, he finds himself in a really bad mood. Other people's demons are the most terrifying demons of all because they do not give a damn about you. They like to scare up your demons and do battle with them. Demons are slow learners and have a full bag of tricks at their disposal. They don't want to die. They want to live, in order to cause more pain and wreckage to those who can be convinced, tricked, or ripped off further. After treatment in AA, they expect to be given accolades for not continuing to fuck people over!

I think it may have been those terribly depressing antidepressant pills that made me more and more dependent on my husband to do everything for me, including, eventually, all of my thinking. I noticed the same thing happened to almost all of my married women friends. In order to bear being married in the last couple of years of misery, the women were always getting on antidepressants. It makes a marriage last two more years on average, I figured out. When the drugged woman regresses back to childhood, becoming girlishly compliant once more, it seems good at first. But what happens is that men never have a limit to the bullshit they need to be fed constantly in order to prop themselves up psychologically. Something is seriously wrong with them. Men cannot ever leave well enough alone, and they, like all children who keep pushing until they have reached the Mommy Limit, must be put in a time-out.

The antidepressant pills only delay the inevitable for twenty-four months after a marriage should rightly have ended. No marriage of any kind should be attempted, ever, between heterosexuals. These days it seems that gays are the only ones who are into marriage, but now having been allowed "the privilege," they will soon tire of it, too. When gays tire of marriage and the planning of big wedding parties and all the accoutrements that come with it, there will be peace on earth, at last—of that I am convinced.

The only part of my brain that still worked properly, après the Anthem, was the part that could write jokes for my sitcom. There was so much daily drama in recovering from the fallout of the National Anthem, and there was so much daily drama in being married to a newly sober cocaine addict, that there was actually no room for anything else in my life, including me. The fact that there was no room for me in my own life was classic codependency, but that's the way it had *always* been in my life—aside from comedy, which was really just about me thinking that I was fighting on behalf of others. I saw my sitcom and my comedy career as: Fighting on Behalf of Working-Class Mothers. My messianic complex was at its apex back in the early '90s.

As a child, I paid the cost *and* bore the burden for everything that ever went wrong in my family; still they called me "selfish," and I will no doubt be called "selfish" for telling the whole story in this book, too. I was the Barr family symptom-bearer, and honestly, that is what makes a person get fat, I think. Carrying the whole family's sins around requires a broad back. I was obsessed with authoring the role of a pop culture mother for television who spoke truth to power. I was always upset at the women I grew up with who never seemed to do that.

I was nursing a grudge against the universe by this time. A lifetime of bitterness about my childhood seemed to surface after I no longer had to work my ass off just to pay my bills and cover the basics. It's funny how things go. Whenever you think you have it made, look out! It's always something, isn't it? If you would have told me as a child that one day I would have my own show and be very rich and very famous, and very unhappy, I would never have believed it. I was sure in my childhood fantasies that fame and fortune would fix everything that had ever gone wrong. During my most famous and prosperous period, upsetting thoughts began to flash through my mind. I thought I had dealt with all the abusive things about my mother and father when my sisters moved in with me and my first husband, back in 1980.

I got madder and madder, and sicker and sicker. Repeated attempts to reach out to my family about what had happened in my childhood were ignored by them, as they became somewhat embittered that I was still unhappy and angry even though I had become rich and successful. They were also angry that I had married a man who they did not like at all, against their advice, in spite of their warnings and begging me not to, and they retreated from me, and vice versa. After one year of letter writing and asking my parents to verify the things I was dealing with, and receiving no response at all from them, I decided to just drop a bomb on them and the entire family. With unwavering support from my husband, I gave an interview to *People* magazine, accusing my father of incest and describing other abuses. My parents denied all the allegations against them.

I was under a therapist's care at the time, and she rightly recommended that I not do that until my therapy was complete, and I had the chance to confront and work through these accusations with my parents. I had lost all perspective and thought of myself as a commodity, a brand, an example, and an avenger. I was angry that my parents never responded to my requests over a period of a year to meet with me, and to talk about the reality of abuse in our family. I exploded.

The word *incest* conjures ideas of sex, but there was never any sex between my father and me. There was violence, humiliation, inappropriate words, "jokes," and rather grotesque displays that never should have occurred between a father and his daughter, but there was no actual *sex*. For someone like myself who dealt with words and the power they have, I should have chosen them more thoughtfully, more carefully, but I didn't really think things through at all, and I was definitely not careful, and I just didn't care anymore about anything but striking out. I was as miserable then as a person can be. I felt tormented and disconnected, had lost myself totally in an often violent and abusive relationship, and felt under attack from every direction. I felt like I had dealt with my father's lack of boundaries toward me and my younger siblings for all of my life, and perhaps because I was living with a man who had less than no respect for me, or my boundaries again, I just went ballistic.

I have attempted to make amends to my family, but it's quite tricky, still. I entertained the excuse that my family had refused to deal with my charges and my problems, and I, at the end of my rope, just decided to drop a big bomb on all of them, to destroy the wall of denial and semantics forever. Ultimately, though, no excuse worked to let me off the hook. I made a terrible, poorly conceived decision that caused an incredible amount of pain and shame for my parents and siblings. They hired Melvin Belli, who was my father's hero, as Perry Mason had been Bubbe Mary's, and they threatened to sue me for libel. Of course, they passed a polygraph test, proving there was no "incest." I still wonder what word would have been better to use. It doesn't seem that there is one that conveys the feelings I had as a young girl in a family that didn't really much value women's needs, privacy, shame, or pride.

I sometimes think that fame turns everything in your life into a photo or publicity op, as it does for many others who are in the grip of the insanity that fame causes. I heard Bill Murray say that everyone freaks out for about two years after they get famous, and there is no way to avoid that or to warn someone about what it's like. I find that to be so true. I identified with and felt compassion for Britney Spears as she walked through reams of paparazzi and shaved her head in public, breaking down completely before being committed to the mental ward.

Every newly famous person will lose their mind for a while; it's just what happens. The brief sojourn to the mental institution provides a most welcome breath of sanity, paradoxical as that sounds! Staggering around under the pressure of unceasing public scrutiny by really hostile people, who really do wish you would drop dead, causes quite a loss of balance. No one is ever prepared to handle the hatred that accompanies being "beloved."

A simple thing like starting a song in the wrong key was key to being keyed in to the reality of singing a song by Francis Scott Key, who may still be spinning in his grave. When asked now for my advice to new singers of the National Anthem, I say, "Know your key and don't start too high and don't be afraid to simply stop and start over again if you need to."

I tried to return to my religion again as a way of rediscovering my sanity and a sense of peace. Attempting to support me in this rediscovery of my Judaism, my husband Tom opened the shower door in our newly acquired Brentwood mansion, where we moved after living at the beach about six months after the unfortunate singing accident, and said, "They said I could convert to Judaism! Then we can have a huge Jewish wedding [our second wedding—the first one being small and only family, with Tom fresh out of cocaine rehab], and apply to join the Brentwood Country Club, too! We will go legit in a big, big way!"

I know now that he had lost his mind, too.

My husband was convinced that once I accepted the trappings

of fame and fortune, we would be able to bullshit our way to the top of showbiz and hit a payday jackpot. When he started with the "It's time that you start getting treated like the queen that you are. We will turn this whole thing around, trust me!" stuff, and telling me who I needed to drop or fire or attack because they were not doing enough of that, I loved it. Anger and getting even made me feel alive; in fact, if not for my giving the Evil Eye, I would have felt lost.

"They are disrespecting *you* when they disrespect me, and that is not befitting a queen of your importance and your stature! Do you think any of these people would treat Camille [wife of Bill Cosby] the way they treat me? No, because Cosby is treated like a king, and Camille is his wife, his queen. It's just utter sexism! I used to think you were just a man-hater when you would drag out your women's lib shit and stuff like that. But now I see you were right, because I am treated so badly by Hollywood, and it's really because they don't like you because you are a woman. You will sing that song again at a bigger venue next time!"

More Klonopin, please, Doc!

We became obsessed with acquiring status symbols, and not just that, but using the popularity of my show to try to get them for free. Like gambling addicts, we wanted to get something for nothing. I marveled at how smart and daring and devious my husband and I could be.

All I really wanted was a clothing line for fat women. I was convinced then, and still am now, that size XL is the American norm. And since I had taken all the flack in the world on behalf of fat women in the tabloid press and from hack comedians who, in addition to making jokes about women's sizes, shapes, and minds, tell marvelously inventive jokes about how our vaginas smell bad, too, I felt I should be the recipient of those revenues reaped directly or indirectly from all that. I figured I would use half of the sum total to start a business, where I would employ other fat and undereducated, underemployed domestic goddesses to sew our own fashions and open our own darling boutiques until I had amassed an army of plump, small-business owners. We would then form our own political party and tear down the walls surrounding the elite, thin forces, who know nothing about insatiable hunger or obsession, or being a woman who gets fat in order to be able to carry more people around on her back and support them all. Then we could begin an American women's army and, for a change, win the wars we start everywhere, especially if we were fighting against women who were thinner than we were.

After the Anthem incident, I became my husband's pet project, and he needed a full staff under him (literally) to rehabilitate my broken and soiled image ("brand") as a hater of everything decent, family-based, and American; only he could do that, despite the fact that it was he who encouraged me to sing in the first place. The fact that a FATwa had been put on my head by George Bush the elder, who called me "disgraceful," did not deter my husband from nurturing endorsement deal after endorsement deal. Employing industrial-strength schmoozing and flattery, he was not about to let my abject humiliation prevent him, high on magical 12-step thinking, from succeeding.

I was a complete lunatic by now, imploding from being pulled in too many directions. Though I had always been the girl who went too far, and was proud of that, the reaction of the right-wing media, starting with Ronald Reagan's son Michael, San Diego's less successful version of Sean Hannity and Rush Limbaugh, was downright scary as hell.

At any rate, when my husband proposed converting to Judaism and securing exalted country-club status, I asked him, "Are you going to learn Hebrew, too?" He sweetly replied, "Of course not. If

I learned Hebrew and did the actual shit it takes to convert, that would take two years! They say that my wanting to be a good Jewish stepfather and husband counts for ninety percent of the conversion anyway. Then we will have your gorgeous, Jewish, dream wedding, befitting a Jewish queen, and a fantastic bar mitzvah for your son Jake—a bar mitzvah worthy of the son of a queen." Can bullshit be of biblical proportions? What can I tell you, it sort of worked on me at the time—did I mention the drugs?

We did, indeed, have a gorgeous Jewish wedding and a fantastic bar mitzvah befitting a queen of my stature. Tom had hired a number of beautiful young women to assist him in the planning of these events, and it never occurred to me at all that he might've been cheating on me with any of them. The guy was quite a good actor, too.

We felt right not-at-home among our A-list neighbors in that lovely enclave called Brentwood, California. What a stellar, diverse group they were: Julie Andrews and Blake Edwards, Martin Mull, Harold Ramis, Meg Ryan and Dennis Quaid, Cindy Crawford and Michael King, Merv Adelson, Phyllis Diller, Marcy Carsey, Robert Iger, all of whom I liked, and others, some too phony and self-absorbed to mention. One thing that seemed to bring them all together, though, including my hubby, was the added pride and privilege they felt as a result of living in close proximity to one Orenthal James Simpson. When we were being "vetted" for membership in the Brentwood Country Club and were allowed to eat a club sandwich in its restaurant, we witnessed "The Juice" golfing on the green. "I would love to play golf with The Juice someday; he is, like, the ultimate businessman," Tom (the business major from the University of Iowa) gushed reverently. "You are going to get some endorsement deals, I guarantee you, as soon as this whole National Anthem thing dies down. You'll see. I won't let you down there, trust me." I could tell he was sincere; the drool always gave it away.

I was trying like hell back then to fit in with the classy folks whose already morbidly obese self-esteem was pumped up even more for having O.J. Simpson as a neighbor. I also busied myself with having tons of plastic surgery (mostly to get the meds) and contributing vast amounts of charity money to buy our way into the best circles of terrific new *friends.* It was during a meeting with one of the many shady, rheumy-eyed CEOs who offered me endorsement deals that the guy actually said, "You will be great selling things on this new network, because as women buy more things from TV, they go outside less, and sooner or later they become shut-ins, which is, to put it bluntly, an actual captive audience. And *you* are someone they trust, so you could sell them anything!" That was the exact moment I decided to flush all my meds and start to become *me* again.

Perhaps because of the offensive way some offensive people misinterpreted my interpretation of "The Star-Spangled Banner," the Brentwood Country Club turned us down for membership four months later and our $50,000 was returned. It was a hard blow to Tom, who sought legitimacy and power as a replacement for cocaine. Speaking of "blow," it was a blow to our three-year marriage, and our seven-year friendship as well. Suddenly, the "you saved me from drugs and made me famous" flattery befitting a queen was no longer forthcoming from Tom. Now, thanks to his stilted sober judgment, it was actually my disgraceful behavior on the baseball field that had prevented us from reaching his goals. In his mind, he was dragging me around behind him, and not the other way around at all.

In the last part of our marriage, as a way of throwing Tom and me a bone, a competing agency who wanted us to leave Wilhelm Moreless and join their client list asked Tom to read for a new Arnold Schwarzenegger–Jim Cameron movie, called *True Lies*. He nailed it. He was so happy at the time. He said that this was his chance to come out of my shadow and take over the moneymaking, so that I would be free to retire and get pregnant, and that made me feel so happy! I had already undergone major surgery to undo a tubal ligation. I followed that with major surgery of every kind. I think I did all that to get the medication and a rest from the constant swirling drama of my life, and also because my husband constantly joked about the way I looked, and I felt pressured to do it. It makes me sick to think about how little self-esteem I had then, but that is the truth. In public, though, I was all feminism and business.

But something was beginning to change for me. Maybe it was because I secretly threw away all of my psychiatric medicine and started to awaken from suspended animation, but watching Tom's flattery of Arnold and Jim was stupefying for me to watch. I started to think that maybe I was full of shit; maybe I was just an overindulged comic who was lucky enough to have landed a television show, and not the Queen of the World. After Tom and Arnold both started to talk about someday running for governors of California (Arnold) and Iowa (Tom), I started to plan for divorce. I couldn't believe the kind of bullshit they were slinging around, but I figured it was never going to happen, so why worry about it. There was no way in hell that Arnold Schwarzenegger would ever be elected governor of California, and no way in hell Tom would be elected governor of Iowa, I thought. (Since I have subsequently figured out that *this is* hell, I am now waiting for Tom to declare his candidacy and, of course, win.)

Once, during that time, Tom and I were standing inside the Governor's Mansion with the governor of Iowa, and I was telling the governor a joke when Tom's foot ground into mine and I stopped, shocked, to hear my husband ask for us to be excused for a moment. We walked away before I got my punch line out, which should have upset me, but I was used to being interrupted by

Tom, from the beginning of our relationship, whether it was a phone call on the day I was reunited with the daughter I had given up for adoption eighteen years earlier (to leave her and help Tom get to a hospital before he bled out through the nose after a cocaine bender) or a hundred other equally dramatic interruptions. Every one of which I excused. So when he whispered to me out of the corner of his mouth with a big smile in the middle of telling a joke to the governor of Iowa, I excused myself.

"Watch what you say here," Tom, the recovering cocaine addict, advised, after he had taken me aside, in plain view of the governor, as I had always to be put in my place in plain view of those around us. He whispered, "I plan to be governor of this state someday! You're gonna have to learn how to act in order to be first lady. You need to go to charm school or something, to kind of refine yourself. You have the funny and ingratiating part down, but you are still kind of rough around the edges." He smiled, continuing, "You'll do fine."

I said, "Are you out of your fucking mind? I do not want to hang around with politicians!" He ignored me, as usual, in that Asperger's way he had, while leering at all the thin girls in high heels that he could see.

He was starting to talk about how inner-city kids need an incentive, and how Arnold Schwarzenegger's Inner City Games Foundation would supply that for children of color. Like the rich do, he began to mouth all that blame-the-victim horseshit. That's when I knew my socialist pal had joined the conspiracy. I know I am not an easy woman to understand, live with, or care about. I can barely stay out of my own way most of the time, unless I am meddling in other people's business and fixing their lives, or seated in front of a computer keyboard. I could portray a character right alongside the one my husband was portraying for a while (which is how I began to see our marriage), in order to bring along some business deal or another for just so long, before the acting became boring, conniving, manipulative, concerned with shadows and lighting, all vanity and pretense. When the reality that you are only acting in a marriage sets in and the accompanying self-loathing for the inherent lack of honest human emotion registers, something has to give. I reached that point, realizing that I was just a prop in somebody else's story and not mine at all, a perfect codependant. I could no longer resign myself to go on living that way, hoping to hit some jackpot on which everything else was riding. I recognized that I was the same type of gambling addict that my dad and both my grandfathers had been.

I dropped the first bomb on my husband, and everything he had built for the two of us to share with his assistants, his family, and his friends, when my maid, Rosario, pulled me aside to tell me she had found one of my husband's assistant's panties in our bed. Rosario and I emptied my husband's closet of the handmade shoes and boots and tuxedos he bought so as to be befitting the husband of a queen into the beautiful pool in our meticulously manicured Brentwood backyard, which Tom, coming from a fairly moneyed family, had designed in order to cheat on me in a manner befitting a queen whose husband cheats on her.

The plot began to thicken into a rich pudding indeed. I then drove straight to my husband's office and tore all of the pictures of him posing with various celebrities off the walls and helpfully dropped them from the balcony, where they shattered below on the concrete. The poor assistant sat wide-eyed and trembling.

As the fear that I might smudge her perfectly drawn lip liner in my rage washed over her dimwitted face, she then lifted the phone and placed a call; within minutes, the guards from the Radford Studios came to escort me off the upper part of the studio lot and forced me to contain myself behind the doors of the *Roseanne* stage set. Once there and newly angered, I enlisted the help of my prop crew to retrieve hammers, nails, and boards, and then marched across the entire four-block lot to nail my husband's office door shut.

As we were doing this, my husband showed up in a golf cart with his childhood friend and fellow Iowan, who had relocated to California and now *worked* for us, and was having sex with the assistants who preferred not to attempt to have sex with Tom. Tom got out of the golf cart and yelled, "Honey, you are mentally unstable and need to go back to Sheppard Pratt mental institution, and I am going to help you do just that! A private plane is on reserve, and you have been given time off from your show." A young woman from the prop crew spoke up behind me and said, "Say, 'Honey, *you* are the one who is sick, and I am firing you from my show!'" Loving the suggestion, I repeated it, loudly. Unbelievable to me, then and now, the guards came back and banned me, not Tom, from the lot where I made my television show. They took down the boards from his office, escorted him inside, and sent a team of people to sweep up the scattered glass and save the glossies of Tom with Arnold Schwarzenegger and the Planet Hollywood crew. Sheppard Pratt is lovely during autumn, as I recall.

Chapter 22

The Great Escape

Tom, in his own mind, had done everything humanly possible to make himself happy, and therefore make me happy, and I was supposedly just too self-obsessed and negative to appreciate all that he had done for himself, and therefore me. At the end of our relationship he said, "There is no pleasing you. You are an awful person!" I actually thought I was an awful person for all the things I suspected Tom of doing, and that made me resolve to be a better wife and stay married to him for three years longer than the three years, six months, and three weeks that we should have been married. I blame the Prozac. After the divorce and the Prozac detox, I found that I was actually right about almost everything that I thought I was wrong about, and I then had to forgive myself for being wrong in doubting that I was, in fact, right all along.

In a matter of weeks from that day, I had finally determined that the demons in me that kept me in this bad and painful relationship needed to be totally destroyed once and for all. I was so mad at them for all of their codependency issues. First of all, they couldn't exist without parasitically living off me, and I couldn't exist without a man telling me that I deserved to be treated like a queen. I needed my ego stroked promiscuously the way that only other people's demons could do. I decided that I would face my demons down and slay them all—a very tricky proposition for any normal woman, but especially for one who had, at twelve years old, sold her soul to the devil for fame, fortune, ego, and snacks.

I recognized that I must first unleash my demons fully, in order to destroy them and that it must happen in Paris, beginning at the Louvre. After having my thirst for wine and cream and edibles slaked, I ventured forth, and passed 'neath the Crystal Pyramid. Inside was all the beauty of the world I had dreamed about since I was a girl. Art makes the "terror of existence bearable," as some old genius once said.

While in Paris, I returned to the Louvre daily, and I also drank and drank and drank, and smoked and smoked and smoked, and then I wrote and wrote and wrote, walking down dimly lit streets, reclaiming my anonymity, swearing, yelling, wasted from feeling hopeless despair and existential angst, unwashed for days, stinking, sitting next to beggar women on the street, reading Henry Miller's *Under the Roofs of Paris,* writing about madness, barefoot, knowing that no one knew who I was or wanted anything from me. I wasted $3,000,000 on castles, boats, hotels, planes, booze, drugs, tour guides, chauffeurs, and sin. I was sinning as big as I could, unleashing the madwoman. "You got to sin to get saved," sings Miss Maria McKee.

I fell in love with my big, blond Finnish bodyguard, Ben, who had helped with my ruse and my escape, and on our first night together I asked him if he would father Number Five, and he said yes. He accompanied me to the greatest museums and architectural marvels of Europe and the Mediterranean—from Paris to Florence, Venice, Rome, Madrid, Marbella, Sardinia, Marrakesh, and Amsterdam. In Nice, inside the museum where the works of the greatest Jew of all, Marc Chagall, are hung, I saw the truth of the longing for God in an upside-down world, expressed by another once living and thinking soul, on canvas, and felt the transcendental shock of it—of psychically merging with the vision and brushstrokes of an avatar. It is the most healing thing that exists.

Ben and I drank, danced, smoked, and partied our way through my divorce/soul retrieval. I got to see Michelangelo's *David* in Florence, where I dropped the second bomb on my husband by pay phone, telling him I was filing for divorce. And I got to eat real Italian garlic bread.

Recipe for Real Italian Garlic Bread

2 teaspoons minced garlic
½ stick (1¼ cup) unsalted butter, softened
Dash of sea salt
One 15-by-3½-inch loaf day-old Italian bread, sliced in half lengthwise
Pinch of sweet paprika on top

Preheat oven to 400°F.

Chop garlic so fine that it disappears when mashed into the softened butter. Add the dash of sea salt and then paint the garlic butter on the inside of both halves of the old bread. Wrap the bread in a moist towel and let sit for thirty minutes. Remove the moist towel, place the bread halves on a cookie sheet, and bake for ten minutes. Sprinkle each half with paprika, and slice before serving.

I saw and studied everything Michelangelo. His work has some nice, bipolar, morbid, thought disorder stuff going on in it. I felt sorry for the guy for having to create those images of damnation and cruelty on the hallowed walls of hallowed halls, where witch burners could relive their crimes while pretending to be innocent of them. The deep fear and loathing in those Sistine Chapel paintings, commissioned of a homosexual artist by an all-male clergy, is apparent in the depiction of women, who are all represented as dead or cringing mothers, bleeding victims, whores, or demons, and not once as stand-up comics, writers, or CEOs of small businesses. I must add that it was during this trip that I heard on Spanish TV, while in Madrid, that one O.J. Simpson had been arrested for the double homicide of his ex-wife and Ron Goldman, a nice Jewish boy who just got in The Juice's way.

I still think about the circuitous irony of that time in my life: how O.J. killed two people and got away with it; how the same rabbi who converted Tom, married us, and bar mitzvah'ed my son eventually married Tom to his new wife, a non-Jewish midwestern blonde; and how I married and got pregnant by the guy Tom had hired to drive me around and protect me, Ben Thomas.

Chapter 23

Buck Stops Here

Getting pregnant by in vitro fertilization wasn't easy. I was forty-three years old and sterile, but thanks to my Brentwood neighbor, a fertility doctor, I had my eggs harvested and mixed in a dish with my husband Ben's sperm, and then I took a bunch of shots to make me artificially fertile. The procedure is called ZIFT (zygote intrafallopian transfer), and I became pregnant on the very first try. The eggs were implanted sunny-side up in my uterus on Thanksgiving Day, 1994, during a three-week break from filming *Roseanne.* I have a picture of me dressed as a ballerina with a smiling Ben seated next to me on that happy day when our son was manufactured. The doctor told me that six fertilized eggs would be implanted in my womb, and that I must stay in bed and be calm for three to four entire days, and not get stressed out, so that they could implant on the old uterine wall.

That was very difficult for me, because on the third day, my new husband, Ben, had to have emergency surgery after breaking his leg. I did not get stressed out by any of these things because I had also learned that very morning that I was pregnant with quadruplets. My first thought was, I am eating for FIVE! Heaven on earth! All the pain of the recent past washed away. Quadruplets were definitely the way to bounce back!

Once I saw all four of them on the screen that was hooked up to my womb, I wanted to know them. I wanted to know people who were born by design. Their mentality would be positively futuristic. They would have to be new kinds of thinkers.

Then, not more than a couple of weeks later, I started to absorb the eggs, one by one, over a three-week period. I burst into tears at the thought of losing them. My doctor told me it would all be all right if I moved as little as possible and did not get stressed. I began to pray for hours and hours each day, I needed the big soul hookup to the big soul battery in the sky badly. I would walk slowly to the car and sit on a pillow to ride slowly to the doctor's office to be hooked up to the ultrasound machine. I watched as, one after another, three zygotes disappeared into the ether. Only Buck was left and he was tearing away from the tissue, hanging on by a thread. I began to breathe deeply and slowly and send my thoughts to the energy in the screen, to the little tiny speck there. I told it that it was okay to come here, and that this was an okay place to hang around for a while. I attempted to make a deep psychic connection with the zygote and invite it to stick around so we could hang out.

I wanted my son to come to earth so badly because I knew that he would be funny and bright, as well as handsome, *and* that he'd make the varsity tennis team in ninth grade—and of course I was right about all of this. Most of all, I think I wanted my son because I knew that having him would force me to change, and though I didn't really know all that back then, I see it now.

At the most crucial fourth week of my pregnancy, my husband, Ben, with his broken leg in a cast, was bedridden right next to me.

One night while we both lay there unable to move, we saw on the news that a hurricane was headed our way. I instantly imagined the worst: being ripped to shreds by Mother Nature, as my husband and I lay there helplessly underneath Ralph Lauren bedding. My anxiety was getting the best of me. Desperate not to miscarry, I decided to call Rabbi Eitan, a friend of my friend Sandra Bernhard, another loudmouthed sister Jewish comic. Sandra told me I would love him, and that he was for real, and righteous. I decided that this was probably as good a time as any to finally listen to what a rabbi-type guy had to say. Besides, the way I figured it, I gave so much money to the Jews in my lifetime, one way or another, that I should at least get something useful in return, when I needed it.

I wanted to be comforted by him, but also I wanted to be able to get *off* the phone before he tried to speak to me about my sins. The poorer rabbis always seemed to bring those subjects up, and it was never as much fun for me to talk about as it seemed to be for them. I was quite pleased when our conversation instead turned to the topic of helping me remain calm. Teaching people to remain calm in crisis is what the richer rabbis do, and I like them better than the pushy poor rabbis who talk about gluttony and selfishness for many reasons, some purely selfish.

Eitan genuinely seemed to want to help me, though, and he asked me if I would like to learn a valuable tool. I asked how much it would cost and was told there was no cost. I reminded him that I was on doctor's orders not to move. "Yes, Roseanne, you have mentioned that quite a few times, but what I am about to teach you requires that you only close your eyes and breathe."

"Hell," I said, "I can handle that!" And he proceeded to teach me the valuable art of breathing in the substance that I then breathed out. The substance that I contained briefly after breathing it in and just before it was breathed out would adhere to my inner workings and construct a spiritual vessel to contain itself. This simple letting-go-of-thinking thing, the meditative-state stuff, was very new to me, and it felt so powerful that I imagined that one day, perhaps, I could achieve the impossible: self-control!

Once I was pregnant with Buck, the doctors ordered me to avoid stress, so I had to back down and turn my show over to other writers and producers. For a huge control freak, the most stressful thing in the world is to give up control. Not to get stressed doing the most stressful thing was difficult as hell. I was carefully driven to the *Roseanne* set and I delivered my lines from a couch or a chair. I left all the worry to other people. Thank God for the O.J. trial, which I watched every single day for the three months I was on bed rest.

Anyway, that zygote wanted to come here pretty badly, and it is now a fifteen-year-old boy named Buck who still cannot believe that I was ever married to Tom Arnold. He says, "You were married to that guy? The one who gets all those hot chicks? Why do you think he went out with you? Did you not know it was just for tha cheddah? Dude, no way! Were you high?"

"I was on the government pills for sure, son," I said. "Now go do the dishes, or I'm grounding you off of Facebook."

Another ironic tidbit is that it was in my son's nursery, while changing his dirty diaper, that I saw on TV that the jury had acquitted one Orenthal James Simpson of murder. It was then that I knew I must move away from Brentwood, where he might subsequently return. Already, it was almost impossible to even venture outside without boatloads of tourists from all over the world driving up and asking you to direct them to Rockingham Avenue.

Being able to marshal all of my will, force, and ability to focus on emptying out and being silent, was indeed the closest thing to heaven that I ever felt here on earth. Being in a peaceful and heavenly state helped to quiet the voices in my mind, and I *was* able to stay calm enough to carry Buck to full term. Meditation became essential to me then, and still is today.

While this newfound tool was successful in enabling me to have my son, I also found that all that focusing became detrimental to me as well. It was no longer allowing me to dissociate and turn a blind eye to my behavior, my decisions, or my past. Now, mind you, dissociative behavior is what allowed me to survive a complicated and at times traumatizing childhood. I had learned to function and even become wildly successful in this state for most of my life. I had multiple personalities and bipolar disorder diagnoses to prove it. I know it is hard to understand how a person on the verge of madness can function as well as I did in a world where portly, loudmouthed, bipolar delusionals are supposed to be locked away, not starring in a successful family sitcom for nine years. I was good at my life when it was a story told through fictional characters that I could make do and say what I wanted them to. My real life was the scary thing, though. I had little control over that.

Rabbi Eitan wanted me to come to meet *his* teacher, Rabbi Berg, at the Kabballah Centre in Los Angeles. He escorted me into a room and said he would be right back. Sitting alone in the room waiting for his return, I was surprised to see the door open and an old hippie guy wearing a dashiki enter. He handed me a book and said it was about me and my show. "This was written by a friend of mine; he used your TV character as the example of the average woman. I thought you might want to read it. I have never seen your 'Little Beaver' show," he said, "but I know everyone else has, so . . ."

I liked him right away, because I like kooks like me—we understand each other's language. So I said, "You mean, *Leave It to Beaver*? That was an old show with a perfect mother named June on it, and many people have said that my show was its antithesis. Is that what you mean?"

He said, "I don't know anything about TV shows or movies, but something is telling me to have you read this book and get back to me on it if you want." Then he disappeared behind closed doors.

Opening the book, to no particular page, it just so happened (as it always seems to) that my eyes fell on the right words: "Roseanne Connor is a character authored and portrayed by Roseanne Barr, a Jewish woman who is questioning the philosophical assumptions regarding the status of women in popular culture. Roseanne Connor as well as Roseanne Barr could be helped along greatly with some deep meditation." It was all true, every word!

I stepped out into the reception area. "Who was that guy and where did he go?" I asked a few of the staff members.

"What guy?" they responded.

"The older guy with the dyed beard and the hippie robes," I said.

"There is no one here fitting that description," they replied.

"He just came out and handed me this book!" I insisted.

They looked at the book, and then, almost in shock, a woman said, "The Rav came out and gave this to you? You are so lucky!"

Needless to say, I read the book and got back to him on it. I told him that it was very good, and almost spooky that I had come there to meditate and was handed a book about how I and my character should do just that. "The Light!" he replied, laughing.

As it turned out, I was lucky enough to become one of the Rav's students. He taught me tons of new angles on Torah stories and meditations that helped me to become not only calmer but more and more aware of things I had done in my life, or that I had blocked out of my mind. I was able to learn to relax enough to experience self-awareness in all of its twists and turns. I told the Rav that I had multiple personality disorder. He showed me the page in Zohar that says we are made up of many entities. Becoming more self-aware put me on a deep and dark yet ultimately illuminating journey of repentance and integration after my son was born.

I was also lucky to have as my psychiatrist, Dr. Colin Ross. He helped me to remove layers and barriers that kept my mind in parts, at the same time that I was learning deep kabbalistic meditations. This took fourteen years of intense therapy, but I am happy to say that after all this therapy I am still crazy, but at least now I remember the stuff I do! My meditations made me realize that material wealth and fame were not what my spirit really wanted. What I really wanted was material wealth and fame and peace of mind. I wanted a game changer.

Chapter 24

True Tales of Ten Turning Spheres

I had become braver and braver in my spiritual journey of making amends, exorcising my personal demons, nullifying all unholy deals, and integrating all of my divided parts. I had moved out of the common frame of mind that people call "forgiveness," and instead moved into a frame of mind more about "repentance." I called my teacher, Rav Berg, and said, "I want to make a confession to you."

"I know you do," he said, since he is one smart rabbi. "Come to my house for lunch tomorrow."

"I will," I said, hoping those young Iranian Jews who cooked for him would make that fantastic lamb dish. When I got there, I saw that we were going to have steak, which smelled delicious. "Did you know that Rebbe Shimon says in the Zohar that dogs are the reincarnations of bad rabbis?" Rav Berg asked.

"No," I said, thinking, How innocent and quaint, and all those things I think when a rabbi talks.

"Yes, that is what it says in The Book. You know my wife's dog, Murray, right?"

"Yes, of course I do," I said. During a synagogue service once, I told my son Buck that per the Zohar Murray was exactly like a human being, as is anything that possesses a spinal column. So Buck got down on the floor (he was only five then) and told Murray that he better start listening to people who were bigger than he was. Buck said to him, "Now, I am bigger than you are, so you should come over here and sit by me right now."

Murray stayed put, so I asked Buck, "Do you think maybe that Murray only speaks Hebrew?"

"I never thought that animals could speak another language at all!" said my son.

"It just goes to show you the things we don't think sometimes, huh?" I said.

"Yeah," said Buck.

The Rav offered me a seat at his kitchen table. The steaks looked like they cost twenty dollars each—really, really good ones. "So," he said, "the Zohar says that all dogs are the reincarnation of bad rabbis. My wife's dog, Murray, here, was a bad rabbi, and I think I know who he was, too. He was a rabbi who turned me in to the authorities during one of my other lifetimes. I was excommunicated for writing books about the Zohar, which was forbidden at one time. So now he has to come back here to be my wife's dog, and you know what I do that really gets his goat?" he asked me.

"No, what do you do?" I asked.

"Watch this," he said, and then he cut out the middle part of the steak, the very best part, called the dog over, and fed it to him off his fork. "That is what I do. It kills him that I am nothing but kind to him. He wants me to get mad and treat him badly, but that would be a terrible mistake. Treat even your worst enemies with dignity and kindness; that's what you need to do, too, my dear," he told me.

In addition to the steak, the Iranian girls served up a tomato salad, olives, and other tasty treats, and they poured delicious red wine for us to drink. It was heaven on earth, sitting there with the Rav, who was watching the Reverend John Hagee on TV. "That guy is good," the Rav said. "He knows a lot about Torah, but . . . unfortunately, he is incorrect in many, many ways."

"Like what?" I wanted him to explain. He told the Torah stories like I had never heard before in my life, and they were fascinating to me.

"Well, Hagee misses the boat because he gets caught up in who is telling the story and which interpretation of the story is more righteous, and all that BS, and he misses the forest for the trees."

"Like . . . ?" I coaxed.

Being a rabbi, he could not be brief. "Well, the *message* is lost, and the message is what matters, not who delivers it!"

"Rav, what's the message, dude?" He loved it when I called him "dude."

"The message is that you must treat others, especially your enemies, with simple human dignity, no matter what they do to you. If only a critical mass of Jewish people could do this, we could summon the Messiah! In the Age of Aquarius, these kinds of Jewish people are to be as numerous as mustard seeds. Are you in the groove or not?"

"Yes, Rav, like most Jews, I think that I am Jesus," I said. We laughed.

"Well, we who want the Messianic Age are *all* Jesus!" he touché'd, being a master, and not a victim, of dogma, like common clerics.

"I must confess, Rav," I said. "I feel bad about a deal I signed with Satan when I was twelve years old. I've laughed it off for a long time, chalking it up to being young and unhappy. And yes, I know the whole concept is archaic and Stone Age, but the more negativity I get rid of since I've started to meditate, and since Buck was born, the more I want to keep ridding myself of *all* of it."

"Let me ask you, Shana Rifke, were you smart enough to make the deal with Satan on Shabbat?" he said.

"Smart?! Rav, I am so ashamed that I desecrated my own deeply held belief system by defiling the Sabbath!" I confessed.

He absolved, "We have all made that same deal in one way or another, Roxanna." The Rav didn't always remember my English name; he mostly called me by my Hebrew name—Rifke—like my family did when I was a kid. "So, Rifke, to answer your question about making a deal with Satan, here is what the book says—the Zohar tells us that on Shabbat, no evil inclination of any kind can exist. It's the day of peace because there is no duality on that day, only unity in the soul. So, there is no deal! Shabbat is Satan's day off—you picked the perfect day with the perfect loophole, and all of the torment you've felt about it is just unnecessary."

I said, like all the newly saved do, "So, I should start a foundation? Build a school, write children's books, do a new tour? What should I do?"

He said, "You should just concentrate on being nice, and actually be nice and nothing else for a while."

Then we had my favorite dessert—chocolate cake with a molten chocolate middle, French press coffee, and a shot of schnapps—as we discussed particle physics, my favorite part of our visits.

So being nice would heal me—how hard could it be? Little did I know that on the one hand, I would better fit into "polite society" for a while and be able to engage in interesting discussions at luncheons with interesting people who talked about interesting things instead of trying to get into arguments with them that ended with me telling them how full of shit they were. Yet, on the other hand, trying to be nice was the hardest thing I have ever done—a descent into hell itself, where I suffered the tortures of the damned, and ceased being able to be funny at all.

The truth was that being nice changed me deeply. I tested myself in thousands of ways, including standing in line to meet George W. Bush. I thought, If I can be nice to *him,* I will know that I have control of myself. When I met him, my mind was racing. I had to think of something to say to the person who I considered to be the worst person on earth. I shook his hand as we posed for a picture, and I said, "Mr. President, I pray for you every day." He answered, "Well, that's the important thing, aren't you a nice girl!" In my mind I said, *I'm fifty years old, and hardly a girl, asshead.* But I just smiled and said, "Thank you, Mr. President!" However, I was still not able to control the Evil Eye, though I had practiced and meditated for a couple of years to be able to do so by then. When Bush looked into my eyes, I felt it launching. I blinked and blinked and complained of allergies.

Soon after, I realized that there was just no way for me to be nice *and* to be truthful. A comic needs truth to be funny. Without the sting that truth brings with it, you are, as my dad said, "funny as a chapped ass." I began to understand that the very definition of *nice* that most people accept is "not upsetting the way things are." I realized that people hate people who tell them the truth. They think it's mean! They only like truth tellers centuries after they are dead, and only if they have died a tortured and humiliating death. Then, and only then, do people like and revere them, but never while they are alive and telling the truth. When they are alive and telling the truth, they are hated and savaged by the same kind of people who later worship them. That is what I realized after being "nice" and "polite" for a number of years, which required holding my tongue and tolerating intolerable people.

Although it was fun to experiment with new things, I came to the realization that I could no longer be polite to impolite people, and I could not be nice to assholes. The truth, I figured, is never really nice, and it always hurts when you don't want to hear it—even though eventually it does set you free. I brought this all up to the Rav years later, and he thought for a few minutes, then said, "Rifke, you have missed my point totally! You can still be the biggest B-word on earth; that is how you were made, but just not toward *people*! None of them are your *real* enemy—you, me, all of us, we have only one enemy. Use what's good in you against what's *evil in you*—give it all you've got, kill the hell out of it, dead, Dead, DEAD! Believe me, you are the one woman who can do it, so do it for all of us!"

Stunned, I knew at last what to do.

Chapter 25

Exorcism: Becoming One

I booked my ticket to Jerusalem. I went undercover, with no hoopla, as I wanted no publicity at all in my quest. At the King David Hotel, I changed into the dress I had inherited from my bubbe Mary—of her own design, it was beige with brown embroidered flowers, a darted bodice, and a lovely bowed kick pleat in the back. It fit perfectly and looked great in the picture that made it into the *Jerusalem Post;* and the wig made of human hair for stylish Orthodox women that I wore made me look like I fit right in! In that way, I took Bubbe with me to the Wailing Wall, where the women of my tribe have prayed for centuries. I called the Rav from my cell phone on the way over, and he said, "Create a new kabbalist for these times," and I assured him that I would.

I walked up to the Wall, and knowing that I would never be the same after I touched it, I raised my hand and held it away from the ancient stones as I began to meditate. Before I touched my hand to the Wall, I said these words: "In departure of all I have learned about religion, I *ask* for nothing, I beg not, I plead not, I bless and curse not. Instead, I *offer* everything, my entire life, in the service of Truth, wherever it is." When I moved my hand away, I was no longer alone. I would never again need to "practice" any religion at all. I was now *free of it all.* With no more imposed limitations on my thinking, and no more fear of punishment for my thoughts, I felt freed from slavery, and therefore filled with Love and Light.

When Jerusalem's then-mayor Ehud Olmert's people contacted me, I agreed to meet him in his office for a photo op and a handshake. As we stood shoulder to shoulder looking out at the city and the Temple Mount, I dared to say to him, "When will we rebuild the Temple?"

He said, "When the Messiah comes."

I said, "Why do we have to wait?"

He said, "Because the Arabs want the same place for their Dome of the Rock! The Messiah will liberate it from them for us."

Turning to look into his eyes, I said, "Why don't we just share it with them?"

He said nothing and looked away.

Chapter 26

Gethsemane

After I went to the Temple Wall and rid myself of all expectations, all superstition, and all excuses for bad behavior and disappointment, I knew it was up to me and me alone to make all my dreams come true.

I was one year into doing a two-year talk show with spiritual themes for King World, the company that distributes *The Oprah Winfrey Show.* When I first started working on the show, I invested everything into coming to New York City to interview my friend Rosie O'Donnell. After we moved our entire staff and the whole production to the Apollo in Harlem, Rosie canceled. I wanted to kill her; I held a huge grudge against her, thinking she was trying to sink my show on purpose. I stopped talking to her for a year, and later, feeling all self-righteous, I confronted her about it at Elaine Stritch's one-woman show. We were standing in the audience yelling back and forth at each other when Rosie said the reason she canceled was that her appearance was scheduled during the same week that she had to give her adopted daughter back to foster care, because of Evil Jeb Bush. I had to ask for her forgiveness, and I must say that when you have to take the Evil Eye back after you cast it wrongly, it really, really hurts your whole body and soul for a long time! Later I would learn from my teacher, Rav Berg, how to focus it. (I have always used my powers wisely since I learned self-control.)

But the day Rosie canceled, I was furious, as we scrambled to find a guest at the last minute, which is impossible in show business. Showbiz tradition dictates that no really big names will ever come on as guests at the last minute, and Rosie was the biggest name in town at that time. But someone knew someone and we moved some mountains and got Gladys Knight to come on in place of Rosie.

On the show, I asked Ms. Knight why "he" (the guy she sings about in "Midnight Train to Georgia") didn't "make it," and had to go back home on the red-eye train, and she looked heavenward and said, truthfully without a touch of show business bullshit, "Sometimes real talented people just don't make it, Roseanne, no matter how hard they try." I couldn't believe that she didn't sit there and bullshit like every single other show business personality I had ever met did, and say the usual lie, "If you just work hard and believe in yourself and trust in God, it will happen for you, eventually." I have an incredible amount of respect for her for saying what she said, as it's pretty much frowned on to ever truthfully suggest that show business is all bullshit. She had told the truth in such a gracious way, and I learned a lot from watching her do that.

Even more memorable, I got to sing with her! It was like dying and going to heaven. I decided that since there was no longer any hope of success, and yet I still had to show up every day to work, I would enjoy every second of the show to the fullest, without fighting, or conflict, or the desperation to turn things around and succeed.

At the Temple Wall, I had merged my small self with the Greater Self; I offered to give something, instead of asking for something, and it started to make a big difference in my life. I began to enjoy things so much more than before. Once I started to really feel more joy, I wanted to be nicer to people, and the nicer I would be, the more I wanted to sing again, though the fear of doing so was staggering and overwhelming.

I decided to start singing one song a week no matter how nervous I got, and no matter how bad and how embarrassing my nerves made me sound! I was going to do it no matter what, and I was going to get better and better at it no matter what, right there in front of the TV audience. The producers I had hired were really supportive of my becoming a rock star on the show. We probably pioneered the entire concept of reality shows when we just took a camera and followed me from rehearsing and putting a band together in L.A., to New York's CBGB club, where me and my band, The DXXX, gave a rock-and-roll show that had slam-dancing and all the punk rock that New York could handle. I sang "Satisfaction" by The Stones at three times the speed they did, and changed the words to be about menstruation and Chernobyl. It was a blast!

I got a lot of letters from people who told me how bad I was. One of them, my favorite, said, "You sound like a drunk singing in a bar at closing time. Stop!" But I didn't let that deter me at all.

I began to book the people with whom I had sung in my room as a kid. I booked and then sang with Lulu, Janis Ian, Etta James, the Monkees, Phoebe Snow, Chaka Khan, Eric Burdon, KC and the Sunshine Band, War, Bette Midler, Willie Nelson, Julio Iglesias, Keely Smith, Patti LaBelle, Merle Haggard, Loretta Lynn, Toby Keith, Jewel, and a lot of others.

My real goal was not really about singing at all. It was about seeing for myself how it felt when everyone around me encouraged me to do what I thought was funny, and also about learning to speak truthfully, in a nice way, without anger—my quest according to the Rav. The classic problem that codependents like myself have, is that it's hard to find a way to be assertive without being aggressive. I could never find that in my life before. I would dissociate from the anger I felt until it overwhelmed me and caused an explosion; I would strike out, instead of merely saying, "I would like you to stop talking to me like that," and simply start over again.

After we sang on the show, I asked all of these great singers on camera what they honestly thought about my singing, and oh, I loved to see that shit fly! Every one of these talented and most gracious people told me the absolute truth about my singing, and they made it all sound so sweet. They told me I sucked in a real nice and gentle way. I modeled that behavior. I took it all in, and I learned how to say true things nicely. As a comic, you need a "sting" to get a laugh, and that had always been my way, until I studied with the Rav.

Wayne Newton is one of the nicest of the nice people. He said, "Your singing is so full of joy, it's positively *infectious*!" Hilarious! Cyndi Lauper said, "I know a guy who can really teach you a lot about harmony and tone that will make you even better!" I graciously accepted all comments. I found that the most talented people are actually the nicest people of all, not just in public, but to everyone, always.

The nicer I became, the less fear I felt, and the less fear I felt, the better I was at singing. I realized that no one could stop me from doing these things. I realized that no one can stop a person from getting better, or improving. I enjoyed every minute of the whirl I took into a world of creative madness on that show, getting out of coffins and diving into vats of candy. One show, I came on wearing a teddy and the Powers That Be refused to air the show out in Portland. That was exactly what I wanted to happen, and I threw a fit on air, saying that I knew I was the *only* teddy-wearing woman *ever* censored from appearing on television! I want that known, too.

I was so sad not to be able to sing with Janis Joplin or Elvis, but I did sing with his daughter, Lisa Marie, and I did hire Janis's best friend to channel our girl back here so that I could ask her if she meant to kill herself or not, and she said, "No, it was a really fun experience that just ended badly." Of course, the greatest thrill of all was singing backup and dancing right beside my idol, James Brown. Mr. James Brown's eyes just about bugged out of his head when I let him see some of what Ms. Barr can do. It was the greatest moment of my life when Mr. Brown looked over at me and said, "Oh, I get it, you're an all-around entertainer! I thought you were just a comic, but now, oh now, I gotcha, Mrs. Barr!" I smiled and said, "I learned from the best, and that was you, Mr. Brown."

Not one of the many subsequent shows that the network put on to replace mine got even half the audience I delivered. I had a 3.8 score, which would now be a monster number, and was then, too, but they measured wrongly. They didn't factor in VCRs or any newer methods of media. I was hearing from many college students that they couldn't stay awake until 2:00 a.m. to watch my show live, so they recorded it every night. I am thrilled to hear that the old Nielsen method has finally been reworked and new methods employed to measure the audiences.

The truth is that the show, which all of cable TV ripped off or borrowed from in some way, had plus-size beauty contests, plus-size talent contests, plus-size queen-for-a-day shows, plus-size prom dresses, a "Date My Daughters" segment, Judge Roseanne, rehab shows, multicultural holidays, hemp cooking shows, lots of God talk, and lots of conspiracy theories. I got used to seeing ideas

I thought of get picked up and copied, and I was actually thrilled about it. Imitation is the sincerest form of flattery, and I was very, Very, VERY flattered by everyone in television. Of course, since then I've been reminded of another version of that old saying that's made the rounds for a long time: "Imitation is the sincerest form of show business."

I also must say one thing about myself as a singer, and that is, I sure did get a lot better! Many singers cannot say that. Many singers wouldn't sing again ANYWHERE after they had a really bad show, like I had once, but I am no quitter. I slew all of my fears when I realized that I could start completely over again, as I wish I had done on that field in San Diego, but was too afraid to just say, "STOP! I need to start over!" After about a decade or so, I regained the pure joy that singing had always been for me, in my real life, not just in fantasies.

As incredible as I know this sounds, one day I got a call from the wonderful Mr. Tony Bennett, and he invited to me to sing with him at the Pantages Theatre for four United States presidents—Ford, Carter, Bush the elder, and Clinton! I walked onstage confident, and I sang the best I have ever sung. When I looked out at the presidents, Mr. President Jimmy Carter smiled at me and gave me the thumbs-up! He was the only one of the four for whom I ever voted. I have the framed *Los Angeles Times* picture in my home of Tony and myself singing together that night. I must say, I did quite well, and I had fun! I must also say that I cannot even remember what song we sang because I was totally dissociating the entire time. I walked off the stage and went directly to a Secret Service agent, who was taking a break and having a smoke behind the curtain, and I said, "Sir, would you be so kind as to give me one of those fucking cigs? I'm about to faint!" I had not smoked for years but began again immediately after that song. I smoked for three or four days before the nervous fires burned out.

Now I realize that I am that Star-Spangled Banner myself, in a way. Tattered and torn after one perilous fight or another, I am still here and still standing on the side of freedom. I don't have to be the very best singer on earth; I can just sing for the joy of it. No pressure.

I sing almost every day now. God enjoys it, so who am I to deny Her?

Chapter 27

The End

Have you noticed how every tale about a little girl or boy on an adventure in a mysterious place, where it's never quite clear if things are real or imagined, seems to return home with a lesson learned? I guess it's fitting that mine should, too. Whether Dorothy comes back from Oz and decides there's no place like home or Alice comes to her senses with vivid memories of Mad Hatters and Cheshire cats (whatever *that* meant), the story is always about self-discovery. It was like that for me, too. There was always a twist or turn to amaze me—what with Hollywood, big-time TV, running around the world and sometimes not knowing if I was running toward something or away from it. You may be surprised that somebody doing all that running can stay so pleasingly plump and then some. But I've had quite a voyage—one that was as crazy and exciting as money and a ticket to Tinseltown can provide.

Although I have to say that the best part, when I look back, was probably the leg of the journey before I got rich and famous. It was the breaking-out part that was the best—the part that started with me taking the saucy little jokes I cooked up at my kitchen table and serving them up to the yahoos in the bars, the lesbians in the church basements, and all the rest of the folks who looked into the funhouse mirror of my humor and either laughed or looked away. And then, finally, there I was, sitting onstage beside the great Johnny Carson—the wizard who sat *in front of the curtain.* That was the total fulfillment of the dream of the little fat girl from Utah, who had sat with her dad on a broken-down couch, basking in the silvery glow of the television in an otherwise empty living room, on that weird little street in that most *enchanted* of cities—the city where I lived under at least two or three spells before I even *got* to la-la land.

Let's give credit where it's due, though. My dad opened the first door by hollering, "Comedian!" whenever a craftsman of that hallowed guild would appear on the tube in the comedian's uniform, the suit you just figured was navy even in black-and-white, and begin to spin his little tales that told the real truth about everything—that there is nothing to do but laugh at it all! Buried somewhere in those short stories of cultural persecution, nagging wives, bad breaks, fat mothers-in-law, pain-in-the-ass bosses, heartburn, hangovers, guys walking into a bar, or dogs that would only talk to them when nobody else was around—somewhere in that briar patch full of haunting laughter, just for a second, I saw the grinning rabbit of happiness. He'd flash me a big toothy one and say, "Come on, kid—this is where you belong. Take your soul, full of sadness, alienation, and anger; add a dash of wry; swish it around; and serve it hot. Yell it back in the world's face and make people laugh while you poke the big guys in the eyes for them."

Watching comedians on that little screen, I realized where my path led. But before there could be deals with agents and publicists and attorneys, there had to be a deal with someone even more evil and devious than they. No, not me, not quite, but the

Devil himself, or at least the one who worked in the branch office of my bedroom in Salt Lake City, and, of course, in the private inner world of this kosher, Mormon, fat, dark girl with no ass and a brain that would not stop asking questions of The God in Heaven or of The God in Hell.

Yep, the day came, years and years later and not so long ago, when I summoned old Lucifer himself, and much to my surprise, He showed up and granted me an audience. This time it was *not* a little girl with a head full of dreams who wanted some of His time and the benefit of His connections. Nope, it was a battle-tested veteran of the ego wars. I was more of a match for Beelzebub after navigating all the ups and downs that come with a big-time show-biz career, fame and fortune, and running the gauntlet from being hailed as the Next Big Thing at one end of the Tunnel of Love and Hate to being dumped at the other end and told, in so many words, "You're played out, bitch!"

So how does one undo a satanic contract, you ask? Well, you must first mix the herbs, hair, blood, and rum together in just the right combination, and then into the mirror you must gaze, jumping through all of hell's hoops to anthropomorphically conjure Lucifer in order to get face time with Him. He's not easy to reach—what with being guarded by the millions of souls who once worked in PR and are now His minions in hell, and having a schedule that keeps Him very, very busy here in Hollywood, as you might well imagine. However, Satan accepted my invitation to lunch, perhaps because I made it known from the start that I would, of course, pick up the check, or simply because He loves Spago as much as I.

At last, the preappointed day arrived. I began to dress for what was perhaps the most important meeting of my subconscious life. I thought about wearing all black, but it seemed so boring to me. I wanted to establish a power look right from the beginning, so I chose an all red outfit—a skirt with little red beads at the hem, a low-cut red bustier, red high heels, red nails and lipstick, and red chopsticks stuck at a jaunty angle in my updo bun, the one I had worn to the Emmys that year.

Are you ready for this, dear reader? I arrived first, and sat down and ordered a cocktail. I wanted to remain clearheaded given the task I had at hand, so I drank only two Belvedere martinis, filthy, with three olives, while I sat there waiting. His people had told my people to tell me that He would find me. It seemed to me that every man in a suit who walked into the restaurant could have possibly been Him, but when none of them looked my way, I finally just gave up anticipating Him at all.

At first, I had no doubt that He would show up, but as the moments ticked away, I was no longer sure. Perhaps this was just one of the games He played with people like me, letting us just sit and wait all alone until it dawned on us that we had been stood up, passed over, and ignored by a powerful source—the worst of all realizations for anyone in Hollywood, being stood up in public. I began to doubt my powers of persuasion. I thought, Maybe my bullshit didn't work on the Trickster Extraordinaire.

My face was beginning to feel hot, and I wished I had worn black instead. I picked up my phone to see if I could get a last-minute replacement guest, just so I wouldn't be sitting there all alone in red, sticking out like a sore thumb. That is a terrible thing for a famous person, sticking out like a sore thumb in public in Hollywood, alone! Everyone and their brother, after stalking you for a moment or two, while getting their pitch together, will commence pushing their screenplay or idea for a "comeback vehicle" on you, and that is almost a fate worse than death.

As if the situation couldn't have gotten any worse, my ex-husband Tom Arnold walked in! I was so horrified and in shock that I wasn't able to pull my eyes away from him in time to avoid his eyes catching mine. He approached my table. "You look thinner than I thought" were his first words to me. Beat. "I thought I would start out with a joke! Zing!" He laughed, shooting me with an imaginary gun.

I was so uncomfortable that I prayed Satan would come to the table right away. Tom stared down at me, waiting for me to say something. "Hello," I finally said begrudgingly.

"Do you mind if I sit down?" he asked.

I wanted to say no but said, "Sure." I sold my soul again in order not to be seen sitting there alone. Calmly, I said, "Please, have a seat." Tom sat down and didn't say anything for a bit. He just sat there quietly. I had never seen Tom sit so still. There was no face pinching, hair twirling, lip smacking, or rocking back and forth at all. "You *really* aren't doing coke anymore?" I asked.

He paused and sat back. "Roseanne, it's me. Cut the crap. What did you want to talk to me about?"

"I didn't want to talk to you at all. In fact, I am waiting for someone very special and I would actually like you to leave."

Tom glared deeply at me. "No," he said. "It's ME—Satan."

My stomach tied up in knots. Here I was face-to-face with the Master of Lies. I thought for a second and said, "I guess I expected You, being the Devil, not to be so 'on the head' with Your incarnation, more disguised. I thought there would be more nuance."

"Nuance is for hacks," He said. "What exactly is it you want, Roseanne? I am very, very busy at the moment, and since I already own your soul for all of eternity, I can't imagine what this is about."

I said, "I won't take much of your time, Satan. I just needed to go over a few things with you."

He seemed to like that I was respectful of His time and loosened up a bit, suggesting we order something to drink. I expected that Satan would order a Manhattan or a Bloody Mary, or, like in the song, a piña colada, but was surprised to find that ice water was His drink of choice, and He could barely get enough of it!

As we sat, perusing the menu, we began to overhear snippets of conversation about Hollywood business deals and box office openings, which were soon eclipsed by the drunken trivial gossip, loudly spoken by non-Jewish second wives in their late twenties, about what assholes their Jewish husbands were, but how generous and caring as well, and what surprisingly good fathers they make at age one hundred.

I muttered, "There but for your grace go I, sir."

He laughed and said, "You would never have found a rich Jewish guy to marry you! They like thin and sexy young blondes, not fat, pushy Jewish broads!" And we both had quite a laugh at that.

"You are pretty funny," I said, starting to shine his ass.

"Coming from you, that is quite the compliment!" he shined back.

"Hey, it's really you—you came!" I said, surprised at my own enthusiasm.

"You noticed," He said sarcastically. His voice reminded me of that deep one that you hear on spooky movie trailers.

"It's been a long time," I said, gathering my wits as I took a deep breath and sniffed a little to see if brimstone had an aroma. It did, I think, and it wasn't pleasant. Or maybe the devil had had Mexican food for breakfast. Either way, He spoke next.

"Actually, it hasn't. You might be surprised how many times I've been hovering just over your shoulder, whispering a tip or two and some encouragement at special times—you know, like when you were reading people the riot act or serving them a boatload of shit, when a little talking-to or a heart-to-heart might have done the trick."

“That was You?” I asked. “I thought that was just me getting in touch with my inner bitch and getting people back for all the times I’d been hurt and talked down to on my way up.”

“Yeah, that was Me, every time you’d look past all the good things life had brought you and seize on some little slight to use as an excuse to blow your mind and scare somebody with your industrial-strength temper and hollerin’ chops. I’ve always been impressed with the way you could rummage around in the haystack of happiness till you sniffed out the needle of negativity, and then use it to pop the bulging balloon of bratty bullshit that you liked to spray all over everybody within raging distance. Hey, I was even there helping you F things up with your family. Did you think you did that all by yourself?”

“Oh my God!” I said, hating to hear it as the wave of recognition and embarrassing, creepy memories washed over me.

“Uh, do me a favor,” He whispered. “Don’t use the G-word in my presence, okay? It’s *way politically incorrect* when you’re in a meeting with my end of the religious symbolism industry. Now, what did you want to talk about? I’m busier than ever these days, what with all the politicians and priests and lawyers and famous cheating husbands I have to, ahem, *counsel.*”

“Do you mind if I order first?”

He nodded, compliant. We decided to try the beet tower and the fatted calf, still listening in as the “girl talk” from the table beside us got louder and drunker and the de rigueur flirting with the obviously gay waiter began. We rolled our eyes at the waiter pretending to be a top when he was obviously a bottom in order to seduce the unhappy, bored, and aging gold diggers who might help him get an audition with one of the many agents they knew.

“That guy, you might be interested to know, is going to make it pretty big, and will be dating Sharon Stone in about eighteen months. He has a red carpet in his near future,” Satan said.

Finally, I screwed up the courage to spill the beans. "Satan, here it is, Guy. I want out of the contract," I said. "You didn't hold up Your end of our bargain. I may have been a little girl at the time, but now, at fifty-eight, and almost beginning to approach middle age . . . I must say that I remember the major deal points quite clearly."

"That doesn't take a genius," He said snidely. "It was mostly a standard boilerplate 'fame and fortune in exchange for your soul, or what's left of it after it's been jammed through the fame-and-fortune meat grinder' contract. We call it 'Form Six sixty-seven.' There are no loopholes, although I must admit, your addendum with the 'stay-fat-and-still-be-able-to-pull-men-under-your-spell' clause was pure genius! Most of my female clients opt for the 'stay-thin-even-with-the-occasional-binge-eating-episode-minus-the-upchucking' amendment."

"Hey," I interrupted Him. "Form Six sixty-seven? What does Form Six sixty-six cover? That's the most famous one, right?"

"You don't want to know," He said with a dismissive flick of His hand, as if brushing off something distasteful. "Let's just say it involves 'men of the cloth' and leave it at that. We've gone through stacks of those. As it is said, where's the last place you'd look for the Devil? Answer: in church! Enough said."

"Oh my God," I said again.

"Hey, what did I just say about the G-word?" He said. "Anyway, what's this about Me reneging? You had your big whirl around the block in the Look-at-Me-Mobile, while everybody watched, year after year, and according to the agreement, everybody was either full of admiration or burning with jealousy or both. What did I miss?"

"The operative word there was *had*!" I snapped, barely letting Him finish. "Yeah, I knocked 'em dead in Denver, had them rolling in the aisles in L.A., and then had a gigantic hit show for nine seasons, and could still rake in some goodies in the wake of all that . . . *but* . . ."

"But *what*?!" my seemingly all-too-real apparition or whatever He was demanded.

"But a ton of it's GONE! Yeah, I made some serious dough back in the day, and I got my attention and all the rest, but I'm *still* a writer and a comic and a thinker and an actor, and now, if I want to work anywhere besides my little studio—which, by the way, is conveniently located just minutes from LAX and is equipped with state-of-the-art Macintosh hardware and editing software and high-tech, industry-standard, top-name audio and video gear and is available for viewing by appointment, call us!—if I want to work anywhere where I'll have an audience of any size. . . . I mean, can You imagine how degrading it is to have to parade what's left of my ass in front of a bunch of midlevel studio drones who went to high school with my kids before they dropped out? (My kids, I mean.) Do You have any idea what that's like? Within a few years of having that gigantic show that's actually been studied in sociology classes in universities for the impact it had on our culture—that show that was a training ground for people who learned enough to go on to massive careers—within a few years of that, I actually started to hear the word *has-been* whispered behind my back!"

"I know the feeling," said the Dark Lord. "I know what you're thinking. I'm not supposed to have feelings, but I do know what you mean about that whole has-been thing. There was awhile there, in the '90s, when the economy seemed to be booming, but I couldn't get a major war started to save My ass. Houses were appreciating like, well, like a house on fire. Most people weren't too miserable. A black man and a fat woman—a feminist, in fact—had big TV ratings. I mean, people were starting to wonder if I was out of business! Those were pretty good times for lots of folks; needless to say, it wasn't good for My brand."

He paused, kind of wistfully for a Devil, I thought. But then He brightened up and shot me a self-satisfied grin, and said, "But then—well, let's just say, thank G-word for religious fanatics, Republicans from Texas, cheap foreign labor, right-wing gasbags on the radio, the Catholic church, Mormons, hatred coming out of both sides of the Holy Land—I *love* that one!" He said it like a kid in a candy store, giving *hatred* and *Holy Land* an extra push. "Shall I go on?" He asked, but didn't wait for an answer. "Oh, baby, one of my biggies: WALL STREET! Yeah, it's all cooking up nicely again, and Devil stock is through the roof. Forget *gold,* kid—invest in war, homophobia, porn, payday loan shops in poor neighborhoods, that BS war on drugs, AND drugs—the legal kind, of course, the ones they push on TV—and anything having to do with insurance. It'll stay bad—I mean good—for Me, of course, for a while, because even suggesting that something may actually be unjust and need fixing is, remember this now: *negative thinking*! Remember that one; it's huge. Take this Devil's word for it: Teach people that it's not the stuff put into the food and the air and the water that gives people cancer or autism, it's their own *negative thinking*! Holy hell, I really knew what I was doing when I cooked *that* one up. You know that book *The Secret*? It was *My idea* to call it that instead of *Blame the Victim.* Nice, huh? And the dopes LOVE it.

"Hell, with a little help from My conservative minions, who luckily don't know what *conservative* actually means, I've got 'em rewriting the Bible and taking out all that 'be kind to the poor' and 'don't think about money all day' thing that the Bronze Age Jew hippie told 'em about! And can I just give a shout-out to the Texas School Board and the textbook companies that kiss their Holy-Roller, snake-handling asses! Yeee-haaw! Let's get evolution out of the schools, and take sex education out while we're at it, and science along with both of them! Oh, baby! 'Scuse Me, while I kiss the sky! The dumber the Taliban-gelists can keep the Americans, the less they are taught to compete for jobs in the international workforce, and the more desperate they will be. And that's makes for a gi-normous payday for all of My subsidiaries."

I was staring, by now, with my mouth hanging open like an inbred, corn-fed white woman at a Sarah Palin rally demanding that the word *intercourse* be taken out of the dictionary, and taxes lowered, while escalating the war in some far-off country that doesn't have the sense to be Christian. The Devil held up a single gnarly finger, like a litigant on *Judge Judy* just before she tells them to put their hand down or she'll bite it off.

I jumped in anyway. "Hey, that's all good, but I did a reality show on a big-ass network about trying to get a show on a little-ass network, and it turned out to be a giant cluster fuck that I had to hemorrhage my way out of. You call that fame and fortune and getting my ass kissed? You broke the contract, Mr. Dark Lord. What's up with that, Homeboy From Hell?"

He said, "You have to realize that sometimes it gets complicated. Yours is not the only deal I try to honor. Believe it or not, a few people have made deals with me that run concurrently and include screwing with YOU! I'm a demon, not a proctologist—I don't always have the luxury of dealing with one asshole at a time!"

"I beg your Devil-Ass pardon!" I said, indignantly.

But He held that finger up again, and said, "Okay, just to make up for a little of your trouble, here's a tip for a shrewd investment while you're getting advice from the original *inside trader*: Reality shows: They've really gotten better, and by that I mean, *worse.* You can't go wrong getting behind marketing during the new amped-up reality shows. I'm talking about the ones where the people on the screen are way dumber than the ones who are watching, which makes everybody involved really feel good about themselves. You can *so* sell things during the breaks—you know: pills that make your ass smaller, your dong bigger, your wrinkles harder to see, your kids smarter, your marriage better, your attitude shinier, your . . ."

I'd heard enough.

"Been there, done that," I said, feeling back in charge of the proceedings. "I've tried to go through the Home Shopping Network drill. That's another cheesy hoop I wouldn't have jumped through if You'd stayed on the case like You were supposed to. That sucked! I had to get stuff made by Chinese slaves, brought over on nonunion asbestos barges, jack the price through the roof, and stand in front of the camera with way too much makeup on, and act like I was happier than I'd ever been in my life, like I was selling the greatest thing in the world! Trust me, it's not as fun as it sounds. I lost my dignity and made a hundred and thirteen dollars! Another example of You not coming across!

"Now, let's get back to the big stuff. When we made that deal, I seem to remember the word *eternal* being in there, as in: eternal soul. Even when I was a kid, I wasn't dumb enough to trade something eternal for ten years or so of being top dog. Do You really think I'd fall for that and sign up for a hitch with You that never ends, without You at least getting me serious face time in the media right up to the end of my role as me? You've gotta be shitting me! Even when I was marrying all those special-needs dudes, most of the time I was thinking, I have to make this last . . . all the way to the divorce! I mean, it makes me mad that You'd think I was that stupid to lock in 'forever' with the likes of You! Even as a kid! You know a little something about being mad, don't You, O Mighty Angel of Anger?" I took a breath.

"Do I?!" He said, with a curled lip and a raised eyebrow and a furrowed forehead (I guess He doesn't like the Botox). "You know what really gets My pointy tail in a knot? When I watch those award shows you showbiz types like to throw, the ones where everybody likes to act all genuine and sincere, while wearing zillion-dollar dresses and tailored tuxes and talking about what an *honor* everything is, and how *thrilled* they are just to be breathing the same air as a bunch of other ego freaks they hope to outshine."

"THAT gets under YOUR skin?" I asked. "I figured You'd love those gushing fountains of swollen self-esteem on steroids!"

"Oh, I DO! Are you kidding?" He said, tossing His head back in disbelief. It was amazing how His face held its shape while smoothly morphing into everybody from Mick Jagger to Dr. Phil to some generic studio head type, to the pope, Oprah, Bono, Suzanne Somers, Tom Cruise, Angelina Jolie, some hillbilly Ayatollah TV evangelist composite, and Dick Cheney—unbelievable! It was a bit like I've imagined LSD to be, but without the peaceful hippie vibe.

"Hey, are you paying attention?" He snapped. "I'm listening to *your* griping—have some respect for *Mine*!"

"Sorry," I said, a little sheepishly, but then I realized I was apologizing to SATAN for STARING! "Go on," I said. "Hell, I'm not getting any younger."

"I can see that," He said.

"Don't piss me off," I shot back. "Finish telling me what pisses *You* off! And then I've got the floor again." I waited for Him to compose Himself.

"What pisses Me off at those cinematic circle jerks is the way some people actually thank GOD for their success. Okay, I said the G-word, just to make My point. And by *success* I mean the ass shining from their peers in the ass-shining business. Can you believe that they're not only vain enough to actually think that the CEO of the Universe, Inc., gives a good goddamn about whether some artsy-fartsy neurotic on a tiny, tumbling grain of sand in the middle of nowhere gets an award for their skills or not? Their skills are entertaining, but let's face it—their craft consists of pretending to be someone they're not, or making up stories, or rapping about how much sex they get or money they make or sex they'll get and money they'll make after everybody sees them on this glitzy spectacle in a tiny corner of a world half full of hungry people in rags. "Oh yeah," He said, somehow even more sarcastically. "G-word just can't get enough of that."

"I don't get it," I said. "I thought You said You love all that crap?"

"Are you listening?" He said, getting hot around His already smoldering collar. "I said it's the thanking God for their success that pisses Me off! Think about it! Do they really think that the alleged author of all that's good and caring and sharing and unselfish would be The One who provides them elbows sharp enough to slice their way through all those tux- and gown-clad careerist attention junkies and *their* rabid, conniving agents and publicists and crap lappers? I'm talking about the same weasels with a phone in each claw who *live* to get their clients' faces blown up on the big screen that passes for reality in this sad charade of a world—the same world I work like a sock puppet! Baby, let Me tell you: In the entertainment capital of the world, like you said, the breasts may be fake, but the assholes are real. All that effort I put into working for them around the clock from the time they go to their first podunk high school drama class all the way to the podium of that massive, monolithic monument to bullshit that is big-time showbiz—and then they have the nerve to thank the alleged Source of Kindness, and selflessness!

"Come on! Has one of them ever had the damn *decency* to look into the camera and out at all those uplifted, face-lifted masks in the audience and say, 'I deserve this adulation like a son of a bitch because I followed Satan's brilliant direction to a T. It was HE who taught me you don't get anywhere in a world where 'money talks and bullshit walks' unless you miss no opportunities to be noticed! They have absolutely no fucking integrity at all, Roseanne, or else they would honestly say, 'It was the Devil who brought me the craftiest, highest-paid people in a crafty, highly paid web to do the pushing for me! Just once, I would like to hear, 'Thank you, Dark Lord, for this moment where everyone is staring at me, me, ME!

"Listen, Roseanne, I agreed to have this lunch with you because I have a proposition to make you that I think will make you very pleased."

"What?!" I shrieked, feeling outsmarted, almost.

He continued, "I want you to be the spokeswoman for my various business entities. I want you to speak for Me, and put a human face on My Brand. There can be a whole campaign, starring you . . . books, tours, television, radio, all media, and then an extended career in politics. Your own commercials, just like you dreamed of as a child."

"Wow, it sounds amazing!" I remarked. "I like saying the things that are true and that no one else has the guts for."

"I know you do, and I think you and I are the right fit," He went on.

"Yeah?" I said. "I have always dreamed of selling out in a big, big way for the right price, but—before I consider Your interesting offer, indulge my curiosity for a moment, please."

"Of course, I will," He assured me.

It just tumbled out of my mouth. "You make things happen the way people ask You to. Then they get famous by selling their souls, and once they realize that they haven't got one, they quickly hit bottom, which is where they always seem to see the Light! It seems that You are the One who brings most of us to God, though in a roundabout way, as if You and God are like good cop, bad cop. You are both on the same team, really. Aren't I right, Mr. God-Devil?" I delivered the shot like David did to Goliath.

Unmasked at last, He smiled and shook His head from side to side, amused and amazed at the depth of my deciphering abilities.

Eventually, He spoke and said, "You have figured it all out, Roseanne. Everything, including Me, ends up working for The Greater Good, yes."

I said, "I have moved out of childish things these days, and no longer care anything about commercials or success or show business or any of that bipolar stuff, so I think You should move on, and ask Glenn Beck to be Your number one disciple, and hawk Your message for You. He will do well for You, I think, better than me, really."

Perhaps as a consolation to me, He said, "You know, you are probably right. That guy really knows how to divide people and as you know, Roseanne, that is how I am really able to control the world, for now. All roads do eventually lead to Rome, of course. You are on the right track of things, but a little bit ahead of the times, as usual. The entire concept of spiritual duality is vestigial, really, like hibernation. And one day, people will just slough it off, but until then, how else can storytellers tell people about the unfolding of Divine Awareness in humanity, huh? If you can come up with a better story, then, by all means, do so!" He turned to look me straight in my eyes.

I saw Those Eyes again, just then, as I did at age twelve—green and black plaid with a stripe of yellow around the edge and a combustible red center. There He was in all His glory, the Fallen Angel of pride and ego, now named Lucifer! He had *showed* Himself to me, *Shana Rifke Bitnam Katz Davidovitz Borisofsky*. We were looking at each other pupil to pupil, and I did not flinch, as His face morphed into an exact copy of my own. I had learned to calm the panic and horror that rose in me, so I could calmly confront the worst of my own ugliness, and I breathed deeply. I was on a mission to create myself over again, in wholeness, and to integrate shadow and light.

"What is it you are doing to Me?" His lips turned a shade of blue. As He searched the mirror of my gaze, I said, "I am giving you the Evil Eye." He was getting pretty scared now. "You are using Law against Law! Stop it! Not the Evil Eye of an Old Jewish Woman, NO!" He began freaking out.

"Oh yes, and I am feeling empathy for You, too!" I said, knowing that He could not exist in the presence of it.

"I am out of here!" He said, horrified, and then fell to dust and blew away.

Chapter 28

The Real Big Super-duper Perverse Reverse Secret

Like most thinking women who have ever lived on this planet, I have been asked repeatedly, "Why are you so angry?" The question is often posed by drunk, drugged women, and it is always asked accusatorially, as if there is—honest to God—no reason *to be* angry. It pisses me off and tempts me to scream back, "Why aren't you *more* angry?" Am I the only one who sees that the world is turning to shit, and that most people are unaware of the constant game of smoke and mirrors that is in play to keep us from realizing what is really going on?

I watch in amazement as the completely restorative power of anger is being demonized in America by those would-be mind controllers who are employed in religious organizations, pharmaceutical industries, the psychiatric association, government, and the advertising industry and all the media it spawns. To me, this is the conspiracy to end all conspiracies, a crying shame of epic proportions. Only the Evil One could have thought of this!

Imagine for a moment that you are the Evil One, old Beelzebub himself. First of all, you are all about the nasty, the vile, and the wrong. Your goal is to persuade as many thinkers as you can to ignore their own rational self-interest and act on your orders. You must cloud their minds, and make them think that they themselves came up with the ideas that ultimately defeat and destroy them. You want to persuade as many thinkers as you can that everything is okay, and for those who do not buy that, and think they can make a difference, you must convince them instead that no matter how much they try to create change, they will not succeed. Your stealthy servants serve up Hope to the Hopeless, in order to disarm them, because you know that the hopeless could become your greatest enemy. Those with nothing to lose are the potential soldiers for Truth.

You know that the racket you are running, if exposed, will go down fast, as all Ponzi schemes always do. Your business is persuasion! You know how to use law against law. Using religion, you have leveraged God against Humanity! That is how smart you are! You have given us complacency and named it Faith! By remaking anger into something that must be numbed and turned away from, your minions, the zombies and ghouls who do your bidding, have rendered the common citizen helplessly paralyzed.

Score one for Big Devil Daddy! The Dark Lord grinds His chops, growing stronger each time a thinker is confounded, each time fact is disregarded. Hoping to render more unquestioning slaves to do the bidding of His minions, who run the banks, governments, diet franchises, and pharmaceutical companies, He seeks to replace public anger at injustice with capitulation or apathy. These methods are His most effective tools against insurrection and overthrow. He *knows* that anger and hatred are the most transcendental of all human emotions, and that they move mountains.

He isn't all that impressed by the everyday evil doings of the everyday evil soul; He knows He will always have them under His craven hoof. But for The Evil One, the critical thinker is like white meat at Thanksgiving. One of those is worth ten thousand of the useful idiots who hang around in Las Vegas and at gun conventions.

Unfortunately, here in Hell, where everything is a mirrored reflection, a perverse reverse, where perception *is* reality, in order for us to finally turn this torment, doubt, fear, and false hope—this damnation—around, we must 1) admit that we are all, in fact, living in Hell when we demonically ignore the suffering of the helpless who are at the bottom; and 2) acknowledge that we have created and sustained the power of Evil by not getting *angry enough* at it or by *not hating it enough.*

The ones who are happy and satisfied here in Hell, are the ones who keep everything awful in place. Silence is indeed eternal, suspended death, the ego run amok.

Keep getting pissed off, even though all those around you may be drugged on antidepressants and drunk on the false power of positive thinking. If you get pissed off enough, you will get off your ass and change things. You will find your depression begins to lift, and your craving for Justice and what is Right restoring every cell of your being. That is what the ONE GOOD GOD wants us all to know! She is our combined just and righteous anger, and nothing less than the restorative power of critical truth. God is the will of the people united on behalf of Good.

Next time a Satanist asks you why you are so angry, answer thusly: “Because God, the author of all critical thought, requires me to be so, you fucking moron!”

Glenn Beck and Sarah Palin's American Prayer

Dear Lord,

We thank you for blessing us *with our hugely disproportionate share of the world's dwindling resources. We're grateful that those* less blessed *than us have no choice but to work for next to nothing so that our profits are maximized. We pray for those who suffer terrible, agonizing ordeals and losses, but we thank* You, *merciful God, for making sure that none of those horrible things happen to* us. *We thank You for the Gift of the Right Religion, so that we never have to run the risk of actually thinking for ourselves, or of thinking at all.*

Mostly though, we thank You for our vastly superior military might, to keep us safe from those who would oppose us, many of whom are jealous and resentful that we have so much more than we need and mindlessly waste, and for being able to remove the resources out from under the ground of those who practice the wrong religions.

We know You're busy, and we thank You for Your time and for time itself, *generally, because we don't want to be with You in Your wondrous, heavenly kingdom just yet, or sooner than we need to. Thanks, again!*

Acknowledgments

First, to the voices, thanks for always being there. Next, to the people who called me crazy my whole life because I talked to G-d, I would like to say: you kept me honest, and thank you. To all the Gods/Goddesses on earth and in the Heavens and Hearts and Minds of so many, I say, thanks for the glimpse into the life and times of Ascendant Masters.

Thanks to my psychiatrist, Dr. Colin Ross; to my editor, Tricia Whatserface; and to my publicist/chef, James Moore. To my life partner, Old John Argent, thanks for caring about truth and justice and the dow/tao.

To my sister Geraldine; my younger sister, Pearl S.; my genius brother, Dr. Ben Barr; to all of their children and their children; to my own five children and five grandsons and three siblings' in-laws; and to all of their loved ones, thanks for laughing when I do the lemon teeth thing at every wedding; I adore doing it for you, as I feel really funny then.

Thanks to my mother, Helen Ruth Davis Barr, an Original Goddess (O.G.), survivor, and mentor. Thanks to Dr. Mary Daly for the education. And last, thanks to words themselves, but especially those that speak the right things to people who need to hear them at the exact right time, which is, as we know, just after reaching bottom.

About the Author

Roseanne Barr (1952–2011)

Roseanne Barr was born, through a spin of the cosmic wheel of misfortune, in what was then the small-minded town of Salt Lake City, Utah. Her father was a brilliantly funny misfit, socialist, atheist Jew, and football player—Jerome Harold Barr—who along with her mother, H. R. Davis Barr, the classic, post–Holocaust, middle-class, first-generation Jewish woman, taught her all that she needed to know to become a compulsive nail-biter, overeating obsessive with social anxiety disorder and a nasty messianic complex that has defied medication, psychiatry, stardom, and sanity. Her mother also taught her how to manipulate men with wit, and thereby subdue their aggressive sexuality, and then rage at them for that. These many influences ensured that little Miss Barr was to evolve a new organ for thought on behalf of women who subsequently emulated her to also become "people *dis*pleasers."

In an age and culture where women largely fell all over themselves to lap up the very small amount of approval that was smeared on the concrete by the soles of the feet of powerful capitalists, patriarchs, and run-of-the-mill priests, Barr stepped up to irritate and insist instead that the owners of those feet kiss her very large, dynamic, and disagreeably combatant ass. She also graciously insisted that they invite their compatriots to take a crack at it as well.

No crap lapper, she was the first of her generation to refuse to explain and apologize for being offensive, fat, and in possession of an altered opinion and an unapologetic (per her father's mentoring) lack of respect for anything that did not come from other resisters, jokesters, and martyrs, lynched on the tree of human pride.

Living as she did in the very last few days of the American Empire, under the occupation of bores and minutiae masters, when freedom of speech in any form by any woman was unofficially illegal, Barr never could find any critique of her work that had any intelligence to it whatsoever, except for John Lahr's piece on her in *The New Yorker,* thanks to Tina Brown, then editor.

Brown and Barr formed a mutual fan club and decided to bring the issue of feminism front and center to America's most conservative liberal weekly magazine, *The New Yorker.* Brown offered Barr a stint as a guest editor of the first Women's Issue of *The New Yorker* magazine, which was really a revolutionary idea whose time had passed and was highly overdue.

Apparently, as always seems to happen in the U.S.A., whenever anything radical threatens to overtake everything out-of-date, the middle caves in on itself. The exact middle of *The New Yorker*'s contributors decided that it was her time to bust a move and use Ms. Barr's invitation as a way to make a grand exit that coincided with her contract not being renewed, or something like that. Even the highly educated can confuse television personalities with the actors who portray them. The contributor in question apparently felt that Roseanne Barr, who created and portrayed a working-class character, "Roseanne Connor," on a television show, lacked the intellectual prowess required to helm a feminist critique of working women's progress in post–Reagan America. To the editor, this was apparently evidenced by the fact that Roseanne Connor lived in a small house in Illinois and worked at a take-out chicken restaurant. It was either that confused, ill-conceived analysis or the tired notion: *God only knows who the hell these actors think they are!* Just because you write a show and portray a working-class female, who fights to break down barriers set before working-class women and is viewed by forty million viewers every Wednesday evening, doesn't mean you have anything important to say! Oh wait, yes, indeed it does mean that! Sorry. Carry on! (I fear I am starting to sound like Jerry Lewis now! Oh my God, I hope not. I must stop bitching! I simply must! But no, not quite yet, amigos!)

Ms. K then riled up the mother of all backbiting, class-ignorant women writers of all time, Maureen Dowd, who agreed in print in the *New York Times* that Roseanne Connor was loud and loose and could not walk from the soundstage to the hallowed halls of *The New Yorker* up in this mothafocka! It just isn't done!

As always happened whenever Roseanne Barr spoke about America's caste systems, most of her sisters-in-arms gave up the ship and fled in horror when it became apparent to them that Barr was interested in revolution, not polite reform. The issue of which she is so proud is framed on the wall of her office, and features writers Amy Sedaris, Mary Daly, Wendy Wasserstein, and Anna Deavere Smith, among others, and has an article in it about a growing maids' union in Las Vegas, Nevada. (Years later, this union became quite a decisive force in the election of Barack Obama.)

Barr went as far as any woman can ever go in the Judeo-Christian tradition that demands thinking women to constantly reassure the powers-that-be and their lackeys that they are not witches to be burned at the stake. After ramming through the concept of class to a segment of middle-class American feminists, who at the behest of their masters are encouraged not to address, name, or be aware of the class system that controls their every waking thought, Barr bought a nut farm in Hawaii, where she retired, which seemed appropriate to any and all who had ever enjoyed the pressure of her company. She spent many happy hours reading and writing books and cultivating and smoking things that she grew in her garden. Her life took a magical turn when she gave herself fully to the idea that the wild pigs that stalked her fenced acreage and trolled her farmland, trying to root mac nuts out of the ground, could themselves be physically outmaneuvered. Riding roughshod over hill and dale and tusked boar on her Kawasaki Mule, Ms. Barr has redefined the has-been in sublime repose.

Her busy life was cut short by an angry, razor-tusked boar while shooting at it drunk on her Kawasaki Mule in preparation for a luau bar mitzvah for her fifth grandson, Buster, named for Buster Keaton. He barely noticed, as he had received a Playstation 9 as a gift, and no one missed her at all. No one attended her funeral, or spoke at any memorial, as all wonderful things had already all been said while she lived, and there was no need.

She is survived by five children and five grandchildren, whom she also survived, and by the handsome John Argent, who continues to write songs but now sings them himself, to much greater success.

Her lesser regrets were that she had not burned even more bridges, pissed off more idiots, fired more assholes, sung more patriotic anthems, and gained more weight.

Her major regret: never having had sex with Elvis Presley.

The attribute of which she is most proud is, of course, her humility.

Her favorite thing about her body: "My eyes," she once said. "I can cast the Evil One like no one else."

Now free of her physical existence, she is able to hang around with her best pal and discuss solutions to world problems uninterrupted, one-on-one, for all of eternity.